The Diamonds of Dixie

The Diamonds of Dixie

Travels through the Southern Minor Leagues

ERNEST J. GREEN

Madison Books
LANHAM • NEW YORK • LONDON

Published by Madison Books
4720 Boston Way
Lanham, Maryland 20706

3 Henrietta Street
London WC2E 8LU England

Distributed by National Book Network

The paper used in this publication meets the minimum
requirements of American National Standard for
Information Sciences—Permanence of Paper for
Printed Library Materials, ANSI Z39.48–1984. ⊚™
Manufactured in the United States of America.

Library of Congress Cataloging-in-Publication Data

Green, Ernest J.
The diamonds of Dixie : travels through the southern minor leagues
Ernest J. Green.
p. cm.
Includes index.
1. Minor league baseball—Southern States. I. Title.
GV875.A1G73 1995 796.357'64'0975—dc20 94-39409 CIP REV.

ISBN 1-56833-043-X (cloth: alk paper)

British Cataloging in Publication Information Available

Dedicated with love
to my wife

Zena

who took me back
after my summer romance
with baseball

I tell you something else and you can mark
this down as a prediction. You give this country
twenty or thirty more years, everybody's got
any sense is going down South.

SATCHEL PAIGE

Contents

Acknowledgments

FOR MORE THAN A QUARTER CENTURY I was lucky enough to have colleagues who shared a fondness for the national pastime: the late Righton Robertson, Harold Guy, Sherman Silverman, Bruce Dudley, my frequent companion to baseball games and a historian who wrote *Distant Drums*, about the 1948 Cleveland Indians, Dennis Sullivan, with his encyclopedic command of baseball data, and Bob Coords. Our offices were all located on the same corridor within a distance about equal to that from home plate to second base (that's 127 feet, 3⅜ inches, for the uninitiated), and if I stepped into the hall and dropped a comment on the latest trade or the current standings, I soon collected a small crowd of these folk. Over the years they all helped to sustain my affection for the game and made me a more informed student of it.

David Lamb was generous in sharing his experiences of baseball travel and provided many useful suggestions. Cathy Burns contributed helpful trip analysis and helped me keep my goals in sight.

I visited thirty southern baseball clubs during the 1993 season. My thanks go to all the players, general managers, field managers, and other club officials who took time to talk with me during the visits, which lasted up to seven days. I invariably showed up at the worst time of day in the midst of a busy home stand, and they were gracious and cooperative.

My wife, Zena, is a lukewarm baseball fan at best. At her most enthusiastic, she says that it is nice to sit in the sunshine or in the cool evening air on a pleasant June night. Yet she has been my companion at more games than anyone else over the years, and her company has been appreciated all the more because it reflects a bond that baseball didn't have to forge.

My sons Michael and Laurence unfortunately inherited more of their mother's baseball genes than mine, but I can usually coax them into going with me to one game a year each. They both encouraged my trip; neither of them ever said there was anything peculiar about having a father who drove away a summer going to minor league baseball games.

I appreciate the extra effort put forth by Julie Kirsch and the other production staff at Madison Books to make the book materialize by Opening Day. And if editors were diamonds, Jennifer Ruark and Jon Sisk would be several carats each. They saw a book in the pages I gave them; then had the skill and patience to help me see it too.

Others to whom I owe thanks for information, assistance or support are mentioned in the text. In a few cases, I have, as promised, provided pseudonyms for protection of privacy.

Introduction:
Seeds of a Summer Odyssey

MANY BOOKS HAVE BEEN WRITTEN about baseball, and many more about the South. Until now, no one book has specifically wed these two subjects. They were, for awhile, reluctant marriage partners anyway. In the nineteenth century, baseball was mainly a northeastern sport spreading toward the Midwest, not the South. Its early icons and images reflected this geography: Cooperstown, New York; Elysian Fields, Hoboken, New Jersey; the great 1869 Cincinnati Red Stockings. When baseball did spread to the South, it was minor league baseball, not the big-time stuff. Until recently, southern baseball meant the Southern Association, the Texas League, and the even smaller leagues and their backwater towns. Baseball has been played in the South for a long time, nevertheless, played well and played badly just as in other parts of the country. I once sat next to a fan at a minor league game in Alabama, a beefy square-faced man who stuffed tobacco from a Red Man pouch into his jaw without looking at the pouch, the tobacco, or his hand.

"How do you think baseball is different in the South than in other parts of the country?" I asked him in my best interviewer manner.

He narrowed his eyes in deep thought. "The players sweat more," he replied finally, slowly letting loose with a large, satisfied grin.

The poet Donald Hall seconds his sentiment: "Baseball is a

country all to itself." Hall is right. Baseball has all the elements of a cultural system, from rites of passage to norms, values, and symbols, and a highly specialized language, which over the years has been collected into general speech. Baseball even has its own creation myth featuring General Abner Doubleday as the giver of life. As a country, however, baseball has national and regional variations and dialects. The total environment is different when it is practiced in Japan, in Mexico, or in the Dominican Republic, and even within the United States. When the Yankee game went south in this country, a different experience was created.

Baseball is different regionally and even from community to community, because baseball is more than the nine players standing on a field. It is a sport, an industry, and most of all a set of ideas in the minds of its fans. When I was growing up in northeastern Oklahoma in the 1950s, professional baseball meant the Tulsa Oilers, a Class AA Texas League team. I never saw a major league game until my twenties. To me, baseball was the Beaumont Roughnecks, the Shreveport Sports, the Fort Worth Cats, and other southern and southwestern teams. While the newspapers carried accounts of major league teams, I could only vaguely envision what baseball was like in faraway places such as Detroit, Chicago, and Brooklyn. Before television, my imagination concocted pictures of the big stadiums and of the men who played in them, imperfect images formed as much by my own psychic interior as from the incomplete information available.

North of the Mason-Dixon line, a major league team was always within travel or radio distance for baseball fans of the 1940s and 1950s. As a consequence, even in villages that had their own minor league teams those northern teams never developed the intense loyalist followings of clubs in the South. Where, in the North, did umpires have to be escorted in secret out of town after a home team loss as happened in Louisiana in the 1950s?

Besides the Texas League and the Southern Association, the South and Southwest were especially rich during those years in delightfully named lower minor leagues. There was the Evangeline League, for which I conjured up young ballplayers, sitting around the lobby of their seedy hotel after a game, still in dirty uniforms, pulling tattered copies of Longfellow's poem by that name from their back pockets and reading to each other. There was the Longhorn League, suggesting baseball games often obscured by a cloud of dust as a huge herd of cattle passed just beyond the outfield fence on their way north to the railhead. In the Sunset League, every game began around dinnertime and the players were always bathed in an amber glow as they raced to complete the game before darkness fell. (There were no lights in the ballparks of the Sunset League, at least in my young mind.)

Memories of my baseball experiences in the early 1950s call up windblown rides in the back of a pickup truck driven by a friend's father. He was a bricklayer, and flying bits of dried concrete would sting us as we bounced along the two-lane roads from Collinsville to Tulsa, about twenty miles to the south. In the early evening twilight, the Tulsa skyline rose solitary out of the prairie as we approached. On hot afternoons, Tulsa's distant spires and pyramidal towers seemed to dance on heat waves, hovering above the horizon like the Emerald City.

The Oilers played at Texas League Park, a wooden structure built as a WPA project in 1934. Entering the county fairgrounds at Fifteenth and Sandusky, we would park within a few yards of the entrance and walk through gates under a three-story wooden facade curved and flanked by pilasters. Inside, we always sat in the right-field bleachers. The left-field bleachers were for black fans, who had their own concessions, drinking fountains, and rest rooms, all designated with the word "COLORED." I turned right in the old park without question, assuming at age twelve that it was the natural order of life.

The park was built with wood and nails and was a wonderful place to watch baseball. Until 1953, Texas League Park had its own restaurant facing outward toward the parking lot on the left field side. Called the Oiler Grill, it was a diner with polished black tile at one end, a white stucco finish, and awnings covering its circular and rectangular windows. It operated as a drive-in when the Oilers were on the road, and a scoreboard outside the diner kept a current account of the game in progress. Fans could order a hamburger and malt and listen to the Oilers on their car radios.

Inside, distances to the fences were 330 feet down each line and 390 feet to center field. A covered grandstand, supported by wooden beams, ran from behind home plate a short way past first and third, and a wooden press box sat on the roof. In left field, bleachers had been erected above the fence for the Knot Hole Gang, where young fans could see games for a dime. My friend John J. Kidd and I were too advanced at ages twelve and up to sit in the Knot Hole section, and proudly paid our thirty-five cents to sit with the adults in the bleachers.

Enclosing the vast green carpet of grass, colorful outfield fences advertised Tulsa commercial institutions: Froug's Department Stores, Meadow Gold Milk, the Golden Drumstick Restaurant. The entrance to the tunnel leading to the Oiler's clubhouse adjoined the corner of the right field bleachers and John J. and I hung around there, hoping to pick up a few bits of wisdom from the players.

We saw gritty second baseman Johnny Temple play two seasons for Tulsa in 1951 and 1952 before moving up to the National League. Johnny was a four-time National League all-star for the Reds and made history by being part of the first interleague trade. On December 15, 1959, he was dealt to Cleveland and three players (one of whom was Billy Martin) came to the Reds. We saw Johnny Vander Meer, famous for his double no-hitter with Cincinnati years earlier, play out his career with Tulsa in 1952. He looked ancient to us, and in fact was by baseball standards, but put together a commendable season, going 11–10 with a 2.30 ERA. More notably, he threw his third no-hitter in professional baseball that season, beating Shreveport 12–0. In 1953, Nino Escalera thrilled us by hitting nineteen triples and by sliding into first base on every close play. Given a long look by Cincinnati in 1954, he couldn't hit big-league pitching but he could run and run and run.

Minor league rosters had more stability in the 1950s than they do today. One of my favorite players was Fletcher Robbe, who played with Tulsa from 1950 through 1952. He never made it to the big leagues and didn't exactly set the Texas League on fire, but as the right fielder he was the player nearest to where we always sat and would sometimes say a few words to us between innings.

Every home game, before the bottom of the first, a shrill-voiced

Tulsa supporter would get on the PA system and roar out the Oiler rallying cry, "Lets goooooooooooooooooooooooooo Tulsa!" His name was Andy Andrews and he became a local institution. By the early 1950s, Andy the fan had become an Oiler employee, and listening to his call, we assumed that Tulsa ball games would forever begin with that booming voice bouncing around the park like an echo.

Attendance at Oiler games in the early 1950s was usually four or five hundred, modest by today's standards but impressive to a boy growing up in Collinsville, Oklahoma (population one thousand). Crowds would swell to five or six thousand for the Texas League play-offs, and all around town people would talk about whether Tulsa would make it to the Dixie Series with the Southern Association winner. Championships were always celebrated with downtown parades and were widely reported in newspapers and on the radio.

Lonnie Kidd, John J.'s father, was a frenzied fan who brooked no flaws in Oiler players, and would often have to calm himself by wringing his hands and stomping up and down the bleacher seats after "another boneheaded play." Even in the pickup bed we could hear him on the way home after a loss, cursing and bemoaning Oiler frailties, bad officiating, and devious tricks by the opposition. The game didn't end when Lonnie left Texas League Park on those warm summer evenings in Tulsa.

The same summer I began attending Tulsa Oilers' games, I made a two-week long trip across the South with my father and grandfather. We visited relatives in Tennessee, Georgia, and northern Florida; it was the first time I had left Oklahoma. I saw Spanish moss, watched families leave early in the mornings to pick cotton, and swam in the dark, tepid rivers of the Florida panhandle. I came home carrying an exotic vision of the Deep South in my mind, a wondrous, mystical set of images that endure still today. I learned separately about professional baseball and the South during my twelfth summer, but they became twirled around each other like the softly spun layers of cotton candy sold at concession stands in Texas League Park.

XV

My love affair with baseball has been intense and passionate at times, but it has never been the constant, dogged devotion I have seen in others. Twice I have broken up with the old game, told her to go away, that I didn't want to see her any more. The first time was in the late 1960s, when, for a time, the game lost its traditional balance as pitchers began to dominate. Then Oklahoma idol Mickey Mantle retired in 1968, and as a final straw, the Washington Senators left my adopted city in 1971, moving, ironically, to a new location between the old Texas League towns of Fort Worth and Dallas. The breakup lasted for a few years, and then like a reformed lover, I began to call again. After we made up, I behaved myself as a fan for awhile. The second divorce was in the late 1980s. Lockouts, salary disputes, monetary concerns, and scandals were then taking precedence over the game itself in the media. Who needs you? I said. My attendance at the nearest major league ballpark, Memorial Stadium in Baltimore, dropped from twenty or thirty games a year to only two or three.

Addictions aren't that easy to cure, however. In 1989 a Carolina League team moved to Frederick, Maryland, an easy drive from where I live. I went to one game in Frederick that year, a late season spur-of-the-moment trip I had somehow talked my wife into making, and arrived to find that the game was sold out. A business organization had bought all the tickets and had given away coupons locally for game admission. The ticket offices weren't even open. We walked up to the gate to find out what was going on.

Yes, it was sold out, the gatekeeper said. He asked how far we had come, decided that it was too far to drive and not see a baseball game, and let us in anyway.

I may not have known it at that exact moment, but the love affair was back on; baseball and I were an item once more. Frederick is a handsome little city, sheltered by the low-slung Catoctin Mountains to the west. Clean, with a busy historic district and good restaurants, the town was once described by John Greenleaf Whittier in his poem *Barbara Fritchie:*

> The clustered spires of Frederick stand
> 'neath the green-walled hills of Maryland

In other words, a perfect town for a ballpark. In 1990, the Frederick Keys—named for famous son Francis Scott Key, author of the *Star Spangled Banner*—opened a new park, Harry Grove Stadium. I went often that year, sometimes with others, sometimes stopping by the park alone after a day of fishing the clear trout streams of the Catoctins to the north and west. I was getting reacquainted with minor league baseball, after forsaking it for almost thirty years in favor of the big-time version. During one game that year, as it began to rain, ushers, front office people (including a woman in a skirt and hosiery), concession stand attendants, and even a half dozen fans splashed onto the field and rather ineffectually began to unroll the tarp. Several fell, got up laughing, and walked off the field looking limp and damp. That year attendance soared, fueled by the fact that the Keys had a good ball team.

Zena and I were present at the concluding game of the Carolina League play-offs in September. The Keys were tied with the Kinston Indians, two games apiece. In the final game, Kinston took an early 5–0 lead and still led 5–3 when the Keys mounted a rally in the sixth. With runners on first and second, the public address announcer said the two short words that were the team's rallying call: "Shake 'em!" Cheering and other noises stopped as thousands of fans removed key chains from pockets and purses and in unison, began to gently jangle them, building a melodic, haunting noise like the sounds of a thousand wind chimes at a yoga *ashram*. Tim Holland, whose name will never become a household word among major league fans, hit one over the left field wall, over the three tiers of colorful billboards, out into the night and the Keys held on to win the league championship. Instead of retreating to the clubhouse to celebrate, team officials hustled champagne onto the infield after the last out. As Kinston's defeated Indians slunk toward their team bus, the Keys began tackling each other on the infield grass, spraying champagne wildly, and after soaking themselves, coaches, and others on the field, ran over and began spraying fans who were clustered close enough to the seat rails to be within firing range.

Baseball fans everywhere know that you have to sit through a batch of routine, ultimately meaningless and anticlimactic games to sift out the one where drama, purpose, and well-timed heroics provide a memorable experience. A few even know that this trade-off is not only inevitable, but worth it. This was the one.

Around that time, a plan began to form in my mind. I had been teaching sociology at a college in Maryland for what would amount to twenty-seven years in 1993. At age fifty-four, exactly half my life had been spent in one job. I applied for a study leave for 1993 and at first intended to use it to go out and experience life, then return to teach with more authenticity, to leave familiar environs and return with more to say than when I left. I intended to head south when the baseball season opened, and to follow the region's minor leagues across the South until the South ceased to exist. I arranged a leave, concluded my preliminary research, and readied my transportation. Then, only about two weeks before the scheduled departure, I realized that I wouldn't be returning to the college. As Thoreau said when he left Walden Pond after being there two years, two months, and six days, I couldn't spare any more time for that particular life. I told the necessary people of my intentions, and although technically still on the payroll while on the trip, mentally I had become a free agent; cut loose, unhired, retired; my tenure had expired. The only work I would have when I returned would be whatever I brought with me from the trip. My realization that I had other lives to live had taken me a quarter century longer than Thoreau's, but it was no more revocable.

By late winter two central questions were becoming fixed in my mind. Was the traditional South with its distinctive subculture still down there, or had the second half of the twentieth century homogenized it? I believed the Old South of my youthful memories was alive somewhere, pulled back from the interstates, hiding behind a forest of television antennas and satellite dishes, and that I could find it. Was minor league baseball still an important southern institution, or had the major league penetration into Florida, Georgia, and Texas eclipsed the region's enthusiasm for local teams? I thought, and hoped, that modern day Lonnie Kidds still left the southern ballparks with the devout ravings I had heard in the back of that old bricklayer's pickup.

Questions formed, plans made, gas tank full, I spent February and March the way baseball fans always spend those months: waiting for Opening Day.

Quiet Nights in the Sunshine State

IMPATIENCE LANDED ME IN FLORIDA while opening day for the minor leagues was still a day away. I stopped in Miami Beach for some sight-seeing, and I spent several hours examining the architecture in the art deco district. I have driven fifty miles out of my way to see one art deco structure, so the allure of an entire neighborhood of these flashy, wildly colored structures was irresistible. The district's one square mile contains over four hundred buildings, almost all built in the 1930s during the heyday of art deco construction. Hotels of Miami Beach have all the usual features of the streamline moderne version of art deco, plus vibrant tropical colors. As they took their livelihood from proximity to the ocean, architects added nautical references like porthole windows and balconies reminiscent of decks on a luxury liner.

When I returned to my truck, parked in front of a curved and blocked hotel painted a brilliant yellow and white, I was struck by how well the vehicle blended into the city's aesthetic. My transportation for the trip was a full-sized 1972 Chevrolet pickup, bought new by my stepfather in that long ago year when the country re-elected Richard Nixon and the Vietnam War continued to cut our society into rancorous fragments. I had become its owner just three years previously, after my stepfather's death, and had driven the truck little. Its bright white and two-tone olive paint remained shiny, and it was a fine piece of machinery. Although it had been state of the art twenty-one years ago, nothing on the inside was LED or LCD. Needles fluttered and pointed at numbers, light bulbs behind the dash shone through pieces of red plastic, and the smooth-riding cab seemed to float along the road like a boat plowing through gentle swells. For the trip I had put a camper shell over the pickup bed, a high riser with screened windows on each side for good air circulation and darkened glass for privacy. The eight foot-long bed, six feet wide, provided forty-eight square feet of living space. A sleeping cot ran down one side, and at the foot of the cot a "kitchen" area consisted of cardboard boxes full of campground cooking utensils and a large cooler. Down the other side I had a large cardboard box for my clothes, and plastic crates containing my files and reference material. Storage under the cot for miscellaneous items still left enough free space to set up a folding chair for reading or watching ball games on my tiny five-inch battery-run television set. The pickup sported a chrome hood ornament in the form of a largemouth bass breaking out of the water and peering anxiously toward some distant shore. Grover, my stepfather, had affixed the bass. He was part Cherokee and all fisherman; the truck had built up most of its mileage pulling a boat to a nearby lake for fishing.

I called her Sweetspot. The word can't be found in any dictionary, but everyone who has played baseball knows where it is. When a batter swings and the ball makes contact at the right spot, a feeling of hitting through the ball occurs because there is no vibration. This spot of maximum energy transfer from the bat to the ball is known as the "sweet spot." In his book *The Physics of Baseball*, Robert Adair demonstrates how a vibrational node, or point of no vibration, occurs about thirty inches up from the handle of a thirty-five inch bat. An antinode produces the distortions that can be felt, sometimes painfully, and even result in a broken bat, as contact is made higher (hitting the ball off the end of the bat) or lower down on the handle. Players sometimes say a ball is "fisted" when contact is made at the lower antinode.

When tuned up, Sweetspot's big engine purrs without vibration. No red-blooded Chevrolet, I thought, with a name like Sweetspot could possibly develop mechanical trouble, even on a three-month, seventeen-thousand-mile trip in hot, demanding weather. Just in case, though, I kept the names Breakdown and Disaster in the back of my mind. The truck was twenty-one years old.

I drove out of Miami heading for Homestead, Florida, on US Route 1. The old north-south route begins, or ends, according to your perspective, at Key West and bends into and out of the South Atlantic region, tilts up through the mid-Atlantic, runs through the Holland Tunnel into New York City, and weaves all the way north to the Canadian border in Maine. In many places it parallels an interstate and has been relegated to hosting strips of marginal economic activity. Nowhere is this fate more pronounced than in that stretch known as the Dixie Highway between Miami and Homestead. Here you see strip development at its worst: mile after mile of seedy motels, run-down fast-food places, windowless cinder-block buildings featuring nude revues and adult bookstores. As I approached Homestead, the stripscape began to show signs of damage from Hurricane Andrew, which had roared through in the pre-dawn hours of August 24, 1992, more than seven months earlier, recording winds of 164 miles per hour before the official anemometer blew apart.

Rebuilding had gone slowly in southern Florida. Many buildings were still unoccupied, roofs blown off or damaged and heaps of rubble piled everywhere. Acres of homes remained vacant, with insurance claim numbers painted crudely on front elevations of homes visible from the streets. In the housing developments, people worked on the unlivable ruins, adding to the huge piles of rubble in the yards. Highway and street signs had been blown away, replaced by wooden, hand-lettered versions stuck into the ground. I passed a new home development that advertised "hurricane proof" houses. They were being built of cinder block.

At a little league baseball field, I stopped to talk with some men repairing the damage. The field was in reasonable shape, but the backstop was missing and the bleachers had been blown far away and twisted into uselessness. New aluminum bleachers had just arrived.

"Can't talk long," one said, "we've got to get these bleachers stacked and covered." He looked at the sky as we talked, as if apprehensive that an unannounced hurricane might drop by at any

3

moment. In fact, another serious storm had come through the area since Andrew, further setting back the cleanup.

Even seven months after Andrew, a sense of disorientation prevailed. Natural disasters not only wreak physical havoc, but also alter people's psychological maps. Landmarks disappear, neighbors leave, boundaries become vague, gone are neighborhood gateways and the sense of security one feels when entering a familiar place. The men worked mechanically and without humor. The people of Homestead would need many seasons before the effects of Andrew no longer dominated their lives.

A week after I passed through Homestead, the community received another serious blow. The Cleveland Indians canceled pre-hurricane plans to build a spring training complex in Homestead. They reasoned that the area could not be expected to recover economically, and now it would not receive the millions of dollars from construction, continuing jobs, and increased tourism that would have accrued if the Indians had followed through on their plans. Homestead was becoming the victim of a self-fulfilling prophecy. Investors were deciding that the area could not become economically viable again, and by their actions were assuring that this prediction would become true.

I intended to begin the minor league baseball season on the west coast of Florida, so I picked up US 41, the Tamiami Trail, at the junction with Florida 997. Before crossing, I stopped for gas and when I returned from paying, found an elderly gentleman eyeing the back of Sweetspot.

"Oughtn't to keep a dog in the back there on a day like this. Heat'll kill him."

Taking a cue from David Lamb, an earlier baseball traveler, I had placed a BEWARE OF DOG sign on the back camper window in hopes of discouraging anyone from trying to enter. No one was paying any attention to us, so I said, "I don't really have a dog. Just the sign."

"You ain't got no dog in there?"

"No. I just put the sign up so people would think there was a dog."

"You got a dog at home?"

"No. I have a cat. Her name is Fingers." This, I realized as soon as it was out, was unnecessary, and served to confuse the man more.

"I hope you ain't got no dog in there. Heat'll kill him if you do."

It was hot, around ninety degrees, but the screened windows were open and the white top reflected the heat. I started to explain this, then remembered that the dog was a fiction anyway, and just got in the pickup. Many people asked about the dog during the three-month trip. I usually found it simpler to lie when they asked what kind of dog I had, especially if it was someone who I knew wouldn't ask to see it. The breed became more ferocious each time I told the lie, and the lie became easier and easier to tell.

Driving across the Everglades, I saw people fishing in the canal that runs next to the Tamaimi Trail for much of its length. Almost all of the black people who were fishing sat on the bank and used long cane poles, their corks bobbing in the middle of the water-course. The white fishermen were too sophisticated for such equipment. They took boats out into the narrow canal, and cast back toward the bank with fancy spinning reels and fiberglass rods, fishing exactly the same water reachable with the cane poles.

The Florida State League is a class A minor league, and is the only baseball coalition in which all the teams belong to cities in the same state. Historically, the circuit goes back to 1919 when it was formed as a class D league, and with only the depression years 1929 through 1935 missing, it existed through 1941 at either the class C or D level. The league reformed after the war, and the present setup has been in place since 1946. Under the classification restructuring of 1962, all class B, C, and D leagues were designated class A, where the Florida State League continues. The league is considered by baseball people to be advanced A, and jumps from the Florida State even to the majors are not unknown.

As a setting for player development, the league enjoys many advantages. Not much travel is necessary because the teams reside so close to each other, and an east-west divisional structure makes for even shorter travel time and distances. Most of the teams occupy major league spring training facilities, so their clubhouses, playing fields, and training equipment are superior to class A teams in other leagues. The weather is good even in spring, so few dates are canceled because of rain. The league is a bonus for major league affiliates, who would have to maintain the facilities for spring training anyway.

As community institutions, however, teams of the Florida State League have many shortcomings. The baseball parks are modern but generally synthetic, symmetrical, and without character. Attendance is by far the worst of any advanced A league in baseball. (In 1992 the average attendance for the eleven clubs that fielded teams in 1993 was 86,667. This compared to an average club attendance of 126,240 in the California League and 187,255 in the Carolina League. By the middle of the Miami Marlins' first season in 1993, the big league presence in Florida had helped drop the minor league turnstile count by 100,000.)

Attendance figures can be misleading because clubs give away tickets or sell them at tremendous discounts to sponsors. The Florida State clubs I visited gave away tickets with the best of them. A fan in Port Charlotte went through the list of season promotions and showed me how it was possible to obtain free or reduced-price tickets for most home dates. Even with giveaways, five Florida State franchises had total season attendance figures lower than one 1993 home game of the new Colorado Rockies when they topped eighty thousand fans.

One problem with Florida State League attendance, as former major leaguer Wally Moon pointed out to me later in the trip, is that the fields were set up for major league players. Average fence distances for the parks in 1993 were left—335 feet, center—406 feet, and right—332 feet. More importantly, power alleys of 380 to 390 feet were common. Fans who go to the park to see home runs leave disappointed often in Florida.

The most important reason for lack of fan support, however, is that Florida has fewer of the traditional communities that exist in the rest of the country. Most people are from somewhere else and have little identification with the area aside from the condominium or housing complex in which they live. In other parts of the country, parents take children to games; here, the elderly are separated from families and if they have any allegiance to a baseball team, it is "up north." Even the names of some towns sound like meaningless creations of real estate developers rather than references to the community's history.

Whether cause or effect of low attendance, most of the Florida minor league teams do little to promote community identification with the local club. At Charlotte County Stadium, home of the Charlotte Rangers, I picked up a copy of the program and the first several pages contained feature articles on officials of the parent club, the Texas Rangers. The parent organizations own most of the Florida State teams, an unusual situation throughout minor league baseball. With the exception of the Fort Meyer Miracle, every other club in the league has taken the name of the major league club. But the name Rangers, which means something in Texas because of the historical connection with the Texas Rangers of the nineteenth century, has no significance in Port Charlotte, Florida. Many Florida teams even wear the uniform colors of their big league counterparts.

Charlotte County Stadium is suburban and county oriented rather than community based. The architecture is postmodern, with a cantilevered grandstand roof so small that it provides fans with almost no protection from sun or rain. Charlotte's diamond is its most redeeming feature: beautiful dark green grass with checkerboard cuts in the infield and outfield, and with striking diagonal lines coursing through the grass along the foul lines. Tom Burns, the head groundskeeper, has won well-deserved awards for the immaculately tailored field. Walking up the ramp to a first vision of the field, green and brown with colorfully painted signs as a backdrop and with earthy smells radiating from the plush grass and moistened dirt, a fan could almost forgive the other departures from tradition. The results of the game, a rather lackluster affair in which players from both teams freely displayed evidence of early season rustiness, appeared in neither the Fort Meyer nor the Port Charlotte papers the following day. All I could find were the final Florida State League scores; even box scores were absent.

After the game I drove back to a campground on an island off Fort Meyers Beach. The campsites were just across the dunes from

7

the Gulf of Mexico and the whisper of the surf drifted through swales in the mounds of sand. Pines sheltered the campsites and grew to the inland edge of the dunes. Playing against the sound of the surf, wind whistled softly through the pine needles. Henry Beston, who spent a year living in the isolation of a small shack on a remote part of Cape Cod in the 1920s, set down an account of his life there in *The Outermost House*. He wrote: "The three great elemental sounds in nature are the sound of rain, the sound of wind in a primeval wood, and the sound of outer ocean on a beach." About three o'clock in the morning, I awakened. The wind, coming out of the west, was blowing harder, bending the pines and kicking up the surf more forcefully. As I listened, rain began to pelt Sweetspot's camper roof and, for the only time in my life, I heard all three sounds at once.

The next evening in Sarasota produced a baseball experience much like the one the evening before in Port Charlotte. The stadium, Ed Smith, at least has a name instead of a geopolitical location for a title. Sarasota, a Chicago White Sox farm club, started major league right-hander Dave Stieb. He was on the major league fifteen-day disabled list and had come down to get in shape before rejoining Chicago. Despite the attraction of a major league pitcher, only a few hundred fans were in the stadium. Stieb was probably just as happy that there weren't more fans, since he gave up four runs in the first inning, two on home runs.

I sat behind home plate next to a boy of about twelve or thirteen, one of three alternating batboys Sarasota employed for home games. We began talking about the duties of a batboy—putting out water bottles, picking up bats and other equipment, taking balls to the umpire—and I made a few notes.

"Am I being interviewed?" he asked.

"I thought we were just talking."

His face fell.

"Okay, you got me. I was trying to be cagey about it but you're being interviewed."

He brightened. He told me that his name was Steve Dubois. When I asked him to spell it, he said "S-T-E-V-E."

Steve worked two of every three home games, one each for the

8

home and visiting teams. The third night, which was this night, was his night off. He made five dollars per game plus fringe benefits.

"Which are?" I asked.

"We get to shag flies during batting practice and they give us some of the cracked bats to keep."

At his age, I would have offered to pay the club five dollars a game for a job like that.

On my other side sat a delightful Irish family, the McClory's, who were on vacation in Sarasota and attending their first ever baseball game. Growing up in the United States, even nonbaseball fans absorb some of the language and a general sense of the game. In Ireland, however, there is no such cultural anchorage. I tried to explain the essentials of the game.

"The catcher is signaling the pitcher now for the location and type of pitch he wants, and the batter isn't supposed to look around at the signal."

"The batter would be the chap who wants to strike the ball?" asked Ashley McClory, age fourteen.

The following day was clear and bright. I drove up to St. Petersburg to visit the offices of the National Association of Professional Baseball Leagues, which is the administrative head and governing body of minor league baseball, and the counterpart to major league baseball. Currently there are over two hundred baseball clubs and nineteen leagues in the association. Each league has its own president and officers, and league affairs are managed by these executives under their league bylaws, the National Association Agreement, and the Professional Baseball Agreement (commonly referred to as the PBA), which covers the relationship between the major and minor leagues.

Minor league teams are classified according to the skill level of their players. From highest to lowest, the leagues are classified as: AAA (American Association, International, Mexican, and Pacific Coast Leagues); AA (Eastern, Southern, and Texas Leagues); Advanced A (California, Carolina, and Florida State Leagues); A (Midwest and South Atlantic Leagues); Short Season A (New York-Penn and Northwest Leagues); Advanced Rookie (Appalachian and Pioneer Leagues); and Rookie (Arizona, Dominican Summer, and Gulf Coast Leagues). Except for the AAA level, the leagues are concentrated in geographic areas, with the location usually indicated by the league name. Schedules for the full-season leagues (AAA through A level) are about 140 games beginning in early April and ending, except for play-offs, at the end of August. Short season A level teams begin in mid-June and play about 76 games, while 68 and 60 games are scheduled for the rookie-advanced and rookie levels, respectively.

Five of the full-season leagues are located completely, or almost so, in the southern United States. These are the Florida State League (advanced A), the South Atlantic, or Sally League (A), the Carolina League (advanced A), the Southern League (AA), and the Texas League (AA). The individual clubs of these five leagues were the focus of my summer's route through Dixie.

In any given year, about 5,500 players perform in the minor leagues. In an average year, major league clubs sign 1,500 new players and assign almost all of them to a minor league club. In 1993, only four active players in the major leagues had not played minor league ball (Dave Winfield, Pete Incaviglia, Jim Abbott, and John Olerud). Of that large number of hopefuls, only 5 percent ever suit up in a major league clubhouse. While all minor leaguers have dreams, the reality is that most exist only to provide competition for the few major league prospects and entertainment for local fans.

The Professional Baseball Agreement (PBA) now in force was signed in 1990 and ratified in 1991. This document makes the major league clubs responsible for minor league player, manager, and coach assignments and pay, while minor league clubs (almost all are affiliated with a major league club) negotiate stadium facilities with counties or municipalities, provide local staff to run the clubs, and pay away-from-home travel expenses. The PBA is a far-ranging document, providing rules for such specifics as television revenue sharing and age limits of players at different levels. The current agreement expires September 30, 1997.

Behind Al Lang Stadium on the bay in St. Petersburg, the National Association resides in a one-story building, which is actually a remodeled clubhouse. As I walked toward the door, the blue water of the marina across the street bore bobbing sailboats whose

10

frapping lines merged with the sounds of screeching seagulls. A soft breeze stirred leaves in the palm trees, and the sky was a brilliant blue. I stopped by to talk with Bob Sparks, the association's executive director for special projects, partly to thank him personally for the substantial support he had given me in providing access to the association's ballparks and press facilities during the 1993 season, and to find out if there were any new directions or issues in baseball I should know about.

In Bob's view, the major issues separating minor and major league baseball had already been negotiated, and little was likely to change the next time the agreement reached the table. I asked him about the new independent leagues beginning play in 1993 and 1994. These three new leagues, the Northern in the central north states and Canada, the Texas-Louisiana, and the Frontier in the Appalachian region were throwbacks to the minors of forty years ago when teams, and sometimes entire leagues, operated independent of major league working arrangements, trying to develop players and sell their contracts on the market to a major league team.

"Will the association make overtures to get them into the fold, or will they have to apply to you?"

"The latter," he said. "The problem is that it's tough to make it as an independent, and there are no more affiliations with major league clubs to be had. Some [major league] clubs are even talking about downsizing more, trying to get by with five instead of six or more farm clubs. Maybe going from two A level clubs to one."

The farm system had already changed dramatically. Before the reclassification of 1962, major league clubs might have had as many as seven hundred minor leaguers under contract and would invite them all to spring training. The St. Louis Cardinals, pioneers in the use of minor league clubs as a farm system, once had entire class D minor leagues under their control.

Despite the inevitable shifts of clubs and experimental new leagues, the minors had carved out a new niche in organized baseball in the past few decades, and little was likely to change in the near future.

11

I left Florida's west coast driving toward the midsection on small roads. In Winter Haven, I passed the empty ballpark that had for years been the spring training home of the Boston Red Sox. Each spring had brought Ted Williams down to show the youngsters how to swing a bat the Teddy Ballgame way. After a dispute with city officials about the stadium, the Red Sox moved to Fort Myers in 1992. The Cleveland Indians trained in Winter Haven in 1993, with their future spring training site still uncertain. Winter Haven's franchise in the Florida State League moved to Fort Lauderdale, and the Yankees, who were affiliated with the Lauderdale franchise for years, decided not to field a Florida State team in 1993. In an unrelated move, the Kansas City Royals entry moved from the carnival-like setting of Baseball City to Daytona. This confusing state of affairs led to what every league tries to avoid, an uneven number of teams for the year. With thirteen teams, six teams played each other on a given day, and the odd team was forced into an off day. It was hard to rotate pitchers, make travel arrangements, and get nonpitchers enough times at bat with so many off days.

I had arranged to have lunch in Orlando with a friend and because I was running a little late, tried to save time by driving the tiniest distance down the wrong side of a divided highway before making a turn. A Florida state highway patrolman, bothered by this creative move, laboriously wrote out a ticket, which made me even later for lunch.

I arrived at the designated meeting place apologetic, and piqued, mostly at myself.

"It's all right," said Ellen. "I'm always late myself when I try to go anywhere in a strange city."

She listened sympathetically to my biased version of the ticket encounter, and with patience and politeness managed to calm me down.

"I should have warned you about the highway patrol in Florida," she said. "They can be so . . . exacting." She was the first familiar face I had seen in over a week, and brought the sudden realization that I had set myself up for three months of interaction with strangers.

"Ellen," I said, "I'm homesick."

Trying to be helpful, she said, "Well, you'll only be on the road for eighty more days or so."

Ellen took me to a Cuban restaurant nearby and gradually her good nature, the friendly ambience of the neighborhood cafe, and the good Cuban food began to turn the day around for me. When we ordered iced tea, the waiter asked if we wanted it sweet or un-sweet, as they do in the South nowadays. Years ago, they just poured it out of a pitcher, thick as syrup.

As we ate black beans and rice, Ellen told me about growing up in a small town in northern Florida, away from the tourist trade, which was Florida's main industry today. She spoke with a soft southern accent, perfect for reinforcing the images of a rural, mostly vanished Florida of the past. One of my reasons for making the trip was to see if the old virtues of charm, grace, and manners that had been traditional still existed, or whether that part of the South was gone. Eventually it occurred to me that there they were, sitting across the table from me, sipping sweetened ice tea.

After lunch, as I drove through Orlando to Kissimmee to see the Osceola Astros play baseball, Sweetspot's AM radio honed in on radio station WHAL, which billed itself as a Christian news station; the newscasters referred to it as "The Good News Station." The good news disc jockey was talking about a traffic jam, which was bad news, but more useful than good news might have been. WHAL broadcast an unusual mix of music, news, weather, and Christian messages. ("We have a travel special this week. A free trip to heaven. See your local church on Sunday for details.") Be-tween thirty-year-old songs, the broadcaster told jokes, quoted passages of scripture, and interpreted their meanings for contem-porary life. Central Florida didn't look much like the Old South, but it was beginning to sound like it.

Since it was still too early to go to the ballpark, I drove into downtown Kissimmee, home of the Osceola Astros. I was early, and decided to kill some time by asking about the local ball team. My hastily designed survey consisted of going into six business estab-lishments and asking the same question: "How do I get to the park where the Osceola Astros play?" The question wasn't entirely gra-

13

tuitous; I had the general bearing from my *Baseball America Directory*, but didn't know the exact location.

The answers:

1. "They aren't here anymore. They left about a week ago." (This was a reference to the Houston Astros having completed spring training.)

2. "I think they're somewhere up in Orlando."

3. "I don't know." (This was a girl in an ice cream store, who then offered to call her boyfriend to find out. She thought he had been to a game once.)

4. "Which school? There are three."

5. "If they play where I think they play, take 192 east and it'll be on your left." (He was right, although he said he had never been to a game there.)

I concluded my highly unscientific survey by asking the question of a middle-aged couple who were leaving a store. They looked at each other blankly. "We're not from here," the woman said. "We're from Orlando." Orlando is about twenty miles north of Kissimmee.

I decided that I wouldn't have a lot of trouble finding a seat at the stadium that evening.

Osceola County Stadium was similar to others I had seen in the Florida State League. Fences were deep (330 feet to left and right, 410 feet to center, twin 390 feet power alleys) and everything on and off the field was symmetrical. Here, though, even the most ubiquitous symbols of minor league baseball were missing. The outfield fence was green mesh instead of the brightly painted signs that everywhere else lend a splash of color and character to the green and brown of the diamonds. Cypress trees beyond the right field fence helped soften the angular, regular lines a little.

I went up to the press box to pick up a media packet of player statistics. The general manager, Tim Bawmann, was on his walkie-talkie instructing an assistant to start checking tickets. A few hundred fans were in attendance, and almost all of them were in box seats, many, Tom guessed, illicitly. Whatever other reasons they might have had, fans weren't staying away because of ticket prices:

$3.50 for box seats, $2.50 for general admission, and $1.50 for seniors and children.

I spent the evening talking with Chris White, an Astros' pitcher who was charting pitches from a seat behind home plate. The next day's starting pitcher usually logs pitches to help familiarize him with the other team's hitters. Chris had worked the opener three days ago, going six innings with no decision, giving up three hits and one run.

"The [pitching] coach has us on a pitch count," he explained. "Eighty pitches and you're out of there, no matter what the situation."

Chris, a friendly, good-looking right-hander with a typical baseball build, six feet even, 180 pounds, had been drafted while in college in the twentieth round of the June 1991 draft by the Houston organization. Just short of age twenty-four, he was in his third year in professional baseball. In the New York–Penn short season league in 1991, he appeared mainly as a reliever. In 1992, as a starter for the Asheville Tourists in the South Atlantic league, Chris had gone 13–4 with a 3.38 earned run average. Both years he had excellent strike out-to-walk ratios, but the Astros were bringing him along slowly. Many of the current Osceola Astros had been at Asheville the year before and had been promoted together.

As we talked, Chris said all the right things about having a lot to learn about pitching but I was impressed with what he already knew. I talked him into playing a game by covering up the radar gun he was using to log the Astro pitcher's velocity and having us both guess speeds. Fastballs, consistently in the upper eighties, breaking ninety occasionally, were fairly easy, but curves and change-ups were harder. I would sometimes misjudge their speeds by up to ten miles per hour, but Chris hardly needed the gun.

"I was only over ninety once in the opener," he offered.

I asked if it bothered him to pitch to empty stands.

"I have to stay focused the same whether they're empty or full," he said. But then he told me about pitching before twenty thousand fans once in a summer league game. "I was pumped," he admitted.

Chris was born and lived awhile in Richmond, Virginia, which made him a southerner. He moved with his family, however, to

15

Greenville, Pennsylvania, in the northwest part of the state. He attended Cleveland State College and was articulate and well informed. At one point, he asked me, "Are you just a writer or do you have another profession?"

I told him that I was a college professor.

"I knew it," he said. "I can spot them." He should be able to; his father is a professor of philosophy at Teal College. Unlike most players I met during the trip, Chris seemed genuinely interested and asked a lot of questions about what I was doing. When I mentioned that I was going all the way to El Paso, he said "Why don't you just hang around Kissimmee all summer and write about the Osceola Astros drive to the Florida State pennant?"

I looked around at the smattering of deathly quiet fans and shuddered. "I'll just mosey on out west," I told him.

The Astros ran a couple of contests during the game. One was to guess the attendance. "Can't anyone just walk around for a few minutes and count the attendees?" I asked Chris. The crowd was announced a few innings later at 327, but by that time I would have challenged anyone to produce more than 100 bodies. Another contest featured the team mascot, Quazzie. Quazzie was supposed to represent something about the space program to reflect Houston's astronaut theme. The mascot wore a large orange fuzzy costume and was on the cover of the souvenir program ("QUAZZIE ENTERTAINS ALL FANS WITH HIS CRAZY ANTICS.") A ten-year-old boy raced Quazzie around the bases between innings. The prize, a free meal at Hooters, a restaurant chain featuring scantily clad waitresses and a full bar, seemed like an odd choice to offer a ten-year-old, but he won it. The kid really ran fast.

The players I met on the trip were a mixed bag, as were the nonplayers. I later exchanged a few words with another young man about the same age as Chris. I was sitting in the dugout during batting practice when he came off the field and threw his glove down on the bench next to where I was sitting. I picked it up and said "Gloves are bigger than they used to be when I played."

"When was that?" he asked absently.

"Oh, back in the twenties." That would have made me at least ninety years old.

16

"Hey. Long time ago," he said, his eyes vacantly following the line drives coming out of the batting cage.

I picked up State Highway 19 north of Orlando and drove through the Ocala National Forest. The rivers and creeks ran dark from the tannin leaching out of the pine tree roots. I stopped for a quick lunch of yogurt, fruit, and granola near a boat ramp on the Oklawaha River. Water lilies covered the surface of the dusky water and Spanish moss draped the trees that overhung the river banks. After eating I walked over to a quiet pool downstream from the ramp. An elderly man wearing bib overalls was fishing there. We talked for a minute and he showed me a spot in the water near a stump where he'd seen a "nigger man settin' here yesterday pullin' 'em in fast as he could throw his line back out."

The word rolled off his tongue as if it were neutral, like any other word in his description. The disturbing part wasn't that there was malice behind the epithet "nigger," but that there was no apparent feeling at all. I cut the conversation short and walked back to Sweetspot. Soon afterwards, I began chiding myself for running away. I had come to see if the Old South was still there, and when one of the darker parts of it had surfaced, had indignantly turned my back.

Ellen and the old fisherman represented, at least for me, two extremes of the southern tradition. And I knew that I wouldn't find an honest answer to the question of the South's character by walking away from any part of the Dixie heritage.

2

Some Georgia Peaches, Past and Present

MY GOAL FOR THE EVENING was Arthur Grayson Stadium in Savannah, Georgia, but instead of driving straight up the coast from Florida, I angled off to the left, going inland on US 1 out of Jacksonville. This route led through Waycross, Georgia, and I wanted to investigate a possibility. Those who love old ballparks, who like seeing the way they were built to snuggle into the neighborhoods surrounding them, seeing their infinite varieties of grandstands, roofs, facades, and fences, imagining past crowds of people decked out in styles that now seem quaint and innocent, those folks have a problem. No comprehensive reference for minor league ballparks exists. The closest thing is Michael Benson's *Ballparks of North America: A Comprehensive Historical Reference to Baseball Grounds, Yards and Stadiums, 1845 to Present*, which covers only 376 cities, including those with major league parks. Towns that have fielded minor league teams number 1,247 in the United States alone, many with multiple ballparks over the years. To discover if a former minor league town has a ballpark still standing and in what condition, you have little recourse but to do as I did: go and look.

Minor league baseball in the South has been subject to the same ebb and flow that swept the sport along in other parts of the country. The minors were notoriously unstable in the nineteenth century, but beginning with the 1902 season, the National Association

19

of Professional Baseball Leagues was in place and order became the rule. Fifty-two leagues began the 1910 season, a high-water mark until the late 1940s. World War I caused an attrition of leagues, but the 1920s produced a postwar boom, which hitched a ride on the prosperous economy and the good fortunes of major league baseball after the lively ball was introduced. The economic depression of the 1930s struck minor league baseball hard; by 1933, only fourteen leagues were in operation. But the advent of night baseball provided cheap entertainment, and the establishment of minors as farm systems and major league ownership of minor league players became permanent during the depression. World War II disrupted minor league baseball again as it did other aspects of life in the country. In 1942, such longstanding leagues as the Florida State and the Evangeline folded in the South, and by 1943, only nine leagues in the entire country completed the season. After World War II, minor league baseball reached its zenith. By 1949, fifty-nine leagues were in operation, with thirty-one, more than half the total, located in the South or Southwest. Georgia alone had entries in three class D leagues, the Georgia State, Georgia-Alabama, and Georgia-Florida Leagues.

After World War II, returning southern soldiers had a pocketful of money but the production of houses, new appliances, and new cars still lagged behind demand, leaving people with dollars to spend on recreation. Every small southern town had a movie theater and a pool hall to siphon off available entertainment dollars, but many towns as small as one or two thousand could also boast minor league teams. They were often at the lowest classification but provided a place to sit in the open air, an important consideration before air conditioning. Postwar attendance swelled, producing a golden age of the minor leagues. Over forty million fans went through the turnstiles in minor league parks annually in the late 1940s, and nationwide over four hundred towns fielded and supported teams. In small Georgia towns like Vidalia, Valdosta, Americus, and Waycross, folding wooden signs would be put out on a main intersection on summer mornings announcing "Game Tonight," with the time and name of the local baseball park. Sometimes the parks had no names; in the small southern town, there was no real need for a formal designation.

The bubble burst with disastrous results for the minors beginning in the early 1950s, in a way that almost no one had foreseen. When I first began attending minor league games in Tulsa around 1950, the infrastructure was already beginning to decay, though few realized it at the time. Gradually, televised major league games drew attention away from local teams, suburbanization drew people physically away from downtown ball parks, and the growing popularity of professional football combined to produce a sharp decline in minor league baseball that lasted for a quarter century. In 1962, the lowest levels of minor league baseball leagues (classifications B, C, and D) were abolished. This was the final admission that small towns couldn't, or wouldn't, support minor league ball. The goal for organized baseball eventually became to have one hundred minor league clubs survive, as feeders of the major league organizations—just one-fourth the number of teams that had flourished in the late forties.

Again, unpredicted, the late 1970s saw a resurgence in minor league baseball's popularity. Many, myself included, became disillusioned with major league baseball in the 1980s and discovered, or rediscovered, the game at a simpler, purer level. For others, it may have been just an extension of a gradual resurgence of interest at the major league level. Attendance picked up once more in minor league parks, but with several differences. By the early 1990s, twenty-six million fans were attending games, but the number of cities with teams was still small compared to the pretelevision years. No longer was simply announcing that a baseball game would be played enough to market the product. Minor league games were now part of an entertainment package, and front office club officials were more comfortable in discussing promotions and target populations than in detailing the caliber of team play.

Waycross, Georgia, had fielded minor league teams periodically from 1906 through 1963, when the Georgia-Florida League folded. In the nineteenth century, it had been known as the "crossing of the ways" because several railroad lines intersected there. I

21

drove into town prepared to spend hours locating its last professional ballpark but was pleasantly surprised to see what could only
have been a minor league baseball stadium standing prominently
off the highway near the center of town. Memorial Stadium reposed
like a grand brick and concrete relic, refreshingly quaint and archaic compared to the amorphous new parks of Florida.

The stadium was in use; its parking lot hosted a used car market.
Sonny Bland, who worked for the city and was in charge of the
stadium, was working there as I drove up. I asked if it would be
okay to wander through and take some pictures, and he gave me a
brief history of the park. It had been built in 1948 and '49 during
the postwar heyday of minor league baseball. The concrete and
steel construction indicated a feeling of permanence and surety that
minor league baseball would always be a part of the city, an understandable feeling in those last few pretelevision years. The grandstand roof was in good repair and steel supporting posts had been
made deliberately thin to minimize obstruction of sight lines. The
most surprising feature was size. Sonny said that twelve thousand
could be accommodated in stationary seats, and up to fifteen thousand when temporary chairs were added. Its major use today was
for high school football but even in a football configuration, the
old park was obviously meant as a place to see the summer game.
Waycross's chamber of commerce had been trying to attract a
minor league baseball club, but had run up against the usual problem. Without a player development contract from a major league
team, professional baseball simply was not realistic in the 1990s.

As I headed up US 84 toward Savannah, the AM radio cracked
and weather forecasters warned of tornadoes in southern Georgia.
Fields had been plowed for planting and dust devils swirled across
the highway. Here on the coastal plain the soil was dark, not the
red clay common to the hill country of northern Georgia. Rain
slapped the windshield, the wind bearing the clouds northeast in
the same direction I was going. I wasn't sure that there would be a
game in Savannah that evening. The clouds were ominous, dense
with vertically developed shapes, like those that can drop a twister
at any time.

An hour before game time, however, the weather had improved

somewhat. The approach to Arthur Grayson Stadium in Savannah was through wide streets lined with live oaks, shrouded in Spanish moss. Beautiful Greek Revival mansions, many of them antebellum, were set back from the street amidst parklike landscaping. The well-seasoned baseball field, built in 1925, was a small, red-brick structure lying partly hidden by moss draped from the many trees accommodated by unpaved squares in the concrete parking lot. Inside, seats were painted red and blue, and beyond the left and center-field walls a large stand of pines formed a backdrop. Because of its picturesque presentation, Grayson Stadium was one of the parks used in director John Badham's 1976 movie about the Negro Leagues, *The Bingo Long Traveling All-Stars and Motor Kings.*

The left-field fence was 290 feet from home plate, but the short distance had been legitimized somewhat by a wire screen about twenty feet high and extending along the fence for approximately 100 feet. The right-field line was 310 feet. Power alleys were not marked but were fairly deep. With a 400-foot drive necessary to carry the center field fence, home runs weren't particularly cheap unless pulled directly down the right-field line.

The Savannah Cardinals, a St. Louis farm club, were not one of minor league baseball's most affluent franchises. Attendance in 1992 was under eighty thousand, which put them near the bottom of the South Atlantic League. A temporary building lying just inside the gates to the stadium housed the club offices. This was the season's first Bleacher Bum Night, a promotion in which for $5.00, "bums" could go to the picnic area beside the left field foul line and enjoy an hour of unlimited hot dogs and beer. Afterward, they weaved over to the left field bleachers and sat down, looking groggy. I went to the concession stand instead and had a jalapeno hot dog (hot!) for two dollars, a beer (tepid) for two dollars, and a box of popcorn (cold) for one dollar.

The press box at Grayson was a flimsy affair reached by climbing stairs at the top of the grandstand and walking across a catwalk to a small compartment with two tiny booths hanging from the roof like a cabin on a dirigible. Three men ran everything. One kept score, the second served as public address announcer and scoreboard operator, and the third played the organ. No press was to be seen, though the *Savannah Morning News* carried an article on the game the following morning.

"Where's the play-by-play person?" I asked.

"No radio," one answered.

Until the game began, they occupied themselves with passing around a pair of binoculars, focusing on various women in the stands, and commenting, usually unfavorably, about their physical attributes.

When the game began, the Hickory Crawdads began crawling all over the Savannah Cardinals. The Crawdad pitcher, Mickey McKinnon, had his slider working well. He kept it at the batters' knees, coaxing groundouts and strikeouts. In the second, a Hickory batter lined a solo home run just inside the left field foul pole over the screen, and they later added an unearned run, blanking Savannah 2–0.

The three club employees began eating boiled peanuts, delivered from a concession stand. They threw the dusky shells on the floor, and in a few minutes the press box looked like it had an infestation of cockroaches. Wind whistled into the small booth, which vibrated and swayed noticeably every time a gust hit it broadside.

"Does it always feel like this up here?" I asked.

"Hell, this ain't nothin," said the scorer.

In a few minutes, and obviously for my benefit, he said casually to the PA announcer, "Did you know this box ain't held on by nothin' but two bolts?"

The combination of the jalapeno dog (hot!) and the sickly swaying of the press box was producing more than a mild nausea. I got up, stomach churning, and tried to navigate the catwalk without looking down.

Solid ground and fresh air brought some equilibrium to my system, so I walked out to the left field bleachers. In the seventh inning, thirty-five or forty "bums" remained, and, surprisingly, considering their red, bleary eyes, were talking baseball. A woman noticing my camera with a long lens and lens hood, started shouting for me to take her picture. I did, and this prompted several other requests. To save film, I just pretended to shoot pictures and

24

faked cocking the rewinder. Everyone was happy and I asked several people about the teams' prospects, receiving foggy predictions filtered through the haze of a heavy beer promotion.

Outside Savannah the next morning, I stopped for breakfast in a truck stop and sat at the counter next to a large, rough-looking trucker. I ordered a cheese omelet, grits, and biscuits, and the trucker ordered toast and coffee. When the waitress returned with the orders she looked at us, looked at the plates, gave him the omelet and me the toast. We sorted out our orders and began talking. More accurately, he told me almost his entire life story in about twenty minutes, while smoking four cigarettes, and I ate breakfast and listened. He was, like myself, a fringe southerner by birth, but had lived and worked in the South much of his life and spoke with a pronounced southern accent. He had the fierce autonomy of not only the southern white male but also the independent trucker, the "last cowboy." The incidents he related from his life all ended the same way. Someone offended him and he summarily told them to "Kiss my ass!" One unsettling story concerned a company he worked for several years ago, which developed a voluntary retirement plan, and he decided that it cost too much. In his words, "I told them they could kiss my ass on that retirement plan. What good is a retirement plan that costs so much that I cain't feed my wife and kids when I'm not retired?"

The *Savannah Morning News* box score announced the attendance of the previous evening's game as 718. This must have included season ticket holders who hadn't attended the game, but it had been a large crowd compared to the Florida State League games I had attended. Furthermore, the Savannah fans, only seven games into the season, had learned the names of the players and were vocal and rowdy, a change from the hushed ballpark atmospheres in Florida.

Savannah is a member of the class A South Atlantic, or Sally League, whose teams I would be visiting over the next few weeks. The league was formed in 1904 and ran, with the usual interruptions for wars and the depression, at the class C, then B, and finally A levels up through 1962. Small cities in Georgia and the Carolinas comprised its main membership, with a few entries over the years from Alabama, Tennessee, Virginia, and West Virginia. In the early 1960s, the old Southern Association folded and the new Southern League was formed from the South Atlantic League's cities. Later a new Sally League at the A level became successor of the Western Carolinas League in 1980 and had been active since. In 1993, the league had fourteen entries divided into northern and southern divisions and stretched from Hagerstown, Maryland, to Albany in southwest Georgia. Some of the oldest, smallest and most unusual baseball parks in professional baseball are in the Sally League, many of which I would see in the next few weeks.

Out of Savannah, I dropped down to state highway 144 and drove across the middle of Georgia toward Macon. In Glenville, I saw my first Confederate flag on the trip, flying in front of the high school. In the small towns, houses had front porches with swings, and sidewalks framed well-kept lawns. The front porch was an almost perfect solution to socializing in the small southern town, a transition between inside and outside. Sitting on the swing in the evening welcomed those who were out walking to stop and chat for awhile, and relieved the hosts from inviting the strollers inside. Many of the houses had huge banks of azaleas in the front yards, and in mid-April they were in full bloom.

Vidalia, famous for onions, had a minor league team in the class D Georgia State League from 1948 through 1956, so I stopped to inquire about the fate of the baseball park. After several false leads, I learned the names of two former players who still lived in town and telephoned them. Nothing remains of the ballpark today, I was assured. Its location was now part of a strip of fast-food restaurants and new car showrooms; the park, which either didn't have a name or the name has been forgotten, was torn down to provide parking for K-Mart and Piggly Wiggly stores. I heard some good stories about the old teams though, including the fact that Mays Dobbins' career ended because of overindulging in ham and redeye gravy before playing on a hot summer afternoon. Richard Herring remembered that the park was shared by a "nigra" team, whose players, he thought, were more talented than those on the white professional team. I didn't like finding out, though, that one of the diamonds of Dixie was buried under a K-Mart parking lot.

Macon, Georgia, was one of the jewels of the South. The city was laid out southwest of the Ocmulgee River, and the older residential sections overlooked the downtown business district from a sizeable hill. Many of the large homes on the hill were antebellum mansions spared by Sherman on his destructive trek to the sea. I put aside my guidebook because there was so much of interest not mentioned, and hiked back and forth across the hill taking in the Old South scenery. The buildings were a broad mix of nineteenth- and twentieth-century styles, from stately Greek Revivals to a snappy art deco launderette at the edge of the commercial district. The azaleas and dogwoods were in bloom, framing the houses with those most southern of blossoms. On Mulberry Street, I passed the Old Cannonball House, which took a Union round during the war, and on High Street the birthplace of Sidney Lanier, Georgia's greatest poet. Macon was a bonus, and reminded me that not all the diamonds of Dixie have four bases and smell like hot dogs.

Luther Williams Field in Macon was the main park used for filming *The Bingo Long Traveling All-Stars and Motor Kings*. The film concerned the period just before integration of professional baseball, and the two main characters, played by James Earl Jones and Billy Dee Williams, were based loosely on Josh Gibson and Satchel Paige. Outfield fence signs were covered in green for the film, and a few other atmospheric changes were made, but the park needed little modification to serve as a period piece. Seating capacity was only 3,700 and besides the grandstand, which ended between home and the corner bases, only a small set of tin bleachers extended down the right field line. Although there were eight light stanchions, each had only eight lights, adding to the quaint, old-fashioned look of the park.

I went out to the field several hours before game time to watch batting practice. The Columbus (Ga.) Redstixx were in town, and looking through their media notes, I spotted the name of a player whose hometown was listed as Potomac, Maryland. Derek Hacopian and I lived only a few miles apart in Maryland, and I looked him up when batting practice was finished. He seemed glad to talk with someone from home. Derek was dark, handsome, and frequently flashed a pleasant smile. This was his second year in professional baseball. He had been drafted in 1992 after establishing solid athletic credentials at Churchill High School in Potomac, then at Montgomery College and the University of Maryland, where he was Atlantic Coast Conference player of the year and an all-American. In the short season New York-Penn League in 1992, he had hit a respectable .311 with nine home runs and forty-six runs batted in. He seemed disappointed in how the current year was going, appearing in five of the eight games with only sixteen at bats, and hitting .250. "And I'm DHing a lot." I promised to stay in touch and follow his progress throughout the season.

Before I even left the Sally League a few weeks later, his name had started appearing in the top ten in batting statistics. At season's end, Derek had a .315 batting average, good for third in the league, with twenty-four home runs and eighty-two runs batted in. He continued to be used in the designated hitter role, however, and by midseason the media were regularly referring to Derek Hacopian as "D.H. the DH."

In Macon, I concentrated on talking to ballplayers' relatives and significant others. Beverly Hatcher attended a game to watch her fiance, Terrence Brock, perform as Macon's starting pitcher. She was a Florida State University student, close to graduation, pretty and blond, and not really a baseball fan at all. She and Terrence had been engaged for six years, since high school. First college and now his career had delayed marriage. She wanted to go to law school, but was uncertain about her fiance's baseball future and whether to postpone her own career. The immediate plan was for her to spend the summer working in Macon where Terrence pitched, and then to evaluate how things were going.

At Florida State, Terrence Brock had been a right fielder. He switched positions after Atlanta drafted him in 1992, in the twelfth round, and went 6–4 with a 2.31 earned run average for Idaho Falls, a rookie league team. Despite Terrence's good beginning, Beverly seemed realistic about the long odds of making it to the major leagues. We were sitting together and talking five or six rows up behind home plate. "I hope he doesn't think I'm hitting on you and let it affect his pitching," I said.

She laughed. "He's so focused on the mound, I don't think he even knows I exist while he's pitching."

She may have been right. He went five innings, allowed two hits, no runs, struck out six, and didn't come looking for me after the game.

Next game one of the staff told me that Terrell Buckley's family was in the stands. I asked his small crowd of relatives if I could sit through the game with them and ask a few questions about Terrell. His mother, sister, cousin, and fiance were in town for the weekend from Pascagoula, Mississippi, a ten-hour drive to Macon. They all planned to see Terrell play as often as possible during the season.

Terrell grew up in Pascagoula and emerged as a two-sport athlete, although his baseball experience was limited. Last season (1992), he had been an all-rookie cornerback for the National Football League's Green Bay Packers. The Atlanta Braves, who seem to be partial to football players despite the Deion Sanders experience, drafted Terrell out of Florida State University in the thirty-eighth round. Their interest was based on his basic athletic ability rather than proven baseball skills, for Terrell had only thirteen at bats and two hits in his college career. After the June draft, there was no time to play him in a rookie or short season A league because of training camp with the Packers, so he missed the 1992 baseball season. He trained with the Braves in West Palm Beach in spring 1993, and they were impressed enough with his ability to assign him to a class A team, agreeing to his reporting for summer camp with the Packers in July. Terrell had signed for a reported $6.2 million with Green Bay. His monthly pay with the Macon Braves was $850.

No one in Terrell's family had any doubt that he would be in the majors within three years. They had seen his success with the Packers and had spent years reading positive publicity about his superb athletic skills, and assumed that baseball stardom would come easily. That evening, however, Terrell was hitting .190 and had struck out six times in twenty-one times at bat. I asked Laura Buckley, his mother, whether she would rather Terrell had finished college before signing with the Packers.

"Whatever he wants, that's what I want for him," she said.

29

His fiance, Denise Ramirez, was a little more forthcoming.

"Frankly, big-time sports is where the big bucks are. They aren't in having a college degree by your name."

As a Ph.D. driving around the country in a twenty-one-year-old pickup, I was in no position to argue with her.

About a week later, I caught up with Terrell in Columbia, South Carolina, and met him after the game in his hotel room. He had a sliding "strawberry," a circular scrape on his hip about two inches in diameter, and had undressed because of the discomfort from clothing.

"Sometimes," he said a little self-consciously, "these things hurt more than real injuries."

Terrell Buckley was a handsome, even featured black man with two wide gold chains around his neck. At 5'10" and a muscular 175 pounds, he seemed to have the ideal build for baseball—compact, powerful, and speedy. In the batting cage, though, he hadn't appeared comfortable that afternoon, fouling off batting practice speed pitches despite his obviously good bat speed and command of the entire plate. He couldn't get in a groove with consistent solid contact, and his timing just wasn't there. I asked if the switch to a wooden bat from the aluminum bats, which were standard in college and high school, had a big effect.

"No, but I didn't play enough in college to get that used to an aluminum bat." He admitted, though, that this year was the first time at any baseball level where the greater precision required by wood was a factor. He had only one extra-base hit and was striking out a lot.

I hadn't seen Terrell play enough to judge his skills in the outfield, but on routine flies during batting practice, he seemed to be nonchalant, even appearing to loaf. When a ball was hit over his head, however, a glimpse of the instincts necessary to make a good outfielder flashed unmistakably.

"I'm a cornerback," he said. "I don't have any trouble breaking back on a ball." The only part of his game of concern, he claimed, was lack of arm strength on throws from the outfield to home plate. "But that will come."

The longer we talked, the more obvious it became that his central identity and interest was in football. Terrell said, though, that he was giving himself three years to make the major leagues, and if he did, he wanted to play both sports as long as possible. He was adjusting to the travel required by professional baseball, but didn't like it. Also, he seemed annoyed at the length of the baseball season.

"Why," he asked me seriously, "is a baseball season so long?"

That was a hard question for me to answer, because I had always considered a baseball season too short.

Things were in disarray at Paul Eames Sports Complex in Albany, Georgia, when I arrived. The previous evening had seen the first South Atlantic League game at the brand new stadium, and the front office staff had just moved into its new offices. I saw unpacked boxes and smelled fresh paint everywhere, the police were meeting in the unpaved parking lot about traffic patterns, and the sod on the field had only been down for two weeks. It hadn't taken yet and the grass was a dull shade somewhere between green and tan. Only on the field did anything seem normal, as the players and coaches followed familiar, reassuring rituals: stretch, jog, hit, field, run the bases.

The Albany Polecats were scheduled that evening to play the Charleston Rainbows in their second home game of the season. This was Albany's second season in the league, and there was high excitement and enthusiasm in the city over the return of professional baseball after an absence of thirty-four years. "Polecats" is an unlikely nickname because of the reputation of skunks, but Albany teams of the past had a tradition of colorful names. From 1911 to 1916, a team in the earlier class B Sally League was nicknamed "Babies" because Albany was the smallest city in the circuit; and from 1926 to 1928, the team was known as the Albany "Nuts" because of the local pecan industry.

Lorie Baran, the director of press box operations officially, and about one hundred other things unofficially, was assigned to sponsor me and probably keep me out of other people's hair. Despite the overall dither, the staff was friendly and was having fun, taking the move in stride and generally laughing about the numerous shakedown problems.

31

Paul Eames had a large playing field. The distances hadn't been painted on the fences yet, but I was told that they ran 325 feet to left, 415 feet to center, and 334 feet to right. The paint on the advertising signs on the outfield was so new and bright that it hurt to look at them in the late afternoon sunlight. One of Lorie's jobs was to run the scoreboard during the game. The board was controlled by a pad in the press box, but it had been left on all night and had overheated. Numbers would stay on the board for a few seconds, then disappear. Random numbers would then begin popping up all over the scoreboard, puzzling the fans, who were pointing and trying to figure out what was going on.

Paul Eames, after whom the park was named, was a fixture around the stadium. Paul had played and managed in the low minors from 1945 to 1955, and was director of parks in Albany. He had been influential in obtaining the current minor league franchise for the city, and in the public relations effort necessary to float $4 million in bonds for the new park. A likeable, good-natured man, Paul had the typical build of a catcher—short and stocky. Now in his sixties, he had bad knees caused by years of squatting behind home plate.

"I never met a man who had a stadium named after him," I said.

He grinned. "Because they're usually dead, that's why."

Paul had had some pop in his bat, one year hitting .317 with eighteen home runs. He caught behind a young minor league Willie Mays on a day when Willie went five for five. He hit against Satchel Paige, or as he said "against the sound of the ball going by."

Paul played when minor league teams had salary caps, when independent teams made their money by selling the contracts of players who had good years. Many owners therefore paid players under-the-table money as incentives for them to excel and increase their market value. "When I played for Smithfield [Virginia], the owner owed me $1,500, a lot of money in those days, and I tried all winter to get it out of him," Paul told me. "Then the Dodgers signed me to come to Vero Beach the next spring, but I didn't have enough money to get all the way there. I caught the train to Durham, North Carolina, where [the owner] lived, and knocked on his door in the middle of the night. He didn't have any money on him, so I grabbed his arm and took him to his filling station he owned, and he only had $700. He said he was going to tell the police I held him up. I didn't think he would but instead of going to the bus station, I caught a cab to the truck stop and paid a driver $50 to let me ride to Florida."

I heard several variations on the same story from old ballplayers during the trip, which indicates that underhanded practices were apparently quite common. When I mentioned going through Waycross to see the stadium, Paul told me that he had been player-manager there in 1954 when the Georgia-Florida League was integrated. Their first black player was an outfielder named Jones, and according to Paul, "He looked like an ink blot in that white home uniform. We packed the stadium during that first home stand. I guess people knew that there were black players on white teams other places, but no one had ever seen it in Waycross, Georgia."

Jones went three for fifty-five because every pitcher he faced threw at him. Paul's theory was that the lower minors eventually folded in the South because teams couldn't find places for black players to stay after integration. "The team bus was Jones's hotel," he said.

Paul Eames was an interesting, colorful part of Albany, Georgia, and well deserving of having a stadium named after him. All those communities with ballparks named County Stadium, Municipal Field, or some such should take note and honor their own local legends.

Paul told me that Americus, Georgia, had an interesting old ball-park still standing from days when they fielded a minor league team in the class D Georgia-Florida League, so I drove up the thirty miles from Albany to see it. The grandstand is one of the few remaining made from wood, most of that variety by now having burned down or rotted away. A police officer sitting in her cruiser near the field told me that the park had recently been renovated, with convicts doing much of the labor. Since almost all stadiums today are owned and maintained by cities or counties, and these political units control a population of prisoners, this solution to holding down labor costs is not at all rare. The field is used by the local high school team and is well maintained, though it falls far

33

short of professional standards. The old wooden outfield fences have been replaced by a chain-link barrier, but distances remain the same and are too long for high school players. Each line measures 330 feet, and it takes 405 feet to carry dead straight center field. The wooden grandstand has exposed rafters visible from the seats, and from outside the stadium, the wooden front has a layer of slanted boards, which gives the top five or six feet a louvered effect.

The old park will live on in film, whatever its fate in real life. In the mid-1980s, a biography of Bear Bryant, the longtime Alabama football coach, used the park for location shooting because it evoked the types of stadiums where Bear coached as a young man.

The town of Americus has a good record in historic preservation. The downtown Windsor Hotel, dating from 1892, has recently undergone a five million dollar restoration. The restored building is an impressive Victorian structure. All brick, it takes in an entire city block with surfaces of various textures, and turrets, towers, tall chimneys, porches, bays, verandas, and Romanesque windows with Second Empire-type dormers. The hotel would show best on a chilly, misty November afternoon, but it is clearly magnificent any time.

Unlike the good folks of Americus, many communities would agree that it is reasonable to restore a landmark structure like a downtown hotel, but would have no compunctions about razing a baseball park. Yet minor league parks have been gathering places for thousands of community residents, often over several decades. History has been made in them. They have been sources of community identity and pride. Many have distinctive architectural details. On the trip, I saw some encouraging interest in preservation of ballparks, even attempts to obtain listings on the National Historic Register, as with War Memorial Stadium in Greensboro, North Carolina, for example, and Rickwood Field in Birmingham. The efforts are hardly a ripple, however, in the main current of thought that says that progress resides in total razing and newly poured concrete.

Back in Albany, Wally Moon was in town for the home stand. The Albany Polecats are a farm club of the Baltimore Orioles and

Wally was one of two roving hitting instructors employed by the Orioles. When I met Wally, he said that he visits each club three times during the season, usually staying for five or six games. Since the Orioles have six farm clubs, he was on the road much of the period from April through August.

In 1990, Wally Moon was manager of the Frederick Keys in their Carolina League championship year. Watching from the stands that season, I had been impressed with his professional approach to the game and the patience and understanding he showed the young players. He was a deeply tanned, silver-haired man with bushy eyebrows and a serene, confident demeanor. Wally is a southerner. He was born in Bay, Arkansas, attended college in Texas where he earned a master's degree, and he still resides in Texas during the off-season. He had an outstanding rookie year with the St. Louis Cardinals, joining that select few who homered in their first major league at bat, then going on to hit .304 and be voted Rookie of the Year. Wally played in the outfield and later at first base. After the 1958 season, he was traded to the Los Angeles Dodgers, who were playing in the Los Angeles Coliseum. The stadium had been built for football and practically every kind of public entertainment except baseball. Left field was originally only 251 feet, though Wally said that they extended it to 276 feet and put up a forty-foot fence during his playing days there. As a left-handed hitter, his opposite field bloops often fell in over the screen and became known as "Moon shots." His playing career ended after the 1965 season with 142 home runs and a career .289 batting average.

I sat through a late Sunday afternoon game with Wally a few rows behind home plate, and he talked while making notes on how hitters handled certain pitches. I asked him what he looked for in a hitter.

"Bat speed," he replied, "plus control of the bat, ability to hit to all fields, and ability to select pitches." Wally said that a .300 hitter had to put the ball in play eight out of ten at bats. If that ratio falls to seven out of ten, averages will be in the .280 range, and if it is six of ten that will drop a hitter to around .250. He said that the roving instructors were there to work with all the players, but everyone knew the prospects and the long shots, and he usually came in with information about which aspect of hitting a prospect needed to work on. As a former major leaguer with a respected playing history, over forty years of professional baseball experience, and a genuine ability to perceive and explain hitting nuances, he seemed to have found a perfect fit of ability and occupation.

I asked Wally what the biggest adjustments were that new professional baseball players had to make. "It isn't just the level of play," he said. "Playing every day is at least as big a problem." He explained that travel, irregular mealtimes, and daily performance take a toll and require counteracting strategies. Players have to learn how to rest their bodies and their minds, and to pace themselves over a season that begins in March and lasts until September.

We talked about the role of colleges in a professional baseball player's career. One obvious difference, Wally explained, is the number of games. Because a college semester ends in May, so does the baseball season, and over a three-year college career, a player may end up with fewer games under his belt than in one professional season. Aluminum bats are another problem. College averages are often inflated because an aluminum bat has a larger sweet spot than a wooden bat; and flares over the infield that show up as hits in college would shatter a wooden bat and become easy groundouts. Wooden bats cost twenty-eight dollars apiece, and the expense could quickly get out of hand because a team like the Albany Polecats could sometimes go through ten or twelve bats in one day. One of Wally's jobs is to teach young players how to handle the bat so that fewer of them are busted. Aluminum bats sell for eighty-five dollars apiece, but are practically indestructible and college budgets will probably never stretch far enough to allow wooden bats. He told me about a company called Baum, which was experimenting with a new bat made of compressed wood and plastic. The product reputedly was almost as tough as aluminum, but still had many of the properties of the wooden bat, such as similar velocity of the ball off the bat after contact. Wally predicted that colleges would eventually switch over to the Baum bat, and that this would make the transition to professional baseball easier for hitters.

As we continued to talk, Wally seemed to realize that my interest was in hitting in general, not in individual hitters, and he became more willing to use the batting activity in the game to illustrate points. I realized, gratefully, that I was getting a graduate course in batting from a master instructor. He showed me how one at bat may necessitate several shifts in strategy, stance, and intent depending on the count, game situation, and presence of runners on base. In a late inning, a left-handed batter swung late on a fastball and drove the left fielder back to the warning track with a high, opposite-field fly.

"Moon shot?" I asked Wally.

He smiled. "I didn't hit them even that hard," he said.

On the morning I left Albany, I woke up in a state park on the Flint River, my base of operations for the last few days. As I was having breakfast, I heard a bird song from somewhere over on the river bottom. The song was vaguely familiar but not recognizable, reminiscent of whippoorwill but different, and not one I was accustomed to hearing near my home in Maryland. I reached for Peterson's field guide but even before I opened it, the name surfaced from the depths of a southern childhood. Chuck-will's-widow. Chuck-will's-widow. The songs of the South were with me still; I had come on this trip to call them from cover.

My full name is Ernest Jackson Green, Jr. My father's father, Thomas Jackson Green, was born in 1879, grew up near Dalton, Georgia, married and had two children there, and moved to Oklahoma sometime in the first decade of the twentieth century. When I was a boy, he told me stories of his father, a Confederate soldier who served with honor. In one battle, my grandfather said, his father carried the regimental colors after two other soldiers had been shot with the flag while advancing toward the enemy. He told me many other stories, which I have either forgotten or which I ignored at the time, being too busy with things important to a young boy. One of my missions on this trip was to make up for, to the extent I could, my inattentiveness of long ago.

I had always assumed that my name was the result of my great-grandfather coming home from the Civil War, as many did, and naming his children (eventually numbering fourteen, twelve of whom lived into adulthood) after venerated war legends. My namesake, I thought, was the brilliant, eccentric Thomas J. "Stonewall" Jackson. His untimely death early in the war, many southerners swore, was the sole reason for the South having lost the war. Before leaving on the trip, I had gone to the Archives of the United States in Washington, D.C., to research my great-grandfather's military record. I found that his name, Isham Jackson Green, predated the Civil War by two decades and probably was derived from Andrew Jackson, whose name was larger than life in the Tennessee region where my great-grandfather was born in 1840. Since I could never generate any affection for the Indian killer Jackson, I rather hoped the name had simply come over from England, but I had been unable to trace it further back.

The archival search had been only partly successful. Confederate records are less complete than those of the Union, and all I was able to establish was that Isham had enlisted on May 16, 1861, in Company C, 3rd (Lillard's) Tennessee Mounted Infantry, with the rank of private, and had been assigned to work for four days at the depot. Nothing beyond those few facts were recorded on the muster roll. The likeliest place for additional service records, I was told, would be the state archives where Isham's widow, Rebecca, might have filed for a pension after Isham's death. The claim would have been supported with facts about his career. By those circumstances I found myself in Atlanta, driving toward the state archives, seeking information that I could have had gladly and with pride if I hadn't been too young or too willful to listen when my grandfather was alive.

To reach the archives from the south, you go past Fulton County Stadium on Capitol Avenue, a few blocks away. The stadium is the home of the major league Braves, the NFL Falcons, and the college Peach Bowl. It was the first site of big-league baseball in the Deep South, and on April 8, 1974, was the launching pad for Henry Aaron's 715th home run. Today the stadium looks uninviting; and though only a mile south of midtown Atlanta, it sits in a barren, nondescript junction of three interstate highways. Built in the mid-sixties, the stadium represents that generation of multiuse municipal complexes referred to as "cookie-cutters." Once inside, you could be in St. Louis, Pittsburgh, Philadelphia, or Cincinnati and have the same visual experience. With the stadium, its surrounding parking lots, and three intersecting interstates, the site is a concrete manufacturer's dream.

In the state archives I ran into another disappointment. Pension files for Isham did not exist. Perhaps his wife Rebecca, worn out from having fourteen children, had predeceased him, in which case there would have been no pension. Or maybe she had just neglected to apply for the eight dollars per month pension, though this was unlikely because that was pretty good money at the turn of the century. I couldn't even find Isham's date of death; incredibly, the state of Georgia only started recording deaths in 1918. The sole recourse was to check local records where the death occurred. A cross-reference did exist citing Isham's name, however, in the pension application of another ex-Confederate soldier, a man named Henry W. Renfro.

Henry had served with Isham and another witness named in the application during the war. Answers to application questions show that by 1897, when Henry made his pension claim based upon "infirmity and poverty," he had indeed fallen on hard times:

8. What is your present occupation?

Answer: I was a druggist last.

9. How much can you earn (gross) per annum by your own exertions or labor?

Answer: Nothing at all.

13. . . . give a full and complete history of the infirmity and its extent?

Answer: I was wounded in my left shoulder, and [illegible] that and other [illegible] since about 1880 or 1881 I have been paralysed and for sixteen years I have been crippled and not able [illegible] to be infirm.

14. What property, effects or income do you possess and its gross value?

Answer: Not one cent.

18. What was your employment during 1895 and 1896? What pay did you receive each year?

Answer: Sitting in a chair on a pillow, when I was not in bed, didn't get a day pay for it.

On a separate page, Isham and another witness, R. F. Hannah, jointly swear to the following answers:

2. Are you acquainted with Henry W. Renfro, the applicant, if so how long have you known him?

Answer: We have known him 32 or 33 years.

4. Do you know of his having served in the Confederate army or the Georgia militia? How do you know this?

Answer: Applicant served in the Confederate army we served in the same company and regiment.

5. When, where and in what company and regiment did he enlist?

Answer: In Oct 1861 at Sweetwater Tenn in Co A of 62 Tennessee.

6. Were you a member of the same company and regiment?

Answer: We was.

7. How long did he perform regular military duty, and what do you know of his service as a Confederate soldier, and the time and circumstances of his discharge from the service?

Answer: For over 2 years he was a good Soldier we dont remember as to his discharge the time and place.

On his application, Henry had sworn that he was in the Confederate army "until the surrender." Other forms attached to the application indicate that it was successful. The deposition for witnesses had been signed by Isham in his own hand, so he had been literate, unlike my grandfather.

In all I had learned little about my great-grandfather's life. No records had been uncovered to document the campaigns he had fought, the quality of his service, or even the military rank he had achieved. Census records indicate that he married Rebecca and began having children after 1865, so he was apparently a Confederate soldier until the surrender also. That, and the fact that he had helped an old army buddy obtain a pension, was all that remained. He had been a hero to my grandfather, that much I remembered, and there was nothing in the records to indicate that this measure of the man was misplaced.

Out of Atlanta I headed east to get back to the heart of the region where South Atlantic League baseball is played. With no clear destination for the night, I drove awhile and stopped to make a telephone call. One of my colleagues in Maryland, Dennis Sullivan, had told me before the trip that Johnny Mize, the big first baseman who hit the long ball for three major league teams from 1936 to 1953, lived in retirement in Demorest, Georgia. I pulled off at a rest stop and called him. I got his answering machine, which said: "This is the John Mize residence. The Big Cat cain't come to the phone right now. Leave your name and telephone number, and if you're calling long distance, I will call you back collect." The Big Cat didn't intend to get stuck with a big telephone bill. Unfortunately, I didn't have a number to leave and decided to drive on and try later.

They called him "Big Cat" because of his agility around first base despite his considerable bulk. His quickness and fielding finesse stemmed from early experiences with tennis. He was good enough to win county championships and may have had a professional career in that sport had the baseball coach left him alone. John Robert Mize began playing college baseball in the northeast Georgia town of Demorest when he was only fourteen. I remembered his early-fifties career with the Yankees, when he was used mainly as a pinch hitter, and when he always seemed to deliver in the clutch. His Hall of Fame statistics were mostly accrued earlier with the Cardinals and Giants and included 2,011 hits and 359 career home runs. Despite a career lifetime .312 batting average, and career highs of fifty-one home runs in 1947 and a .364 batting average in 1937, he wasn't elected to the Hall of Fame until his twenty-third year of eligibility. At the induction, he said: "I had a speech ready but somewhere along in 28 years, it got lost."

I wanted to ask him about the early days when he played baseball in the South, before the big leagues. Although I finally reached him and he listened politely to my story, when I suggested coming by Demorest to talk with him, he firmly declined. "I just don't fool with it anymore," he said. John Mize was eighty years old, had been a public figure for sixty years, and had certainly earned the right to pass on an interview.

A month and a half later I read in *USA Today* that Johnny Mize had died the previous day of cardiac arrest at his home. I regretted all the more that he hadn't felt like talking when I called him. He had been a strong, small town boy from the Deep South, who ended up playing in the most yankee stadium of them all.

Almost out of Georgia, I was close to Royston, the hometown of the greatest southern baseball player of all, Ty Cobb. Considering Cobb's reputation for fierceness, I thought it would be interesting to see what the townsfolk thought of him. Cobb had died in 1961 and was buried in the cemetery there.

Cobb's father had been a turn-of-the-century community leader in Royston, serving as mayor, county school superintendent, and state senator. His aspirations for son Tyrus were traditional and he was disappointed at Ty's inclination toward baseball. Cobb's initial experiences with baseball were hampered by several other unfortunate circumstances. In August 1905, the Detroit Tigers bought his contract from Augusta in the Sally League, but as Cobb was leaving for the big time, he learned that his mother had mistaken his father for a burglar and had killed him with two blasts from a shotgun. Rumors raced around the small town, claiming that Ty's father had been trying to catch his mother with a lover. Ty's mother was indicted for involuntary manslaughter. Although she was later acquitted, this event staggered Ty during the spring of his first full season. His teammates also subjected him to an especially severe hazing period when he was new with Detroit.

Native southerners were still oddities in the big leagues in the early part of the century, and Cobb had little in common with his yankee, Irish-Catholic teammates. The feud became so bad that Cobb began sleeping with a pistol under his pillow.

Whether these early experiences were enough to transform Cobb into a loner, or whether his ultracompetitive personality was the main determinant, Cobb played for twenty-four years with almost no friends on the field or off. His autobiography, titled *My Life in Baseball: The True Record*, is a relentless defense of the way he played the game. On the advantages of choking up on the bat, Cobb wrote: "I used to love to choke up and smash them at Hal Chase at first base for New York—the kind that carom off the knees of an infielder and leave him limping for days." Yet on sportswriters who painted an image of him as a maniac who ran the bases slashing and cutting, he offers: "I want to say this: I forgive them. They have long since passed on, and there is no anger left in my heart."

Cobb was the embodiment of the strategic, play-for-one-run dead ball era before 1920. He was prideful, fiercely independent, and a master strategist. Indeed, he spent most of his retirement years railing about the negative changes in baseball after the advent of the lively ball and home run hitters in the 1920s. In non-baseball pursuits, Cobb used the same drive to acquire considerable wealth through shrewd investments. When he retired in 1928, he held over forty major league or American league records. Most have been surpassed but his career batting average of .367 will probably stand untouched, for the era Cobb dominated is long and permanently gone.

I decided to stop for the night, and checked in at a state park a few miles west of Royston. Needing some supplies, I drove toward town. At an isolated intersection in the country, I saw two state highway patrol cruisers parked, the patrolmen standing in traffic lanes. I looked at one of them, and he made no sign so I started to drive on.

"HEY!" he shouted. I hit the brake.

He walked up to the side of the pickup, looking in the back through dark sunglasses, which effectively hid his eyes. He was short and thick, with close-cropped hair. "I'm gonna need see your driver's license and registration."

I produced the documents and he perused them. "You had anything to drink today?"

This was my first indication that they had set up a sobriety checkpoint. "No," I said.

He looked at me. "Nothing at all?"

"Nothing."

"Where you staying at in Georgia?"

"State park."

He studied the driver's license again, as if he was sure that some incriminating evidence would show up there if he just concentrated hard enough.

"Where you going to right now?"

"Into Royston, to buy some ice."

"How long you going be in Georgia?"

I paused. These questions had nothing to do with checking for sobriety, and the tone was belligerent.

"I'll probably leave tomorrow."

"Sure you haven't had nothing to drink?"

I didn't answer. To hell with this, I thought. Let him arrest me for not answering the same question three times. He gave my identification one more canvassing and handed the two cards back.

"Sir," he said, "you'll git to Royston faster if you go to your right." His pronunciation of the last two words sounded like "Yore-rot," which I thought at first must be another town in Georgia.

"Where is that?"

He leaned back. "You don't know where your right is at?" He looked across the road at the other officer, as if in disbelief, and then pointed. "Take that road there."

I took the road on my right, but I didn't thank him for the information.

Royston was a small town surrounded by farms. Tractors bounced along the roads and pickups were the most numerous vehicle types in town. The main street was lined with one- and two-story brick buildings, the brick chipping and crumbling under the force of Georgia summers, approaching the same color as the red clay hills just beyond the city limits. References to Ty Cobb abounded in the town. A memorial granite bust stood in a sort of breezeway between two plain buildings used by the city. Diagonally across the street was Cobb Memorial Hospital, donated by the ball-player late in his life in memory of his parents. I drove down Cobb Street, past small homes with wooden front porches and backyards plowed and readied for planting vegetable gardens. A dead opossum lay directly in the middle of the street. Cobb's name had obviously not brought hordes of tourists to Royston; I saw only one run-down motel on the outskirts of town.

No one interested in architectural style can possibly be bored in a new town. Even the smallest places boast one or two commercial buildings or residences of character and visual dignity. I had begun to think that Royston was an exception when I turned a corner and

44

saw a delightful American foursquare. The hipped-roof, two-story house had four rooms on each floor and a front porch running the full width of the house. Two large dormers punched out of the roof. This boxlike house type was common from the 1890s to the 1920s, but this was an unusually fine, unaltered specimen.

I reached for my camera lying on the seat in the pickup cab, and as I did, my peripheral vision picked up a city police cruiser moving slowly toward me. Two officers were staring intently, undoubtedly speculating about my motives in looking over the house. I left the camera on the seat and eased on down the street, hoping they wouldn't turn, flip on the blinkers, and pull me over. The conversation, I knew, would be predictable.

("Officer, I wasn't casing the joint. I was just admiring that colossal American foursquare."

"Well, sir, how about if we haul your colossal ass down to headquarters and talk about it.")

They kept driving slowly down the street, looking my way in the rearview mirror. I had been in Royston less than an hour and had been scrutinized by the police twice already.

Railroad tracks ran behind the row of stores on the eastern side of Main Street, and a carnival had been set up in a grassy field just beyond the tracks. After having dinner at my campsite in the state park, I drove back into Royston to see the carnival. At dusk the bright lights beckoned Royston's young, and the smells of corn dogs and cotton candy floated over the midway. Calliope music flowed from the mechanical rides and barkers hawked their haunted houses and exhibits of oddities.

City police were stationed at each end of the midway. I walked past one, carrying my camera, and he eyed me suspiciously. For a moment he looked as if he was going to stop me, but he said nothing. I was beginning to accept this as an unavoidable aspect of being in Royston. They were there, I suppose, for crowd control. The "crowd" looked to be about twenty people.

Grubby, haunted-looking teenagers worked the booths with games, extolling the virtues of their chalk animals and stuffed toys. I took a few pictures of the general scene, and was accosted by laughing teenagers offering to pose.

45

The carnival manager came over, probably assuming at first that I was a local reporter. He was a thin, grey-haired man of seventy-one, easy to talk to, with a keen sense of humor. He was surprised, he told me, to see so many people turn out because he hadn't been able to arrange advance publicity. After we talked awhile about the carnival business, I asked him about the working conditions of the young people. He said that they were much improved over the past. He tried to keep the same people for the season, but there was a lot of turnover. "I want it to be like a family," he said, "but they still come and go." He claimed that the trailers that hauled the equipment were converted to comfortable sleeping quarters during their stayovers in small towns. "They got a nice living space now," he said. "The truck trailers are fixed up, they got bunks, got a nice set up. Used to be they'd sleep wherever they could, under the trucks sometimes, wherever. Not like that any more. Like it was in the old days."

"When were the old days?" I asked.

"Not too long ago," he said.

I had felt uneasy since arriving in Royston. Not only had the police gone that extra mile to make me feel uncomfortable, but also other townspeople looked at me as an intruder. Yet I seemed to have all the right credentials—I was white, male, and drove a pickup truck. I could imagine the fear that would have been produced by driving into Royston forty or fifty years ago without those credentials.

Victoria Bryant State Park sits on a hilltop two miles west of Royston. The night was cool but clear and the stars were beautiful. Visibility out over the surrounding countryside was good, and I could see just how physically isolated Royston was. The xenophobic little town had shown me something interesting, though, after all. Tyrus Raymond Cobb's psyche, formed by the mosaic of life in this slice of rural Georgia, was now more understandable. The "Georgia Peach," probably the most ironic nickname ever affixed to a ball-player, was no more admirable to me as a person but Royston had been like a looking glass reflecting his personality in all details.

Next morning, I looked at the road map after breakfast. I wanted to take state highway 17 to Elberton, then pick up 72 to South

Carolina. There was no realistic way to avoid driving through Royston again. I buckled my seatbelt, pulled on a billed cap that said "Scout" over the visor, and when the signs said SPEED LIMIT 30, dropped back to twenty-five. I drove slowly and soberly out of Georgia.

3

Bombers and Barbecue

BEFORE HEADING TO THE BALLPARK in Columbia, South Carolina, I had a pilgrimage to make. I had long been an admirer of the writings of Mary Chesnut, the preeminent literary diarist of the Civil War. Her book, *A Diary from Dixie*, was written as the war was in progress but wasn't published until 1905, long after her death. In the book, her personality emerges clearly. She was an outrageous flirt, a gossip, a sensitive, feeling person of considerable intellect, an honest, accurate writer, and a woman of charm and beauty. If I could pick one person as the personification of the southern belle, Mary Chesnut would be she.

A cottage where Mary and her husband, Confederate general James Chesnut, lived for a while during the Civil War still stands on Hampton Street in Columbia. It is a simple, white-frame, one-and-a-half-story house with a central dormer containing an attractive arched window, a small porch with four octagonal columns, and an unusual ironwork balustrade. Jefferson Davis visited once while the Chesnuts lived there and addressed a crowd from the porch. Today, the cottage is a bed-and-breakfast.

As the daughter of one U.S. senator and the wife of another, Mary was well connected. Her husband became an aide to Jefferson Davis and Davis's wife Varina was a close friend of Mary's during the war period. She was at Charleston when the war started and witnessed the firing on Fort Sumter: "We go on the house top and see the shells bursting. They say our men are wasting ammunition." And with that necessary immediacy of the diarist, she wrote

49

of trivia on the same page, "Today Miles and Manning breakfasted near me." She was at Montgomery when the Confederacy was born, traveled to Richmond during many crises, and underwent the Reconstruction years in the South, writing of nights "when I could tear my hair and cry aloud for all that is past and gone." Although Mary was the daughter of one of the South's largest slaveholding families, she was, at least intellectually, opposed to slavery. Diary entries also show that she was an early feminist. She was an admirer of the writings of Mary Wollstonecraft Shelley, and she saw the similarities between slavery and marriage: "The Bible authorized marriage and slavery—poor women! poor slaves!" Another entry recognizes the economic dependence that was the lot of nineteenth-century women: "Douglas is dead—killed by the times I think. The lovely Mrs. Douglas is *free*—and *poor* I am afraid."

Mary Chesnut was also, in terms of the current vernacular, a doper. Her doctor had prescribed opium for relief from emotional upsets, yet at times Mary used the drug either directly or as a mixture with alcohol (laudanum) just to relieve boredom. Traveling to Richmond, she wrote: "Long and tedious was the way. Relieved the tedium by taking Laudanum." Opiate use was not uncommon in the nineteenth century even for upper-class southern belles, and it remained legal until the early twentieth century.

Mary's South vanished with the Civil War, "literally kicked to pieces," though she adjusted and coped, through necessity, with Reconstruction. She died in 1886, the year Ty Cobb, a very different breed of southerner, was born.

In 1942, American morale was low. The attack at Pearl Harbor had been followed by bad news of the war in the Pacific. But spirits soared when General Jimmy Doolittle led a dramatic air raid that became the first significant victory in the Pacific during World War II. Eighty men formed the squadron of B-25 bombers known as "Doolittle's Raiders," and they trained for the mission at Columbia Army Air Base, South Carolina, now Columbia Metropolitan Airport. In 1993, in honor of the men who carried out that famous and heroic raid, the Columbia Mets became the Capital City Bombers.

The Bombers play at Capital City Stadium, a baseball park that first saw professional baseball in 1927. Since then, the park has been renovated, rebuilt, and renamed several times. In its present form, the exterior is an unimpressive view of the underside of grandstand seats fronted by a fence that is too short and topped by a maze of telephone and electrical wires. The grandstand is concrete with a flat, aluminum roof, which looks like an oversized carport cover with two skinny poles supporting it. Railroad tracks run a few yards outside the left field bleachers, and a water tower looms over the left field wall.

Because of the extensive renovations, Capital City Stadium is not listed in *Baseball America* as one of the oldest ballparks in the country despite its having been in use since 1927. To qualify, parks must still have their original grandstand on the original site from the first year of construction. The Capital City field still retains its character, however, unlike most renovated ballparks. From the Marlboro man striding in from right center to the two rows of brightly colored outfield signs and the short, uneven dimensions (left field 330 feet, center 395 feet, right 320 feet) required for home runs, the park conveys a sense of connection with baseball's past.

Watching the Bombers' batting practice, I was reminded by one of the players of the game's interesting contradictions. Coaches choke on their tobacco wads over the sharp contrasts between some players' offensive and defensive games. In the American League, the designated hitter rule has partly removed the entertainment provided fans by lock-fingered, scissor-legged fielders stumbling around on defense and pounding hell out of the ball at bat. Jose Flores, the Bombers' starting shortstop in the early 1993 season, presented the classic quandary. He had good range, a quick, powerful arm, delicate balance, and graceful footwork. Defensively he could shine. In the game that evening, he executed a play I have never seen duplicated. From medium depth at short, he charged a ground ball, took it on a wicked short hop, and had it pop from his glove. Momentum carried him onto the infield grass, but he managed to keep the ball in front of him. With his right, ungloved hand, he reached the bouncing ball and dribbled it, like a basketball, across his body and into his gloved hand. His throw got the runner by the proverbial one step.

At game time, Jose was hitting .087. One of the coaches told me that Jose was tied for the team lead in errors. That was not a particular worry, he claimed, since the shortstop reached so many hard-to-play balls that his error percentage was always going to be high. At the plate, he admitted, Jose was "struggling." This much-used word deliberately camouflages meaning. In baseball language, no one screws up anymore, or lacks the ability to hit or pitch. If someone isn't performing, he is "struggling." Jose, hitting ninth on a team whose combined batting average was .198, scratched out one hit in two official times at bat that evening. The discrepancy between his elegant fielding and his inability to hit was too great for the Mets organization, however. Within a month he was gone.

After batting practice, I asked one of the Bombers' staff where the best barbecued ribs place in Columbia was. She was from Georgia and said you couldn't get good ribs in South Carolina, and went on for a long time about the problems with local ribs. She finally recommended a spot, which I half expected would be the worst place in town just to make her point about inferior South Carolina ribs.

Piggy Park was an imitation log cabin in West Columbia, just across the Congaree River. The tables had recipes and newspaper reviews laminated onto their tops. One review said that *People* rated Piggy Park the "best all-in-one-barbecue restaurant [in America in 1989]: eat-in, take out, drive-through, mail-order and Bible study mission." Surely enough, you could order ribs and literature on the Bible at the same sitting.

I had read that barbecue sauce in this South Carolina area was different. Knowing this intellectually and being faced with it on your plate are not the same, however. When my ribs came, they were covered with sauce that was bright yellow. Barbecue sauce, as I knew it in Oklahoma, was dark, reddish-brown. But everything smelled good and the meat was done perfectly, so by looking out the window while eating, I was able to enjoy the meal. One of the owners told me that the unique color of South Carolina sauce came from apple cider, soy sauce, peppers, and other spices. The owner was friendly and I asked her how common the yellow sauce was in South Carolina. She believed that everyone within about a sixty mile radius of Columbia would serve ribs that looked like hers. However, she told me, the specific spices which went into Piggy Park's sauce were a secret. I tried to look disappointed, but couldn't envision my future including yellow barbecue sauce anyway, no matter how good it tasted.

Back at the ballpark, an old-time trolley shuttled fans from the parking lot. The trolley had a PA system, which was playing "Talking Baseball." The ball game between the Bombers and the Macon Braves was a slowly played affair with no suspense after the bottom of the first, when Capital City scored six runs. It added five in the bottom of the sixth and eventually won, 12–2. Since there were only four extra-base hits in the game, no home runs, and four errors, the Bombers spent a lot of time churning up dirt on the base paths. Their starting pitcher, Craig Bullock, dove for a grounder and dislocated his shoulder. The entire team gathered around the mound, and with the trainer, manager, coach, and two umpires made quite a crowd. Craig was hauled carefully off the field on a cart pulled by a John Deere minitractor.

At minor league games, promotional contests and games keep the evening lively no matter what is happening on the field. After the third inning a young boy in a tuxedo ("Rockin' Robert") climbed to the top of the first base dugout and tap-danced to hard beat music. Players spilled out of the home dugout to watch. In the middle of the fourth, a small child chosen from the stands raced the team mascot around the bases. Bomber the Mouse, whose head was a large baseball with ears, was the mascot but no one could say for sure why a mouse was an appropriate symbol for the Bombers. The mouse was allowed to start at second base, while the child ran from home plate, but Bomber had to walk and got blocked by the third base coach, so the child won. In the middle of the fifth, two girls on the Bomber staff rushed onto the field with lawn chairs, umbrellas, and refreshments for the umpires. At the end of the sixth, the first base dugout tops were used for dugout bowling. Several children rolled balls across the concrete dugout tops, trying to win prizes by knocking down pins. In the seventh, the crowd attempted "the wave," spurred on by the PA announcer. In the middle of the seventh, Rockin' Robert returned. This time he danced on the third base dugout, again to great applause. At the end of the seventh, a man in a Bombers uniform climbed on top of the first base dugout and led fans in singing "Take Me Out to the Ball Game."

After the top of the eighth, two contestants were chosen from the stands and were given bats. They were then required to put the ends of their bats on the ground, lower their foreheads to the knobs, and spin around ten times before running from home to first. They got dizzy, ran into each other, recovered somewhat, and began to pump their legs toward first but veered off sharply toward the dugout. This "dizzy bats" contest was one of the most popular at minor league parks. Although I wasn't sure why, I laughed hysterically along with everyone else each of the thirty or forty times I saw it happen.

Before the bottom of the eighth, the PA announcer told us that several three- and four-year-olds would dance on top of the third base dugout. They were called "Students of Rockin' Robert," who had himself been all of eight years old. As the "students" started tapping away to fast music, one tapped over dangerously close to the dugout edge. An adult lunged frantically to grab the little girl, then draped himself along the dugout edge from the other side to keep the children from falling off and ending the event in disaster. The kids tapped on obliviously, receiving enthusiastic applause.

Contests do sometimes end unfortunately. Later, during a dizzy bats race at a Double A park, I noticed club officials guarding the dugout entrance. I was told that on opening day a man had lost his balance after spinning around the bat and fell onto the concrete lip of the dugout, causing a concussion and requiring many stitches. Although the club might have been blamed, he didn't sue the organization. Fans at minor league games are participants in the evening entertainment in ways that are foreign to those who go to only major league games. Suing the ballclub would be like suing a good neighbor.

After the game, I caught the trolley to the upper end of the parking lot. The old car heaved and rocked, and parents kept protective arms around their sleepy children. Older children examined souvenirs and young lovers held hands. Another minor league evening was winding down.

I read an account of the game in the local newspaper the next morning. There was nothing minor league about players' abilities to handle baseball language. When asked to assess the game, Donnie White, one of the batting heroes in the 12–2 laugher, said:

"We started off slow [this season], and we're still struggling a little hitting the ball, but we're putting it in play and beginning to play much better."

How about their pitcher?

"Their pitcher was struggling."

Ron Washington, the Bombers' manager, was asked if it's easy to let up when leading 12–2. Ron said:

"It doesn't matter what the score is. You go out there with one attitude, and that's to play the game for nine innings."

4

Tobacco Fields of Dreams

WORLD WAR MEMORIAL STADIUM in Greensboro, North Carolina, was billed by its South Atlantic League baseball team, the Hornets, as the oldest minor league ballpark still in use in the country. This claim was, however, disputed. The major point of contention was that although the stadium opened in 1926, the first professional baseball game wasn't played there until 1930. Both Luther Williams Field in Macon, Georgia and Silver Stadium in Rochester, New York, opened for baseball in 1929 and were still in operation.

The field was built for football and track, and early distances down right- and left-field lines were very short. Originally, the foul pole in right field was only 248 feet from home plate. A half-mile dirt track ran down the left-field line and the original seating was in the form of a reversed J, with the stem paralleling the track.

The essential features of the park remain untouched. Fans enter under three Romanesque arches flanked by solid towers with pyramidal tops. The single-decked grandstand is concrete and seating capacity is 7,500. Distances are now a more conventional 327 feet down the lines and 401 feet to center. In 1993, two hundred gallons of paint and a cleaning of the interior cement had made the old park gleam without changing its intimacy and ambiance.

One aspect of the park is, at least to my knowledge, unique. A creek runs through it. Actually, the creek runs underneath it, entering under right field from about half way between first base and the foul pole to emerge outside the right center-field fence. The right fielder's normal position is almost exactly over the creek run-

57

ning a few feet below. I walked around the outside wall with John Frey, the Hornets' general manager, to see the phenomenon. The stream had deep cut banks so the builders had just laid the field over it from one bank to another. Outside the fence, where the watercourse emerged, John pointed. "Home runs often end up in here." Right on cue, a soggy baseball bobbed by in the current.

A few hours before game time, I met John Horshok, one of the Hornets' new owners. He walked up as Frey and I were sitting in the stands watching the ground crew work on the field. Rain had fallen earlier and washed out batting practice. John was a dynamic, energetic man who delivered one-liners in a sharp, staccato rhythm. He had been on the business end of the sports world for years in merchandising, promotion, and more recently, ownership. Before coming to Greensboro, he was in the restaurant business in northern Virginia with former Washington Redskin quarterback Joe Theismann. He told me that the buying price of the Greensboro Hornets had been $2.5 million, and that they had settled on April Fool's Day, just three weeks before.

"Do you think you bought in at the right time?" I asked him.

"Hell no. The right time was when the team cost $25,000, not two and a half million dollars."

The PBA required that every team have a single individual who was responsible for club decisions. This owner attended minor and major league meetings and was the community's visible symbol of ownership. The actual ownership structure was usually more complicated, however. The Greensboro team was owned by American Baseball Capital, Incorporated. The seven corporate members owned various amounts of the team. They were all checked out by the national association before settlement to assure that none of their other businesses—say, a local concession enterprise or one that had any connection to gambling—would represent a conflict of interest. Sufficient money was not the only criterion the association used to evaluate potential owners. Even the limited owners were invited to participate by the major money people because they had some connection with baseball. Tim Cullen, the executive vice president of the Hornets, was a former major league player with the Washington Senators. In the case of better-known celebrities, who have bought into several minor league teams (in Memphis, for example, movie actor/director Ron Howard is an owner), being a lifelong fan seemed to be connection enough. The association recognizes the media value of having a movie star or sports personality own a team.

As John Horshok said, the ideal time to buy a minor league team was in the past. The world of baseball is rife with stories about visionary entrepreneurs who bought franchises in the late seventies or early eighties for a few thousand dollars—or sometimes for simply taking over a team's debts—and sold them five years later for a few million. Even class A teams today sell for several million, and the consensus is that the big growth and appreciation in minor league clubs value has already occurred. However true this may be, John Horshok did not look unhappy to be an owner. He looked downright delighted.

His investment included a park alteration project, which had already started, and would be unique among baseball parks. The project, located beyond the left field bleachers, was the addition of a combination food court and museum.

By game time, rain had been falling off and on for an hour and a half. Baseball rules say that the authority to cancel a game rests with the home team until the lineup cards are exchanged, and then shifts to the umpires. After receiving the evening's cards, the umpires dutifully took a cursory walk through the sodden outfield (where water was standing several inches deep) and called the game. No one seemed in any hurry to leave, especially me, so I sat in the press box drinking beer and talking baseball as long as anyone would hang around. When you live in the back of a pickup truck, rainouts spawn feelings of boredom and claustrophobia. Owners like John Horshok see them more ominously, even as minor disasters, biting chunks from an already too skinny profit margin.

The rain had been pushed in on the leading edge of a cold front, and by morning the temperature had dropped noticeably. I found a laundromat in Greensboro and unloaded my bulging laundry bag. A restaurant across from the laundromat caught my eye because it resembled the homey cafe where I meet my fishing partner Doyle for breakfast before hitting the trout streams. The Greens-

59

boro place was called the Coliseum Cafe, at the corner of Florida and Clapton. Grandiose name aside, the interior did not even vaguely suggest a coliseum. The booths were covered in Naugahyde, the barstools were covered in Naugahyde of a different color, and the table chairs were in a third, sharply clashing color of Naugahyde. The lone waitress greeted me with, "Sit where you want to, hon." Eggs sizzled on the grill, but I knew intuitively that I was in a first-class pancake haven.

Although pancakes weren't exclusively a southern dish in centuries past, the major symbol of premixed ingredients had been the black southern "mammy." Aunt Jemima was a real person, or at least the Davis Milling Company hired a woman to personify the stereotyped image. Her name was Nancy Green, and she cooked pancakes for the company at a concession stand during the 1893 Chicago World's Fair. More than anyone else, Nancy helped establish and popularize the food in the United States by touring the country as Aunt Jemima. Unfortunately, the image of a hefty black woman with a red bandanna and apron also helped stabilize and perpetuate racial cliches about Afro-American women.

Ask a southerner where to find good barbecued ribs, and almost everyone will have an opinion. Asking about pancakes is likely to elicit only a blank stare. Nonetheless, a proper pancake has a complexity and set of nuances that can be appreciated or disdained, like most foods. Texture is important and can be provided with the taste and feel of the various grains. A definite hint of egg and dairy flavors should permeate the pancake. It should be tender and slightly moist but with enough denseness to remain intact after syrup (pure maple, the other sugary, berry-flavored syrups overpower or disagree with the pancake experience) is poured on. Pancakes that dissolve on the fork, or are leathery, or taste like raw dough are common miscreations.

When the waitress brought my breakfast it was simple: three plain pancakes (places that add berries, nuts, or chocolate chunks are usually trying to mask their inferior batter); two thin, crisply well-done patties of sausage; coffee; and orange juice. The prominent flavor in the pancakes was buckwheat, and they were as close to perfection as I have ever tasted. Like barbecued ribs, pancakes require a certain setting for full enjoyment. The Coliseum was busy, service was efficient, and the waitress knew the names of her customers. I paid my bill and complimented the owner on his pancake batter. He was of the opinion, as I have long been, that the batter actually improved and was superior on the second day. His batter, he said, was a combination of commercial mix and his own ingredients, which he didn't offer to divulge. No mind. Finding someone willing to seriously discuss pancake construction was an accomplishment in its own right.

North Carolina may not have a major league team, but it was serious baseball country. Ten minor league franchises were located within the state's borders, from Asheville in the west to Kinston in the east. Since arriving in North Carolina, I had been hearing about an unusual baseball phenomenon located out in the country east of the Raleigh-Durham area: a team without a city. The Carolina Mudcats, a class AA Southern League team, played baseball in something called Five County Stadium. The nearest town was tiny Zebulon, boasting a population of three thousand plus. Fans drove in from cities like Smithfield, Rocky Mount, Wilson, and Raleigh, ranging from twenty to thirty miles away. Distances aside, the team violated one of baseball's traditional expectations about team-community interdependence. How, I wondered, did they manage to sell advertising under these conditions? And how did they manage to entice 263,141 fans to drive out to see them play in 1992?

Five County Stadium was located in a former tobacco field a few miles east of Zebulon. At a crossroads, two dilapidated tobacco barns stood on the northeast corner, an open field was on the northwest, the ballpark was on the southwest, and an old family cemetery was on the southeast. The cemetery was the resting place of members of the Bunn family, according to a handpainted sign nailed to a tree. Therein lay the remains of Bud, Susan, Samuel "and 1 more," whose name had apparently been lost through the years. If a more isolated ballpark existed in the South, I didn't see it.

When I had called Joe Kremer, the Mudcats general manager, he told me to come on out but warned me that he was considering

canceling the game because a low windchill factor had been forecast for the evening. The stadium was new and still unfinished. The
grandstand had a steel frame with no facade. The seats had no
cover and were bright new aluminum and plastic. Parking lots were
still unpaved. The club offices and concessions stands were in temporary buildings. Everything had the look of quick construction
and impermanence.

Inside the club offices, a catfish named "Muddy" swam around
in an aquarium. While we talked, Joe kept the radio tuned to a
weather station. He said that the disadvantage of the Mudcats' situation was having to market in three major areas and a few more
minor ones. The job required a full-time staff of fifteen, a large
number for a class AA team. The players lived in either Wilson or
Zebulon, but fans drove in from all over the five-county area. The
team spent $150,000 each year in marketing.

I didn't get into the specifics of returns for the advertising dollar
with Joe, but a typical minor league team gets a sizeable hunk of
its gross receipts from ad sales. Signs on the outfield fences sell for
$1,500 to $3,500 each depending on size, and companies pay for
full- or half-page ads in the souvenir programs. Radio and ticket-
back advertising also contribute. What the Mudcats were up
against was convincing companies in Raleigh, for example, to buy
signs that would be seen by fans coming from Wilson, fifty miles
away.

Joe showed me the products of a thriving mail-order business
featuring Muddy in the team logo. The catfish head has become a
hot item on baseball caps, tee shirts, cups, batting helmets, and
other souvenirs. Like other minor league teams, the Mudcats were
cashing in on the whimsical nature of their team name.

I went out to the field to take some pictures, and when I returned
to the office, Joe had canceled the evening's game. "Too much
chance of players pulling muscles in the cold this early in the season," he explained. I was disappointed. The only engaging part of
the stadium was the playing field, and I wasn't going to see it used.
The Mudcats were leaving for a long road trip the following day.

The Mudcats were a team without a history (1991 was their first
year), playing in an Erector set stadium and wearing a colorful

logo. They were a good example of baseball as marketing and mail-order merchandising. Would the fans keep streaming into Five County Stadium without the sense of community pride and identification that a home city provided? The whole setup looked as unnatural as seeing their catfish swimming around in the crystal clear water of an aquarium instead of plowing through the silt of a cloudy river bottom. On the other hand, Joe Kremer may be just taking a new trend in baseball to its next logical stage.

The name Carolina Mudcats deliberately promoted a wider than city market base. Other teams, such as the Florida Marlins and the Colorado Rockies, had names that reflected the same reasoning. The Baltimore Orioles had dropped the city name from their promotional literature to acknowledge the fan support from nearby Washington, D.C. All these teams, however, were still located within cities. The Mudcats sit out there, mailing out notions and waiting for their fans to commute, in their tobacco field of dreams.

Since my evening's entertainment was cancelled, I drove into Smithfield, North Carolina. I called Amby Foote, a former minor league baseball player and father of major leaguer Barry Foote, to ask about the location of the old baseball park in town. In the late 1940s, Amby had pitched in the class D Tobacco States League for the Smithfield-Selma Leafs, whose name was a reference to the main cash crop of the area, tobacco.

As did other former minor leaguers, Amby remembered having no rights as a player and being treated as merchandise.

"I read about a big league pitcher this winter," he said. "He pitched 185 innings last year and they called him a workhorse. One year I pitched 240 innings."

He was a twenty-game winner in his prime but the overuse took its toll and his arm burned out while he was still a young man. "We weren't a Dodger farm club but had a working agreement with them. The owner's objective was always for a player to have a big year so they could sell his contract."

Amby was offered under-the-table money, a common practice for getting around the salary cap and enhancing the sale value for top players. He recalled, "I was 9 and 1 in the middle of one season and the owner asked me if I could pitch better if he slipped me more money. 'I don't know,' I told him, 'but I would sure feel better.' One fifty or two hundred [per month] was top salary for first-year men. I remember those payments now when I look at my social security records. There was no tax on the money, of course."

Five years after burning out his arm, Amby could still get a pitching job in professional baseball. What might have been, with today's knowledge and training methods, was interesting to speculate. His son, Barry, played on the little league and high school fields of Smithfield and was drafted third overall in the United States (the second high school player chosen) in the 1970 baseball draft. In one of those coincidences that sometimes occur in small towns, Amby's former manager in class D baseball was Barry's high school coach. Barry played ten years in the majors and after retiring in 1981, managed in the minors for several years. He eventually returned to the majors as a coach, and in 1993 was first base coach with the Mets.

While the old minor leaguers like Amby still rankle at their exploitation and say that professionally, if you don't make the big leagues, your career is meaningless, regret isn't something they convey in their stories or in the tone of their voices. They were paid for playing baseball, and my guess is that few would give up those years even if they somehow could.

Following Amby's directions, I drove to the old field, off Pitchi Road, and saw that it was now used for American Legion baseball. When Amby had played, the outfield fences had been wooden, had proper power alleys, and had measured 340'-390'-340'. Stands were larger then; for one play-off game in 1948, four thousand fans had attended. The park had no name, or at least none that Amby could remember. In 1954, a hurricane leveled the field and no baseball was played there for years until it was fixed up for amateur use. Crowds today are closer to forty than four thousand, and the crack of baseball on wooden bats has been replaced by the clang of aluminum, but the little field, still unnamed, clings to its original purpose.

The New Bull in Durham

THE CAROLINA LEAGUE HAS A shorter history than others in the South, but has been a stable and successful baseball confederation. It began as a class C league in 1945 and has operated in twenty-six cities. Two of the charter members, Winston-Salem and Durham, North Carolina, still field teams. In 1949, the league moved up a notch to class B, and in the 1962 reorganization gained a class A designation. Over time, it has evolved into a high or fast A league, as compared to the low A South Atlantic League. The current eight teams have a northern division comprised of Frederick (Maryland), Lynchburg (Virginia), Prince William (Virginia), Wilmington (Delaware), and a southern half of Durham, Kinston, and Winston-Salem (all in North Carolina), and Salem (Virginia).

The league's image was celebrated in the 1988 movie *Bull Durham*, filmed in Durham and other southern minor league cities. Some even credited the film with the resurgence of interest in minor league baseball, but attendance figures showed a healthy number of fans coming to minor league parks throughout the 1980s. Even if the film was primarily a reflection of the already rising interest in minor league ball, it helped make the Durham franchise one of the most famous in minor league history.

Grainger Stadium in Kinston was built in 1951 and still evokes the feeling of the 1950s. Blue is the theme color, covering the short fence around the front of the park and the steel girders that support a blue grandstand roof. The box seats are folding chairs. Distances run 335 feet to left and right and 390 feet to center. The whole field slopes distinctly from left to right, perhaps to encourage drainage. Also, the field orientation seems off. At Grainger, players peer more directly into the sun than usual, with the field running more west to east from home to center field than is customary.

Kinston's small size was reflected in the club's attendance figures. In April, the team was averaging 1,265 fans per game, the worst in the Carolina League. Billy Johnson, the assistant general manager, told me that cheap beer on Thursday nights would help pump up the figures when the weather got warmer. Three nearby military bases helped bolster the area's mainly agricultural economy. The minor league stop in Kinston was not a favorite of the players, since the town was essentially lifeless after nine at night. Until a few years ago, there were only two fast food restaurants in town; now there are five.

I sat in the sun at Grainger and watched batting practice. To the sounds of rock music piped through the PA system, some of the players swung at pitches thrown underhand from a few feet away, hitting the ball into a net. This exercise helped build wrist strength and bat speed. Often the players would switch to a one-handed swing to help with bat control.

Pete Rose's son was the Kinston Indians starting third baseman in 1993. His name is Peter Edward Rose II, but the local media handouts listed him as Pete Jr. I had followed his progress for parts of two seasons at Frederick in 1989 and 1990, and he had since been hanging on but never rose above class A ball. The previous year had been his most productive, with a .253 average. In the field he was steady but unspectacular. So far in 1993, he was hitting a typical .224 and, at twenty-four years of age, the string of professional baseball seasons seemed about ready to play out. Taking infield, he struck poses reminiscent of his father.

While examples of sons following fathers with successful baseball careers are common, so are failures. Lee May, Jr., was cut from the Memphis team in 1993. Mickey Mantle, Jr., played for the Alexandria Dukes in the Carolina League in the early 1980s, but he hit poorly and quit after only half a season. Juniors don't automatically have it made in baseball.

I saw two well-played ball games in the pleasant Kinston stadium. Small crowds of about 1,500 came each night and had a good time. The team mascot, which was supposed to be a pelican but bore little resemblance to that bird, provided a diversion for small children who would run up behind the thing, pull its tail, and call it a chicken. "I'm not a chicken!" the mascot would protest. Despite the bucolic atmosphere, I was ready to move on after two nights. The town was dead. Closed up, put away, and locked up dead. The morning after the second game, I was drinking a cup of coffee in a local cafe and saw an article about a groundbreaking ceremony for the Durham Bulls' new ballpark, about a two-hour drive away. Escape time, I thought, and a chance to learn something about stadium architecture. I felt a lot luckier than the players, who were stuck there for the whole summer.

New minor league ballparks are built for three reasons. One, perhaps most common, is to replace existing structures that have deteriorated and no longer provide an attractive place for baseball. A second is to attract a minor league team to the city or to recruit for one of a high classification. A third reason, which may be combined with one of the first two, is for the sake of the community. A new park may help redevelop a deteriorating inner city area or follow a population shift to the suburbs. In Durham's case, it is a combination of the first and third reasons.

The Durham Bulls played at a field called El Toro Stadium from 1926 to 1939, when they moved to the Durham Athletic Park. The latter park had become one of the most famous in minor league baseball. Its snorting bull was a familiar image to fans far beyond Durham or even the Carolina League. In 1991, however, the national association agreed to a new set of standards for all minor league parks throughout the country. Clubs were given until 1994 to renegotiate local arrangements and meet the new criteria. Some of the key specifications for minor league facilities included minimum space for the home team dressing room, number of lavatories for women, dugout length, number of parking spaces, candlepower for infield and outfield lighting, handicapped access to park facilities, and press box amenities. Durham Athletic Park met fewer than 10 percent of the new standards. Even if the park were demolished and rebuilt on its present location, parking and access to a major thoroughfare would still have been lacking.

For even so famous a franchise as the Durham Bulls, stability had not been a given. Nearby Raleigh, part of the research triangle, threatened to draft the territory for a class AA team in the late 1980s. This procedure, which may seem unsportsmanlike, was perfectly within the rules of organized baseball. Fortunately for Durham, the move of the Mudcats to Zebulon in 1991 put a class AA team within a thirty-five-mile radius of Raleigh but not Durham, and provided protection against being drafted out of a team.

In 1990, however, voters of Durham County defeated an $11 million bond proposal to build a new stadium in downtown Durham. While city residents narrowly approved the bill, county residents overwhelmingly voted against it. In 1992, the Bulls threatened to move to Wake County. Without the push from the new standards mandated by organized baseball, the old park would probably have stayed in use indefinitely.

Durham, like many other southern cities, had undergone a transformation of its economy. The main business had shifted from textile mills and tobacco processing to service and research. Durham suffered a serious blow when Burlington Mills and the American Tobacco Company closed about twenty-five years ago. Like other southern cities, Durham had made a concerted effort to keep governmental agencies in the center of town. However, every city needs weekend and evening traffic to remain vital. Arts institutions and entertainment centers are integral to attracting people and dollars, and a minor league park can be a key link in the redevelopment chain.

When I arrived in Durham, groundbreaking activities for the new stadium were getting underway. A Jiffy John had been thoughtfully placed approximately where home plate would be anchored, so prospective fans could get oriented to the park's layout. I was in time to pick up a temporary press badge. This got me a packet of information, an aerial view poster of Durham Athletic Park, and free hot dogs. More importantly, the pass provided access to a representative of the architectural firm that had designed the park. Tom Tingle, the project manager employed by HOK

Sports Facilities Group of Kansas City, was young, bright, articulate, and possessed an unforgettable name. I followed him around, listening to him explain design details and pestering him with architectural questions.

His firm, HOK (Hellmuth, Obata, and Kassabaum), had been involved lately in the design of several high visibility ballparks, including Oriole Park at Camden Yards. It was working on fields for Cleveland and the Colorado Rockies in addition to Durham and other minor league projects. From blueprints, artist conceptions, and Tom's explanations, I began to form a mental picture of the new park.

Added to the usual "state of the art" baseball accommodations were less-typical features. The park would have the largest cantilevered roof in minor league baseball. The old warehouse off Blackwell Street adjacent to left field would furnish details and brick color for the new facility, including a brick restaurant over the left field wall. The park would fit not only into the existing street grid but also into the atmosphere of the larger area. In Tom's language, it would "speak" to the other area buildings.

To keep fans from missing any game action while standing in line for snacks, the plan called for a four-foot elevation for the second tier of grandstand seats and inclusion of two concession stands on the cross aisle. Twelve skyboxes were to be built under the ballpark roof, and a new mechanical bull would breathe fire along the right field wall. Tom seemed most enthusiastic when describing the playing field. Left field was to have a "green monster"-like fence twenty-four feet high with a built-in, hand-operated scoreboard. Left field would also have a hard-to-play ninety degree angle in the corner where balls would likely die and have to be dug out. Deep power alleys would encourage triples. Two forty-five-degree angles in the right field corner would send balls off in unpredictable directions. The park would have an old-time feel and some features that were grassroots Durham, such as ironwork seen on the city's warehouses.

The groundbreaking celebration had a festive atmosphere. Kids played games and had their faces painted; politicians threw a few shovelsful of dirt, and we all sang the chorus to "Take Me Out to the Ball Game." I said hello to Crash Davis of *Bull Durham* fame, who was a real person and a former ballplayer. Lawrence "Crash" Davis was a utility infielder for the Philadelphia Athletics during World War II, and played for Durham for one season in 1948. Crash was a singles-hitting second baseman who, with typical Hollywood license, was portrayed as a home-run hitting catcher by Kevin Costner in the movie about the Bulls.

Listening to Tom Tingle, I was lulled into accepting his premise that a new stadium was necessary and forgetting that I generally appreciate older baseball parks for their character and charm. The Bulls were playing out of town—I would have to wait to see them play an away game in Salem, Virginia—but I drove up to the old field, only ten blocks away, to make a few comparisons.

Though attendance had slipped a little in 1992 (to 281,000 from 301,000 in 1991), the class A Bulls had still outdrawn every AA team except one, and eight AAA teams. The place had a mystique. College students packed the stands nightly, drank, and yelled raucously. The old plywood bull, leftover from filming *Bull Durham*, snorted steam beyond the right field fence after every home team home run. Could a new stadium generate the same fervor?

What exactly, I wondered, were the most important factors for building an edifice for "ballists and cranks," as players and fans were once called? Major and minor league ballparks were originally single-decked, wooden bleacher constructions. At the turn of the century, crowds became too large for these stadiums, but new building materials like structural steel and reinforced concrete made possible a revolutionary change in ballpark design: the upper deck. Fans could sit closer to the action by moving upward. Downtown major league parks like Shibe Park in Philadelphia (1909) had stylized facades with towers and turrets, arches and columns. They were downtown but parking was no problem because fans walked or took the streetcar to the game. Parks were asymmetrical because physical barriers existed in the neighborhoods where they had to be fitted, not because architects wanted to drive the outfielders crazy with contrived angles in the fences.

During the 1960s, the multipurpose stadiums arrived. Modernist architecture provided the form that followed the function, and new

70

admixtures made concrete stronger and easier to pour and cure. Candlestick (1960), Dodger Stadium and R.F.K. (1962), and the nearly identical Busch, Three Rivers, and Riverfront Stadiums before 1970 were testaments to the ability of concrete to support massive, circular, free-standing giants isolated in the center of parking lots that looked like concrete versions of the great American desert.

The modernist parks have not been popular with baseball fans. Recently, architects have returned to classic facades, natural grass fields, and uneven wall heights and fence distances. HOK has been in the forefront of this "retro-park" movement, with designs that merge the parks with their surrounding environments in coherent, attractive manners. Camden Yards is their showpiece and serves as the model and standard for the new "old-time" parks.

Building a minor league park requires different thinking, however. With only a few exceptions at the AAA level, minor league parks are single-deck constructions. Single decks can hold twenty thousand, a number few minor league parks can be expected to exceed regularly in the near future. Without the upper deck to cover the lower one, minor league parks need a supported roof rather than a cantilevered one, even if that means blocking a few seats with the supporting poles.

In a double-deck stadium, skyboxes can be built into the upper deck. In minor league stadiums, they have to sit on the top of the single deck for support or have some more expensive arrangement on or under the roof. Twelve skyboxes seating only 120 people take out a sizeable number of prime seats or force fans into a claustrophobic cave under the boxes. This moves the general seating farther afield, thus accentuating the difference between the skybox "haves" and the general admission "have nots." The major function of skyboxes, or loges, in a single-deck stadium is social distinction and not advantageous viewing. Skyboxes are not close to the action on field.

In minor league parks, press boxes, which are usually on the same level and distance from the field as skyboxes, also have distant views. I always took binoculars when I sat in a press box. Major league press boxes, sitting over the field from perches under or outside the facing of an upper deck, have much better vistas.

71

When minor league parks copy their big league progenitors, they nullify some of their built-in advantages. The best minor league parks I saw were pure and simple, erratic but democratic. Looking around the old Bulls' field I decided that, although the future Durham park would be photographed, written about, and marveled at, the new concrete bull just wouldn't snort quite the same as that rickety old plywood creation.

Next morning, a Sunday, I was driving along Stafford Road in Winston-Salem, North Carolina, looking for a place for breakfast when I saw three neon words glowing red. HOT DOUGHNUTS NOW. Actually, the word "now" was slanted across a doughnut between the words "hot" and "doughnut," so the sign read HOT NOW DOUGHNUTS. I jerked Sweetspot around in an illegal U turn and headed for the Krispy Kreme parking lot. I expected the drivers behind me to shout curses and flip me the bird, but they must have been familiar with this maneuver when the sign was red.

This was the first Krispy Kreme shop I had passed on the trip and I had the good luck to hit it when fresh, hot doughnuts were coming out of the oven. For those who only know Krispy Kreme doughnuts as the stiff, dated products sold by the Girl Scouts, reverence for the hot product may seem undue. The parking lot was crowded with cars of the educated, however, and had everything from a pickup even older than Sweetspot to a sleek black Lincoln Continental. I ordered a cup of coffee and a six pack of glazed and ate four of them in the shop. The waitress topped off customers' coffees and traded stories with the regulars. The glaze dripped and the sugar and fat melted like butter with every bite.

I told an assistant manager there was a Krispy Kreme shop in Alexandria, Virginia, not far from where I lived. He told me with some pride that the company was founded in Winston-Salem in 1937. The founder, Vernon Rudolph, bought a secret recipe from a Creole in the French Quarter of New Orleans and turned the yeast-raised results into a legend with a cult following spreading across the South. Now the one hundred plus shops dotted the Southeast in more than seventy cities, moving as far west as Memphis. The newer places had succumbed to modern trends—drive-through windows and standardized baking times. Traditionally, the doughnuts came out at unpredictable intervals and the red sign would flash randomly. Something will inevitably be lost, of course. The little shop sparkled with friendliness that Sunday morning, with chatter obviously as important as the sugar and carbohydrate-loaded objects that ostensibly brought everyone together.

Before leaving with my two uneaten doughnuts, I said to the assistant manager, "You must get a lot of questions about the history of Krispy Kreme."

"Not really," he said. "Most people just eat the doughnuts."

Swinging at the first pitch he was offered, Motorboat Jones of the Winston-Salem Spirits hit it on a line over the left center field wall at Ernie Shore Stadium. I was in attendance at a Sunday afternoon Carolina League game between the Spirits and the Wilmington Blue Rocks. Ernie Shore had proved to be one of the hardest to find baseball parks in the South. It was buried in a large complex with the huge Wake Forest football stadium, a coliseum, a fairgounds, and acres of other buildings. It had the look of an ampitheater: the grandstand was built into the side of a hill so fans walked down to their seats. The grandstand canopy was wood and, in another old-fashioned touch, a brick wall *à la* Wrigley Field ran behind home plate from first to third.

Motorboat's home run was his first of the year. Before spring training, he had been projected for assignment to Cincinnati's AA team in Chattanooga, but ended up in its Carolina League class A farm team. A native Alabaman, he had been in professional baseball since 1987, playing in rookie and class A leagues. He had speed, but hadn't hit with much authority. 1993 would prove to be a breakthrough year, at least at the class A level. By midseason, Motorboat had eighteen home runs and was hitting .330, figures good enough for a July call up to Chattanooga. Uncharacteristically, he had only six stolen bases for Winston-Salem when he was called up. Apparently Motorboat either ran *or* hit, but not both in the same season.

I was just as interested in Motorboat's nickname as in his developing skills, though. I kept a separate page in my notebook for

73

player nicknames, intending it to be a colorful, interesting list reflecting creativity and imagination. At the end of the trip, however, my disappointingly short list contained only three names. Besides Eugene "Motorboat" Jones, there was "Pork Chop" Pough in Kinston and "Pokey" Reese in Chattanooga. I heard other nicknames used in clubhouses, but only those three were self-applied or used consistently enough to be listed in the media handouts.

Nicknames are a dying art in baseball, and not only at the minor league level. Baltimore pitcher Mike Mussina (pronounced "Mooseina") is called Moose. Old-timers were more resourceful. Commonplace last names seemed to provoke colorful nicknames. The Philadelphia A's had a pretty good pitcher in the twentieth century's first decade called Boardwalk Brown, and the Yankees later weighed in with 295-pound Walter "Jumbo" Brown. The nicknaming custom in baseball can be traced back to the nineteenth century. My own favorite was Bob "Death to Flying Things" Ferguson, the captain of the Brooklyn Atlantics during the 1870s.

Nicknames hadn't always been kind and affectionate. A Phillies pitcher, during their worst prewar years, lost eighteen games in 1937, twenty in 1938, sixteen in 1939, and peaked at twenty-two losses in 1940. He probably felt lucky to escape into the military service during World War II, having long since been known as Hugh "Losing Pitcher" Mulcahy. Athletics' pitcher Lynn "Line Drive" Nelson and Phillies' pitcher Walter "Boom Boom" Beck earned those names because opposing teams teed off on them. Earlier nicknames could also be insensitive derivatives of the racist attitudes in the country. Jay Justin Clarke, a catcher who became famous for hitting eight home runs in a 1903 game for Corsicana, Texas, was called Nig, which was short for "nigger." He was not the only white player to wear the epithet in baseball's early years, but he carried the appellation through an eight-year major league career and baseball encyclopedias still list him as Jay Justin "Nig" Clarke.

Curtis Pride moved up through the minor league ranks and made his debut in the majors for the Montreal Expos on September 14, 1993. Curtis became only the fifth deaf player to reach the major leagues. Of the four who preceded him, two were nicknamed

"Dummy": outfielder William Hoy, 1888–1902; and pitcher Luther Taylor, 1900–1908. Love it or leave it, baseball has never been a model of sensitivity.

Ernie Shore Field opened in 1956, one of the last ballparks built before everyone understood that minor league baseball was on a sharp downward slide. The field was named after Ernest Grady Shore, a major league pitcher for the Giants, Red Sox, and Yankees between 1912 and 1920 and onetime roomate of Babe Ruth. He was also involved in the weirdest perfect game (of sorts) ever pitched. On June 23, 1917, the Babe started a game against the Washington Senators. When the first batter walked, he argued so long that the home plate umpire tossed him out of the game. Ernie Shore came on without warming up properly, the catcher threw out the base runner in a steal attempt, and Ernie retired the next twenty-six batters. While his career was short, he retired with a 63–42 record and an enviable 2.45 ERA. After baseball, he moved back to North Carolina and went into business. The depression broke him, as it did many others. Ernie ran for county sheriff in 1936, won the election, and served in that post until 1970.

I watched as a batter hit a squib, which squirted over to the home team dugout. Following one of baseball's most ironclad rules, a coach picked up the ball, slowly turned it and examined it carefully, then tossed it toward the dugout. The rule says that when a ball is batted or thrown out of play, whoever first impedes its progress must examine it carefully before further dispensing with it. This rule holds for everyone from fan to batboy to coach. I have, however, seen field managers pick up baseballs and casually toss them to trainers for the required inspection. What this inspection is supposed to reveal is one of baseball's great secrets. I sat in the sun, drank a few beers, and felt lucky to be able to ponder such weighty issues.

On page twenty-eight of the Spirits' souvenir program, I saw an interesting picture. Mount Airy, a town about thirty-five miles north of Winston-Salem almost on the Virginia border, was having a reunion for the 1948 Graniteers in June, 1993. Mount Airy had once fielded a class D team in the Blue Ridge League, whose teams were scattered around the North Carolina-Virginia mountain region. The team picture showed seventeen young men, including the manager, in flannel suits. Small rosters were common in that period at class D level. They carried five pitchers, two second basemen, two catchers, one player listed as "utility," and a manager who probably played in a pinch. At all other positions, the roster listed only one name. The team posed in the classic three-tier sitting-kneeling-standing formation. In the background, bleachers and the backs of several buildings hinted at the field on which they played. Since I was driving up Route 62 into Virginia anyway, I stopped off to see if the old park was still there.

Even on a Sunday afternoon the downtown Mount Airy area was busy. Andy Griffith had grown up in the town; several businesses referred to Mayberry or to one of the characters in the popular television series. It was one of the best examples I had seen in the South of how to keep a town alive. The stores had been recycled into specialty shops but had not folded up when core business activity had shifted to the strip on Route 62, over to the west of town.

The village movie theater now housed a visitor's center. The blue-green and white paint was faded and chipped, but it still looked much the same as when Andy got his first taste for the movies.

Inside, a woman stood behind the old concession stand, which now held pamphlets and posters instead of popcorn and Super Duds. She bore a striking resemblance, so help me, to Aunt Bee. When she told me she had grown up in Mount Airy, I asked if she remembered the old ballpark.

"I went to ball games there when I was a young girl," she said. "The town really supported the teams in those years right after the war." The park had been torn down, though, to make way for a police station.

The old theater, on the other hand, had remained practically untouched. Aunt Bee showed me the inside, seats still in place, and on the screen a mural that was continuously projected, of an idealistic, small town America. It was Mount Airy's past the way it is remembered but of course never was.

Mount Airy had recently been voted one of the one hundred best spots to retire in the United States, which will probably be its kiss of death. Only the day before, Aunt Bee told me, Oprah Winfrey had been in town filming her television program there. The late afternoon sun was hazy and about ten miles to the northwest, the Blue Ridge Mountains gave off that azure glow for which they are named. Forty-five years ago, walking through the quaint streets to watch a ball game with the mountains as a backdrop must have been a very Mayberry kind of experience. Maybe they overdo the Andy Griffith shtick a little in Mount Airy, but there you can see what is still alive and positive in a small southern town. The 1948 Mount Airy Graniteers may have lost their ballpark, but their city has stood well against the second half of the twentieth century.

A full house at Texas League Park, c. 1950, during the golden age of minor league baseball. (Courtesy of Tulsa Drillers Baseball Club)

The Oiler Grill, located alongside the left-field line facing outside Texas League Park, in 1948. Patrons could drive in, order food, and listen to Tulsa Oiler away games while they ate. (Courtesy of Wayne McCombs, Claremore, OK)

Overhead view of Texas League Park, at Fifteenth and Sandusky, Tulsa, 1953. No game is in progress, but the Oiler Grill has a little business. (Courtesy of Wayne McCombs, Claremore, OK)

Sweetspot at a lunch stop in Georgia. A combination office, living space and reliable, smooth transportation.

Paul Eames, for whom the park in Albany, GA, is named. Wally Moon is watching the action during batting practice.

Jose Flores, shortstop for the Capital City Bombers , Columbia, SC.

World War Memorial Stadium, Greensboro, NC. One of the oldest diamonds in Dixie, built before world wars had numbers.

Groundbreaking for a new stadium in Durham, NC.

Waiting for the pitch, Ernie Shore Field, Winston-Salem, NC.

A police station now graces the field where the 1948 Mt. Airy Graniteers played. (Courtesy of David Beal, Mt. Airy, NC)

1948 "GRANITEERS" – BLUE RIDGE LEAGUE.

1ST. ROW – ZWELLING – 1ST. B., TEER – 2ND. B., TREECE – P., HOLMES – S.S., YEARICK – C.,
2ND. ROW – MARSHALL – R.F., WILLIAMS – P., SOLTERS – UTILITY, NIXON – R.,
3RD ROW – HALL – C., HOLT – L.F., KING – P., DAVIS – 3RD. B., ESSIC – 2ND. B., AKINS C.F.
JACKSON – P., CASBIER – MANAGER.

ECKEROO PHOTO

Watt Powell Park, Charleston, WV. Railroad tracks beyond right field tempt left-handed hitters when a train rolls by.

Nashville's quirky Sulphur Dell, 1908, with Butler choking up on the bat. Note the dirt lane from home plate to the pitcher's mound. (Courtesy of National Baseball Library & Archive, Cooperstown, NY)

Scoreboard at Herschel Greer Stadium, Nashville, TN, paying homage to "Music City."

Artificial turf infield at Tim McCarver Field, Memphis, TN.

6

The Night the Lights
Went Out in Lynchburg

I PICKED UP THE BLUE RIDGE PARKWAY down near the North Carolina border and drove along the spine of the Blue Ridge Mountains to the Roanoke Valley in Virginia. The parkway connected the Shenandoah National Park in Virginia and the Great Smokey Mountains National Park in North Carolina and Tennessee. At high elevations, the road gave a sensation of gliding along a mountain path. Mountain laurel crowded the pavement and the white pines grew close enough to form a canopy overhead. On a Monday morning, I had the road almost to myself. It was not a commuter highway and tourists came only on the weekends to look at the scenery.

As I dropped in elevation from three thousand feet to the valley floor, which lay at about one thousand feet, the redbud maples went from bare to new buds to full bloom, as if I were watching time-lapse photography. The great valley, which contained the Salem-Roanoke area, extended from New York to Alabama and where I descended was bounded by the Alleghenies on the west and the Blue Ridge Mountains on the east. In the springtime it was lush and green. Tiny Salem, in the middle of the valley, had a team in the Carolina League.

Municipal Field in Salem has enough idiosyncrasies to satisfy even the most nostalgic baseball fan. I drove over to meet Sam Lazarro, the Salem Buccaneers general manager, and to watch batting practice. The club offices were located upstairs from a karate school in a small, two-story white frame house owned by the city and adjacent to the ballpark. As Sam and I walked around the field, he filled me in on the history of baseball in the Roanoke Valley.

Baseball was first played on the site now in use in 1927. The grandstand and bleachers of Municipal Field were built into the side of a hill, but originally, home plate was in what is now center field. Batters would try to hit the ball far enough up the hill to make it around the bases before the ball came back in. Roanoke, just to the east, and Salem alternated with teams during most of the century, but Salem had sponsored professional baseball continuously since 1955, first in the Appalachian League and since 1968 in the Carolina League.

The Blue Ridge Mountains formed a panoramic backdrop over the outfield fence. The most prominent peak, called Twelve O'clock Knob, visible over left center, was so named because in plantation days slaves knew it was noon and time to take a break when the sun was directly over the summit.

The ballpark takes up a full city block, but has dead space in several places because of the hill. The field was originally set up for football, so the bleachers don't wrap around. No bleachers run down the first-base line, leaving an enormous amount of foul territory fanning out to the fence. Since the grandstand backs into the hill, fans enter from beside left field or at the top of the hill at about first base level. Streets run immediately outside the outfield walls all the way around. There is no room for light stanchions outside the park, so they stand inside the fence and are in play up to the transformers. The fences are an irregular 316 feet to left, 408 feet to center, and 302 feet to right. Power alleys are crouched a claustrophobic 323 to 327 feet away. Not surprisingly, Sam told me that Salem was always near or in the league lead in home runs. The outfield walls are cinderblock with signs painted directly on the concrete. The short right field fence has a forty foot screen running along the wall for about twenty yards, affording some protection for the row of small clapboard houses just across the street.

Fans are close to the action at Municipal Field. The distance from home plate to the backstop is only thirty feet, about half the distance of most other parks. Concrete ledges form the bleacher seating and had been poured extra wide; many fans bring their own folding lawn chairs for seating.

From a business viewpoint, Sam had a handful of problems. Parking was limited to the streets and one very small lot. Concession stands were inadequate. The press box, a small enclosure sitting on top of the grandstand seats, had recently been expanded but was still cramped. The only cure for these ills was a new park, but the outlook for one was uncertain.

As batting practice was winding down, I left the park to find a place for dinner. Walking outside the left-field fence to the small parking lot, I saw a ball sail over the wall. I jogged a few steps, turned and fielded it cleanly on the seventh bounce. After the mandatory examination, I installed the ball on Sweetspot's dashboard. This park, I thought, must give the club a fat bill for baseballs.

The evening's game between Salem and the Durham Bulls confirmed my first impressions. Baseballs flew out of the little park like terrified geese looking for a safe haven after hearing a shotgun blast. Weather conditions had been reasonable at game time, but when the sun slipped behind the ballpark's hill, a teeth-chattering chill descended on the few hundred patrons. After two innings, I could hardly hold a pencil to keep score, and climbed up to the press box to see if it was any warmer. The enclosure cut down the windchill factor by a few degrees, and a heater was going, which helped a little.

The scorer, Brian Hoffman, told me that he had spent over twenty years in his job. I didn't meet any scorers with greater longevity, though a few came close. While we were talking, a player bashed one off the Marlboro man's saddle. I started to pencil in a home run on the score sheet but the player was scrambling for second base and the umpire hadn't signaled home run with the familiar circular motion. Brian laughed. "He's in play here, all the way to the top of his hat." I looked through my binoculars and saw that the slender pole supporting the advertisement was inside the fence. The nearness of the road outside didn't provide enough space for even that narrow pole.

Brian, whom everyone called "Hoop," was a popular figure in Salem. All evening friends and acquaintances trooped by the front of the open press box to talk sports. Brian was sports editor for several weekly publications in the Salem-Roanoke area, and was a rich source of baseball information.

The evening got colder and colder. In the sixth inning, we looked down into the Buccaneers' bullpen and saw an open fire burning, with several pitchers warming their hands over the blaze. Sam Lazarro came into the press box a little later with the information that they were burning broken bats. He looked nervous because the fire was near the tarp used to cover the infield. He didn't make the players douse the blaze but continued to look warily toward the bullpen all during the game.

The Buccaneer pitchers had a few fires on the field to worry about, as well, as Durham worked them for thirteen hits and eleven runs. This barrage included four home runs and two triples. Despite the almost nonexistent power alleys, center field was deep (408 feet) and permitted frequent triples over the center fielder's head. Caroms off the cinderblock walls gave the outfielders fits, and the scoreboard, located only about 330 feet from home plate, suffered a broken bulb despite being covered with a net.

Rocky Bridges, employed by the Pirates as a roving infield instructor, was working with players during pregame warmups the following day. Rocky, a Texan who played eleven years in the majors during the fifties and early sixties, had celebrated his sixty-fourth birthday the week before. He was a popular figure in Salem, having managed the team a few years before. According to Sam Lazarro, he got mad only twice all year, both times because the beer wasn't in the clubhouse fast enough after games were over.

Rocky was the epitome of that much underappreciated role player, the utility infielder. In an era known for player stability with teams, he played for seven teams in eleven years. He had over four hundred at bats in only one of those years, but hung on with a .247 lifetime batting average and little home run power because he could play three infield positions. Now, despite having arthritis in his hands and, apparently, in his legs, Rocky traveled the Pirates' farm circuit hitting grounders to young infielders. I asked him about how fielding skills develop compared to hitting ability.

"Hitting skills actually develop earlier. I just look for glaring errors. Sometimes I come to work out something about a specific player." Rocky, at five feet eight inches tall and 170 pounds, talked around a mass of chewing tobacco that significantly increased his weight. He shot grounders out with precision, grunting slightly if one was a foot or two from its intended trajectory.

By game time that evening, conditions seemed perfect again. The temperature was in the sixties with no wind. At 7:00 P.M., the sun cast long shadows across the grass and the lights were on. Behind home plate I could smell the grass and the damp infield dirt. The Blue Ridge Mountains stood half in shadow, half in sunlight. By the fourth inning, however, the temperature had dropped again and I headed for the press box.

A plaque inside the ballpark at Salem contains a poignant message. Under a bronze relief of a ballplayer's head, it reads:

Dedicated to the Memory of
Francisco Alfredo Edmead
1956–1974

Who on August 22, 1974
was fatally injured during
a game played at Salem, Va.
United States, between the
Salem Pirates and the Rocky
Mount Phillies in the Class
A Carolina League.

He was one of the most
highly regarded players in
the Pirate organization and a
credit to the Dominican Republic,
but even more important, he
enjoyed the reputation of a
kind and decent human being.

I asked Brian Hoffman about the incident. It had happened during his first year as scorer with the club. Edmead, the right fielder, came in on a pop fly as the second baseman faded back on it. He dove for the ball and his head hit the second baseman's knee, which was covered by a metal brace. The right fielder crumpled and lost consciousness. He was rushed to the hospital, but later that evening, died. Unbeknownst to his team, Edmead had been born with a paper-thin skull, and what would have produced no more than a headache or a concussion in another player had been fatal to the young Dominican. No PA announcement was made, so that the manager could tell the players after the game was finished. His playing manager, Pablo Cruz, had been the second baseman involved in the collision.

Baseball parks, like persons, have personalities. You can get a feel for them, like meeting someone new, after a few hours, but deeper patterns and traits emerge slowly. Municipal Field had such a quirky personality that I couldn't imagine seeing a routine game there if I had stayed all summer. This one saw fifteen total runs with four home runs, three of which were really routine flies. Managers almost never ran anyone, because even the weakest hitter could lift a fly over those cozy walls.

I felt sorry for the pitchers. During the second game, a Salem pitcher sent word up to the press box that he thought a run scored the previous inning should be unearned. Occasionally, situations occur in a game in which the scorer's judgment determines whether a run is earned or unearned. In this case, an error allowed a runner to go to second on a single. The next batter doubled, and Brian ruled that the runner could have scored from first and therefore was the pitcher's responsibility. The pitcher had relayed a detailed message containing his viewpoint, and Brian was trying to evaluate it. "Can you see his point?" he asked everyone within earshot. While the debate was going on, the pitcher hung a curve and the batter hit it over the fence and off the roof of a house across the street. The press box erupted in laughter. "He should concentrate on the batter at the plate," Brian said. "One earned run doesn't mean a hell of a lot in this park."

Lynchburg, Virginia, is Falwell country. While cousin Jerry sees to the spiritual needs of folks in this city of seven hills, Calvin Falwell makes sure that baseball fans have a place to meet their needs for the American pastime. Calvin is president of the Lynchburg Baseball Corporation, which owns the Lynchburg Red Sox, a Boston affiliate. I sat through a shortened Carolina League contest between Lynchburg and the Winston-Salem Spirits with Calvin, his wife, and his adult son Terry, who had been a batboy for the Lynchburg team in his youth. Calvin is a distinguished-looking gentleman who was honored for his contributions to Lynchburg baseball in 1992 with a plaque, which now resides at City Stadium.

Falwells had lived for two hundred years on the same piece of land in Lynchburg. Formerly a dairy farm, the property now housed several businesses and had been annexed by the city. Calvin Falwell first organized a group to buy a baseball franchise for Lynchburg in the 1950s. His lifelong interest went back to boyhood when his father drove a bus for prewar semipro baseball teams in Lynchburg. Teams of that era played at the same location where City Field was later built.

"In those days," Calvin told me, "people would drive to the field and park their cars around where left field and the clubhouse are, and watch games from their cars. Sometimes the afternoon sun glancing off their windshields would blind the hitters, and the umpire would make them move their cars. And I saw at least two car windows broken by line drives."

Calvin Falwell had always been a hands-on owner. In 1959, the umpire ejected Lynchburg's manager from a game. There were no other coaches so the players continued the game unmanaged. Unfortunately, a long-simmering cauldron of bad feeling over playing time erupted and a free-for-all broke out among the Lynchburg players. The bench emptied, as it were. The other team watched in amazement as the Lynchburg players pummeled each other, and waited for the melee to end so the game could continue. Falwell and a police officer finally restored order and sat on the bench to maintain tranquility for the rest of the game.

Lynchburg was without baseball in 1960 and 1961 but in 1962 events connected with civil rights unrest brought a team back for a few games at the end of the season. Savannah had an entry in the class AA South Atlantic League in 1962, and late in the season was in a pennant race. But the racial tension in Savannah had become potentially explosive. The franchise sought a new home to avoid

85

violence even though only one week remained in the season. Falwell saw a chance to lure a team to Lynchburg and acted quickly.

"I remember Deacon Jones [a former pitcher with Detroit from 1916 through 1918, then a coach with Savannah] saying to me, 'Mr. Falwell, before the team moves I need to know one thing. How did the city of Lynch-burg get its name, anyway?' " Deacon must have been mollified, because Lynchburg has been home to a professional baseball team ever since.

As we were talking and watching the game in the sixth inning, a transformer fuse blew and the stadium lights went down. Auxiliary lights on a different circuit provided dim visibility for fans in the grandstand, but play stopped. As we waited for the repair crews to get the banks of lights working again, I realized what the term southern gentleman really means. At least five fans came by and made the same banal remarks about the club not paying its electric bill. Calvin laughed as heartily and discussed the situation with as much animation at the fifth comment as he had at the first. After about twenty minutes it became apparent that the repairs couldn't be made quickly and the game was suspended, to be continued the next day.

Next afternoon I went looking in the Lynchburg clubhouse for a new ballplayer. Dan Gakeler had arrived just that day and hadn't put on his entire uniform yet. He was waiting for a numbered jersey, and his number was a high fifty-six.

Dan was a ten-year veteran who had worked his way from the 1984 draft through every level of baseball in the minors, finally arriving at Detroit in 1991. He appeared in thirty-one games for Detroit that year, starting seven. Then, in 1992, every player's worst fear became reality for Dan Gakeler. A muscle tear in his shoulder forced him to miss the entire season and to undergo off-season surgery. In the spring of 1993 he trained with the Philadelphia Phillies, but the Phillies released him before they went north. Instead of looking for a nonbaseball job, or just waiting for the phone to ring, the big pitcher took things into his own hands and started looking for a minor league team.

Dan and I sat in the bleachers and talked before the team took the field for pregame warmups. He was an imposing 6'6" and 220 pounds. In two days he would be twenty-nine years old.

"After I was cut in spring my agent couldn't place me. I kept throwing at a college trying to stay in shape. Monday I finally called Ed Kenney [Boston Red Sox Player Development Director] and he arranged a tryout for me here Tuesday." Dan had originally been drafted by the Boston Red Sox and was later traded to Montreal and then to the Tigers.

At the class A level, baseball rules allow two veterans on a team. I asked Dan how the rules defined "a veteran." "I don't know what the rules say," he said, "but I'm pretty sure I am one."

Dan couldn't pinpoint the reason for his injury. He speculated that it could have been overuse, bad mechanics, or just the effects of ten years of professional pitching.

"How bad is it?" I asked.

"This kind of muscle tear, full recovery is a year, year and a half. It affected my speed."

On Tuesday, he had pitched for Jim Bibby, the Lynchburg Red Sox pitching coach. Bibby was a former major league pitcher himself. He had thrown a no-hitter against Oakland while pitching for the Texas Rangers, and in 1980 won nineteen games for the Pittsburgh Pirates. After the tryout, Bibby said Dan "was around 86, 87 [miles per hour] and was over the plate, had a real good breaking ball, and good velocity." According to Dan, his fast ball was still under par because of the injury. They decided to put him in the bullpen and see what happened.

I asked Dan if he had started looking at other options like managing or coaching. "I've been afraid to take a job and then have an opportunity in baseball open up. Whatever the job was I'd leave it, so the better the job the worse it would be."

His plans were focused on the here and now, and while ballplayers always say they're taking it a game at a time, in Dan's case it was really true. He was married, had a young daughter, and his wife was pregnant. He had no way of knowing how far an injury-weakened arm would take him. But he was in uniform, or would be as soon as they got him a numbered jersey. I wished him well

87

and told him I would check back with him before the season was over.

After my trip, I drove over to Prince William's County Stadium in northern Virginia to see the Cannons play Lynchburg in the last minor league game on the Carolina League schedule. I especially wanted to see how Gakeler was doing. His season, as I had followed it through accounts in *Baseball America,* had been both promising and frustrating. By late August he had worked only forty innings because of recurring physical problems. When he worked, however, he was effective. His ERA was a team low of 1.56. I walked out to the bullpen to talk to him but looked at the media handouts on the way. His name wasn't listed.

"Did Gakeler get released?" I asked one of the pitchers.

"He just left for AAA," the pitcher told me.

Dan was probably sitting in Pawtucket at that very moment, waiting for a uniform jersey, wondering if his shoulder would make it long enough for another off-season of rest.

Lynchburg was a nice city, but I had driven within that radius where home was pulling at me like a magnet. I planned to go home for the weekend before continuing the trip. I drove up Route 29, took Route 66 into the heavy traffic of the Washington, D.C., metropolitan area, crossed the familiar American Legion Bridge and turned up alongside the river. I was on a three-day homestand in the middle of a ninety-day road trip.

The stop had been planned as a means of resupplying and discarding superfluous items. Actually, little rearranging was necessary. More important was a mental accounting. The South had been coming at me without letup, with continual movement and new experiences leaving little time for reflection.

At one time the Old South was "down there" as a single entity, once you crossed the Potomac River or the Ohio River. That was no longer true, but I kept finding traces of it as strong and real as in my boyhood memories—Calvin Falwell, Mount Airy, the fisherman in Florida. I hadn't yet decided whether these episodes were leftover fragments of the past or evidence of a solid continuation of the southern mosaic.

Minor league baseball in the South was not the same experience as when I was young. Young men like Chris White and Dan Gakeler were as dedicated to the game as any generation of players in the past could have been, yet the crowds watching them play were different. Many of the fans I had met were more concerned about giveaways like Refrigerator Magnet Night than the quality of play onfield. The promotions and contests were surprising to me, because when I was young, the only things we were ever given were doubleheaders. Yet the parks were friendly and homey, and I was charmed by the informality and good nature of minor league club officials. Perhaps, I thought, the Deep South and western South had held more firmly to traditional baseball than had the populous Southeast.

Monday morning I left for Charleston, West Virginia, to see its Sally League team play. Intending to break up the ten-hour drive with some trout fishing in western Maryland, I made several stops along the way: a Maryland winery in the foothills, where I carefully sampled everything on the shelves before buying a bottle of chenin blanc; a roadside stand to buy fresh strawberries; the old Casselman Hotel, which has done business on the National Pike (now Route 40) since 1820, to buy some fresh raisin bread from the Mennonites who run the place.

In the mountains, I parked next to a branch of the Savage River, put the wine in the chilly water, and walked up a fire road carrying my fishing gear. I went about half a mile up the stream, saving the first part of the creek for the morning. It was fast moving and rocky but not easy to fish because it lacked cover. I caught and released a few small brook trout and finally, as dusk fell and provided better cover, landed two medium-sized brown trout.

It was almost dark when I made it back to Sweetspot. I rolled the trout in seasoned corn meal, cooked them on my single burner stove, one at a time, and ate them with strawberries, fresh raisin bread, and cold Maryland wine. After cleaning up, I backed Sweetspot carefully behind a screen of mountain laurel. The little battery-operated television wouldn't pick up anything in the mountains; even the radio didn't register a signal.

I was homesick again, having cleverly arranged the trip so that I

89

had to adjust twice to being on the road, rather than once. Listening to the trout stream, I tried Hemingway's old trick of mentally fishing it, moving carefully up through the pools and riffles until I went to sleep.

Appalachian Spring

THE TRADITIONAL IMAGE OF A minor league baseball club owner is this: he or she owns 100 percent of the team, has no other businesses, lives in the town of the team, knows everyone who attends games, and makes a hardscrabble living by attending to every last detail of the team's operation. When I left on my tour of the South, that was my notion; but I soon accepted that it was outdated, and might never have been true. The owner I envisioned exists only in nostalgic mists and in Charleston, West Virginia.

The Charleston Wheelers (short for stern-wheelers, the paddle-boats that used to ply the Kanawha River) were owned and operated by Dennis and Lisa Bastien. They constituted one of the few mom and pop baseball operations in the United States today, but the term hardly conveys an accurate picture of this dynamic couple. Dennis had recently turned forty years old when I met him and was suave, intense, and self-assured. Lisa, his partner and executive vice-president, had given birth to their first child, Wyatt, the previous fall. Wyatt had been appointed director of youth activities and, safely ensconced in his combination crib and office, he was being raised in the old baseball park on MacCorkle Avenue.

Watt Powell Park had a bright blue and green paint job, but there was no hiding the fact that this was an old, decrepit ballpark. Dennis showed me around, lamenting that I had missed yesterday afternoon's sellout crowd of eighth graders and would see games in which the number of fans was expected to be small. By concerning himself with such public relations details, he had brought 135,000

91

fans into Watt Powell the previous year, the second highest attendance in the South Atlantic League, despite having a small market
and antiquated facilities. The concrete grandstand was cracked
and had so many leaks that Dennis had to install indoor gutters to
channel water when it rained. The national association had recently sent a letter threatening to revoke the franchise because the
clubhouse, concessions, and handicapped access to the press box
did not meet PBA standards. Dennis's other woes included perennial bad weather in the spring and having to share the field with
the University of Charleston part of the year. "Charleston is better
suited for a short-season league," Dennis admitted. "There isn't
enough flat land in the Kanawha Valley to build a new park, and
the place is too far gone to meet standards for class A."

According to Dennis, Watt Powell once had the largest dimensions of any professional park in the United States. Though baseball had been played on the site for most of the century, the present
facility dated to 1948. The original dimensions were 360 feet down
the left field line, 466 feet to left center, 527 feet to dead center,
528 feet to right center, and 330 feet to right. Present dimensions
had been scaled back to 340 feet (left), 406 feet (center), and 330
feet (right). The power alleys were still an impressive 390 and 384
feet, however, and a sixteen-foot wall surrounded the immense
green outfield. Dennis and I walked behind the present fence to see
the old outer concrete wall, which was still in place. He told me
that Ted Kluzewski had hit one over the old centerfield wall in an
exhibition game. Given the height of the wall, the total distance
would have to come close to six hundred feet. I said that I had
never heard about this singular feat before. Dennis replied that he
had heard the story from a reliable source, but he stopped short of
vouching for its accuracy.

Dennis had a history of taking on down-and-almost-out baseball
situations and turning them around. He started in 1979 in Gasto-
nia, North Carolina (SAL), where he won a minor league executive
of the year award. He moved to Macon, Georgia, and took over a
team whose previous owners had skipped out on $85,000 worth of
debts. Dennis repaid the debts and made $15,000 net profit. He
moved to Spartansburg, South Carolina, next and revived an al-

most equally numb franchise. Dennis had often ended up having to undertake construction projects single-handedly, like building an office facility in Winston-Salem, his next stop, by himself. By then Dennis was an owner. While living in the locker room in Winston-Salem's park, Dennis married Lisa and acquired a partner in his baseball franchise masochism. In 1987, they moved over to the present situation in Charleston, West Virginia.

Dennis obviously was a marketing and sales virtuoso, but he upheld strict policies about advertising. I remarked that the familiar Marlboro man sign was missing. "I think it's ridiculous to talk about baseball and clean living and take money from cigarette and beer companies," he said. He showed me a large family seating area where smoking and drinking were prohibited. Such areas are not unusual in the minor leagues, but these seats had a prominent placement in Watt Powell Park.

Dennis began telling me about plans to field a AA team in Lexington, Kentucky, by 1995. It became apparent that a few things were still missing. Dennis didn't own a team to move to Lexington; Lexington didn't have a ballpark and hadn't made a commitment to build one; and Lexington hadn't sponsored professional baseball since 1954. For someone with less of a track record, these problems would have seemed insurmountable. For Dennis, they seemed almost matter of fact.

When Dennis excused himself to go spell Lisa in taking care of Wyatt, I walked onto the field. The groundskeeper was working on the batter's box. "You should get extra pay for an outfield that size," I suggested. He agreed. For all its size, however, Watt Powell looked like a hitter's park. I stood at home plate, looking over the center field fence at a large, heavily wooded hill punching up about three hundred feet and beginning about fifty yards beyond the fence. I could imagine a white, spinning spheroid coming out of the dark background and mentally made good contact. Just beyond the right-field wall, train tracks ran along a ten-foot elevation, and I could see the cars of a train from home plate. A left-handed hitter must feel a tangible temptation when a train chugs past because it seems reachable.

Later, the scorer told me that several balls had been hit into moving coal cars. I had read differently, that Rudy York and Luke Easter had come close but hadn't actually reached moving trains. The only case that was fairly well documented was that of a ball hit by Randy Bush of the Toledo Mud Hens of the International League on April 14, 1982. It landed on a moving coal train behind and above the right-field fence and was supposed to have traveled two hundred miles. I liked Watt Powell. In this ballpark, fact and fiction blended the way dusk became darkness.

During my Charleston sojourn, when I wasn't at Watt Powell I stayed at Kanawha State Forest, south of town. In April and May, by traveling north I had stayed in an extended spring, where the azaleas and dogwoods and redbuds were always in bloom. I backed Sweetspot into a small glen, ringed by wooded hills and serenaded by a small brook leading back into a dark hollow. Spring wild-flowers glittered in the bright sunshine. Their whimsical names— Dutchman's breeches, bloodroot, pink lady's slipper, jack-in-the pulpit—had been assigned in simpler times, even before spring in Appalachia meant the beginning of another baseball season.

My second night at Watt Powell, the Wheelers brought in a relief pitcher named Pickett in the top of the third. He had just joined the team and was not listed in the media handouts. He immediately walked the bases full, then struck out two, then a batter reached on an error, and then they began to hit him. The immense power alleys were in shadow and the outfielders almost disappeared on balls hit into the gap. The lighting was the worst I saw on the trip. To add to Pickett's problems, the scorer was unusually generous in scoring dropped flies as base hits, probably because of the dim lighting.

Pickett then hit a batter, who had to leave the game for X rays. The next batter hit a double. Pickett's fastball was in the mid-eighties, but had little movement on it. He had a slow, roundhouse curve, which he used as a change-up, but had trouble getting it over. He was most successful when he was "sneaky fast." A moderately fast pitch would be followed by one with a slower motion but last-second follow-through made the pitch faster than the previous one. Unfortunately, they were hitting his setup pitch a mile.

Pickett was taken out in the top of the sixth. I was still marveling over the worst pitching performance I had seen in a long time, when the scorer announced his line in the press box. Despite walking five, giving up three doubles and a single, having one error committed behind him, hitting a batter, and allowing two long outs that would have been home runs almost anywhere else (including most major league parks), he had given up only two earned runs (plus three unearned) thanks to the timing of the error.

Unlike in life, things have a way of balancing out in baseball. A week and a half earlier, I had sympathized with pitchers as routine flies disappeared out of cozy Municipal Field in Salem, Virginia. Watt Powell Park had been a guardian angel for Pickett, but sooner or later he'll end up pitching in a park where the devil will get his due.

Before the season was over, I read in *Baseball America* that Dennis Bastien had acquired an option to buy the AA Southern League Nashville Xpress and planned to operate the team out of Lexington, Kentucky, in 1995. To do so, he traded in the class A Wheelers, in much the same way that other people trade in an old car on a new model. The owner of the Xpress planned to sell the Wheelers back to a local Charleston group, so Watt Powell will resound with the cracks of wooden bats for the foreseeable future.

Pete ("The Old Gladiator") Browning, who played baseball in Louisville, Kentucky, was one of the early tragic figures of the game. One day in 1884, he broke a bat (the least of his misfortunes) during a game attended by John Andrew Hillerich, who worked for his father in a woodworking shop in Louisville. The young man took Browning back to his father's shop, put a piece of white ash on a lathe, and turned it as Pete directed. Next day, Browning used his new bat, and had three hits. Not long afterward the Hillerichs decided that there was more money in bats than in butter churns.

Pete Browning had the reputation of being ignorant and illiterate. He gave his bats biblical names and thought that each one had only a certain number of hits in it. He was a good hitter, despite this eccentric thinking, and other players began to believe that he was onto something with the new Louisville bats. Unfortunately,

95

Pete also suggested that drinking helped him hit, and his beer consumption was legendary.

In truth, the Old Gladiator suffered from a condition called mastoiditis. The disease left him almost deaf, contributing to his appearance of stupidity, and probably eventually led to a brain infection. Drinking may not have helped him hit so much as to play through pain. After his baseball career, he was committed to an insane asylum and died at the early age of forty-four.

By the first part of the twentieth century, J. Frederick Hillerich and Sons were pioneering the concept of athletic endorsements. Honus Wagner was the first player to be paid for allowing his signature to be branded onto bats, followed by Larry Lajoie and Ty Cobb. Today about 70 percent of current major leaguers are under contract for bat signatures, and the company has eight thousand metal inscriptions (both past and present) in its files.

I had driven across Kentucky to see how bats are made. The first thing I learned was that the Louisville Slugger is made not in Louisville but across the Ohio River in Indiana. The huge production plant has 250,000 square feet (almost seven acres) under one roof. Inside, the noise level is high, but the wonderful smell of wood being worked permeates every corner and helps to compensate.

Bats are made from northern white ash harvested in New York and Pennsylvania. The company has tried hickory and hackberry, but ash is clearly the strongest wood. The trees have to be at least sixty years old before they are cut. After arriving at the plant, the wood is stored four to six weeks, until a 12 to 15 percent moisture content is achieved. The wood is weighed and graded three times on a scale of one to four. Only the highest grade is used for professional bats.

Semiautomatic lathes spin out a bat every fifteen seconds. One aspect of bat making has changed little since the days of Pete Browning. The trademark is still burn branded into the wood and then the wood is sanded to remove yellow scorch marks. In early stages, a peg or knob protrudes from the grip end of the bat for ease in turning and working. After branding, the bat goes through a finishing machine that removes the pegs, stamps numbers on the end and flame tempers the bat to make it darker.

Some bats then are mechanically hollowed out at the meat end to make them lighter without altering their length. This modification is legal according to the baseball community. Finally, the bat is hand dipped into clear lacquer and hung to dry for thirty minutes.

Hillerich and Bradsby, as the company is now called, is an integral part of baseball tradition, and is sensitive to its role as bat maker. While electronic lathes and tracer lathes partly automate the general production, some bats are still hand turned. If a persnickety player shows up with peculiar specifications, he can watch the same process Ty Cobb observed eighty years ago.

I asked a worker why players are always told to hold the bat with the trademark up. He said that the wood's strongest course was bound by the visible grain, running lengthwise under the trademark. The sweet spot produces greater power not only because of physics but because the wood is stronger there. Contact with that point, he added, produces a tenor sound instead of a toneless thunk.

Aluminum bats are made in the company's California plant. I asked my tour guide if she was aware that another company was making bats composed of plastic and sawdust. She said no, apparently truthfully, as the alarmed look on her face suggested that I had just ruined her day.

Before leaving the plant, I stopped at the souvenir counter to claim the custom bat I had ordered before my tour. It was a beautiful piece of white ash, 36 inches long, newly turned and lacquered, and had my name forever burned into the business end. I had vowed not to collect souvenirs on the trip, and this was the first item I had bought. Still, Sweetspot's cab was beginning to look like a teenager's bedroom. I had collected a few errant baseballs while watching batting practices, had been given a few caps, and had colorful press passes hanging from the visors and mirror. I walked out with my new bat to add to the collection, fondling it along the way.

Even apart from the manufacture of baseball's most famous bats, Louisville was closely connected to the early development of the game. The Ohio River city fielded teams in the American Association, an early big league rival of the National League, from 1882 through 1891, and for the 1892–1893 season was admitted into the senior circuit. One year the team nickname was the Night Riders, a reference to participants in Kentucky's tobacco raids of that period. The name probably didn't increase attendance by African-Americans, however, who were watchful of Klan activity around this southern city. Another label of questionable taste was applied to the 1890 team, which was called the Cyclones because a tornado hit Louisville in March of that year. The tornado had killed seventy-five persons.

For most of the early years of baseball, the game penetrated no farther south than the banks of the Potomac in the East. In the Midwest, the Ohio formed a similar barrier except for Louisville, which was just across the river. For all the seemingly long association of the South and baseball, the national pastime's beginnings were distinctly northern and eastern.

Baseball has actually had two beginnings, one dramatically invented and idealized, the other real and more evolutionary than revolutionary. Neither, however, had anything to do with the South. The mythical origin of baseball can be traced to the need to fit the national pastime into an American framework, and to believe that its origin came out of the fiber of the new nation. A commission was appointed in 1907 to fix, once and for all, the beginnings of baseball. Solely on the written testimony of one elderly respondent, the commission accepted the idea that Abner Doubleday had laid out the game in its essentials in 1839, in Cooperstown, New York. Note that the witness, a Mr. Abner Graves, was recalling events of sixty-eight years before. General Doubleday himself never mentioned baseball as one of his interests. His childhood interests seem to have been mapmaking and reading, and the critical events of his adult years included four years spent getting the southern rebels back in line during the Civil War.

In the early twentieth century, when the commission met, sentiment against immigration was peaking. Earlier immigrants from northern and western Europe had blended rather easily into the new nation. Feelings were turning against the new immigrants from southern and eastern Europe who were streaming through Ellis Island with foreign languages, religions, and customs, because they were assimilating slowly. This sentiment, which broadened to a general antiforeign, nationalistic fervor, would peak in 1920 with the adoption of restrictive immigration quotas to slow the torrent to a trickle. To imagine baseball, the most American game, as having a foreign origin became unthinkable. Besides, anyone who has ever been to the quaint village of Cooperstown, New York, can easily see that baseball *should* have been invented there, whether it was or not.

Baseball's true origins have been traced most convincingly by Harold Seymour in *Baseball: The Early Years*, a thorough if somewhat grouchy review of the game's roots. Baseball developed from the English game of rounders. Published accounts show that rules for the two games were the same until 1829, and gradually began to diverge. The term "base-ball" was published in a rhyme as early as 1744 in England, and the journal account of a revolutionary soldier in 1778 reveals that games of "base" were played at Valley Forge. No doubt, other antecedents of the game can be found in other cultures, because the game simply evolved as an organized means of having fun with a stick or club and something that was round and could roll or fly through the air. Games played in early nineteenth-century America included barn ball, where one boy would throw the ball against a barn and another boy would bat it; and "one old cat," in which one boy would throw to a batter, who would hit the ball, run to a designated point, and try to return to the base before the second boy could field the fall and "soak" the runner, or plunk him, with the ball. As settled areas became more dense in the northeast, the games became more elaborate, and two, three, and four old cat were born. As players were added, rules became more fixed and extensive as needed.

If a single frozen instant and a solitary creator is needed against which to mark time and celebrate baseball's birth, the year 1846 and the name Alexander Cartwright are the logical candidates. Beginning in 1842, a group of New York gentlemen had been meeting to play baseball. Rival teams would meet irregularly at a vacant lot in Manhattan near Madison Avenue and Twenty-seventh Street. Cartwright, a bank teller and volunteer fireman, eventually suggested forming a social club with baseball as its major focus. The Knickerbocker Club was formally organized, and a set of rules and regulations was drawn up to pattern on-field play and to elaborate proper manners and baseball decorum. While rules would continue to evolve during the nineteenth century and undergo modification thereafter, the crucial elements of Cartwright's game are easily recognizable by the modern fan. More importantly, they were substantially different from the "Massachusetts game," which held sway in and around Boston. Instead of using a diamond, Bostonians favored a horseshoe-shaped arrangement inside which the pitcher, catcher, and batter (or "striker") were centered with four bases at corners of the squared-off horseshoe, or U, placed sixty feet apart. This strange looking arrangement, also called "town ball," would be no more familiar to the modern fan than the appearance of a cricket pitch. It was eventually displaced by the Knickerbocker Club version.

As part of the formalization of the game, the Knickerbockers secured a more-or-less permanent playing field in Hoboken: Elysian Fields, a ferry ride across the Hudson River. From the first, then, baseball has carried mythical allusions. The Greek poet Homer described Elysium in *The Odyssey* as distinctly other-worldly—it is at the world's end, the weather is always mild, and the west wind always blows "bearing refreshment for the souls of men." Eight centuries later, Virgil added athletics and a distinctly Arcadian element to the paradisiacal conception in *The Aeneid*:

> then at last they came to the happy places, the pleasant green glades of the Woods of the Fortunate, the home of the blessed. Here air that is more pure and abundant clothes the plains in soft-colored light, and they have their own sun and their own stars. Some exercise their limbs on the grassy wrestling grounds, vie in sport, and grapple on the yellow sand. Others dance in a chorus and sing songs

A field of dreams has existed in the human imagination for as long as poets have recorded thoughts and images, and baseball has more successfully appropriated this link to an imaginary utopia than any other sport.

The first playing field was fittingly called Elysian Fields. An early drawing of the site by Currier and Ives showed a large, grassy expanse ringed by trees with the Hudson River just visible behind them. Men in antiquated baseball costumes poised on well-defined base paths, and spectators, all standing, ringed the outfield. The men wore knee-length frock coats, balanced stovepipe hats atop their heads, and the women were draped in long, flowing dresses. Horses and buggies waited beyond the ring of spectators, under the trees. The scene is at once dated yet timeless. A plaque commemorating the first official game of baseball now rests in a granite slab on the grassy median strip between the two lanes of what is now Eleventh Street:

BASEBALL

On June 19, 1846 the first match game of baseball was played here on the Elysian Fields between the Knickerbockers and the New Yorks. It is generally conceded that until this time the game was not seriously regarded.

Before the 1850s had ended, baseball's popularity had eclipsed anything the Knickerbockers could have predicted fifteen years before. This popularity did not extend much beyond New York City, however, as far as organized baseball was concerned. In fact, by 1857, twenty-four amateur clubs had been formed and all but one were located within the present limits of New York City's greater metropolitan area. Quickly, though, teams began to spring up farther afield and by 1859, the first club on the West Coast, called the San Francisco Eagles, had formed. Cities on the fringes of the South had clubs before the Civil War, most notably Washington, D.C. (whose first club was called the National, and then renamed for the 1860 season the Potomac) and Baltimore (the Excelsiors, not to be confused with the well-established Brooklyn Excelsiors, the team that made the first road tour in 1860). The game was not unknown in the South; New Orleans was in particular a hotbed of baseball activity. Even earlier, private school students in South Carolina had played town ball. In 1861, however, the Civil War began and baseball had to take a back seat until political issues could be settled.

The popular view has been that Union soldiers who ended up in Confederate prisoner of war camps, as a means of filling up leisure time and providing discipline and exercise, demonstrated the game to their southern captors, who then spread the essentials around after hostilities ceased. No doubt awareness of the game expanded through such contact, as did other aspects of northern culture. One wartime game, played on Christmas Day in 1862, featuring a team from the 165th New York who picked nine players from other Union regiments in Hilton Head, South Carolina, was witnessed by forty thousand spectators. Records show, nonetheless, that southern soldiers played baseball among themselves during the war. Baseball "artists" from New Orleans may have had as much or more to do with spreading the game to other Confederate soldiers as did northern soldiers. Al Spalding, the pioneer pitcher whose name lives on in sports equipment, wrote an early history of baseball in 1911. He repeated stories about a series supposedly held between Union and Confederate troops when hostilities were in abeyance before the campaign leading to Richmond. While Spalding could not find anyone who had played in these matches forty-five years earlier, other contests such as horse races were held between opposing forces during lulls in the war and the story of a baseball series is at least plausible.

The war may have temporarily slowed the growth of baseball, but that is all. Postwar baseball clubs began to show up in the South, many predictably named after Confederate war heroes. Norfolk fielded a team called the Stonewalls in 1866, and continuing the bad luck of the Confederates during the recent unpleasantness, they lost their first game 65 to 19. Washington, D.C., still had the National Base Ball Club, which used the Mall as their playing field. Unlike the hapless twentieth-century Senators, the amateur Nationals were a powerhouse. In 1867, they made a road trip west and played in Louisville, another fringe southern town, and in St. Louis, but had to report that the "western" teams weren't much of a match. The Nationals beat St. Louis 113 to 26.

In the late 1860s, a second team called the Mutuals emerged in

Washington, D.C. This team had rooms at the Willard Hotel and elected President Johnson an honorary member of the club. President Johnson returned the compliment by inviting members of the club to the White House. Interestingly, in his remarks to the team, the president said that he had played baseball as a youth, which would have been in the 1820s or even earlier.

By 1868, teams had begun forming not only in the larger southern cities, but in smaller ones also. Wetumpka and Prattsville in Alabama formed their first teams that year, and Pennsacola, Florida, fielded the Seminoles. As baseball spread throughout the South, however, changes in the northern sport were occurring that would have pervasive and long-term effects.

Baseball's umbrella organization in the formative years of amateur clubs was the National Association. In 1868, the organization for the first time recognized professionals. The following year, the famous Cincinnati Red Stockings, the team of all paid professionals, toured the nation and swept to an undefeated season with but one tie. The excitement generated by the superior play of the professionals reversed baseball's direction. Amateurs withdrew from the association during the spring of 1871 to form their own organization and, thereafter, amateur clubs soon ceased to be of any importance on a national level.

Beginning in the decade of the 1870s, the South began to attract the interest of northern baseball clubs because of warmer weather earlier in the season and preseason. In 1871, the Chicago White Stockings went to New Orleans in March to play the Lone Stars, the Southerners, and the Robert E. Lees. They beat the Lone Stars by a score of only nine to six. The Mutuals played exhibition games in the vicinity of Charleston and Savannah that same year, trips that could be seen as precursors of spring training. In 1888, the Washington club became the first team to train in Florida in the spring. The amateur Savannah club visited New York and New England in August of 1871, losing all their matches badly to northern amateur clubs. This was, however, the first time a club from the Deep South traveled north.

While baseball obviously had a foothold in the South before 1876, the activity was a drop in the bucket compared to that in the

North. Why was baseball so slow to develop in the South? The Civil War allowed as much opportunity for the learning and spread of baseball enthusiasm for southern soldiers as for northerners. Reconstruction was a hindrance, to put it mildly, but in the North, baseball had grown out of infancy and had supplanted contending games such as cricket as the national preference some time before the Civil War and its aftermath left the South in chaos.

The sparse population of the South helped keep baseball from developing quickly there. In *Cotton Fields and Skyscrapers*, David Goldfield establishes that in 1860, only New Orleans among leading southern cities had a population greater than one hundred thousand. Not coincidentally, New Orleans was the leading baseball city in the antebellum south. Only the development of cities made the growth of baseball possible. One of the many paradoxes about baseball is that agrarian society didn't allow baseball to develop, yet its dominant images are bucolic, and much of the argot has rural, not urban, origins. Players stand in the field, pitchers warm up in the bullpen, runners slide in the dirt, while flies are chased on the grass, and batters try to pummel the old horsehide (which, since 1974, has been a cowhide). As if to consciously reinforce the superiority of urban baseball, players are seasoned on the farm and called up to the big show in the cities when their skills are well-honed.

In the agrarian South, traditional outdoor pursuits such as hunting, fishing, and horse racing remained possible long after they had ceased to be practical in or near places like New York and Boston. Furthermore, the plantation-owning aristocracy in the South set the trends in leisure activity and favored established sports such as fox hunting. These trendsetters were slow to relinquish traditional pursuits and reluctant to allow a new, vulgar sport such as baseball a foothold.

The more rapid growth of baseball in the North was also aligned with industrialization, which was underway in the North at least two generations before it had a significant impact on the South. Baseball's growth in popularity at a national level depended upon the railroad to transport players across city, state, and regional boundaries. The first "tour" by the Excelsiors predated the Civil

War in 1860 and included various locations in New York and the mid-Atlantic states of Pennsylvania, Maryland, and Delaware. The South lagged behind not only in concentration of population to develop players and audiences, but in railroad transportation to make such team tours possible.

A second way industrialization was linked to early baseball was explained by Warren Goldstein in *Playing for Keeps: A History of Early Baseball*. The agrarian society needed generalists, people who could do many things well on the farm. Industry demanded specialists who could contribute a single specific mastered skill toward total product output. At first, baseball players were generalists but as the industrial revolution proceeded, so did specialization in baseball. No longer could one person master all the skills necessary on a ball field. The more agrarian South did not provide the reinforcement for specialization that was present in the North. Gradually, too, the work ethic of an industrial society began to be mirrored in baseball's paid performers. They were called "players" but expectations grew for practice, punctuality, commitment, in short, the same attributes that constitute productive work in an industrial society. A final link between industrialization and baseball was that factories forced a concentration of population for their workforces, and this also provided an audience for leisure activities.

One reason for baseball's growth in appeal was that it bridged a cultural gap between the middle and lower socioeconomic classes. Among the masses, baseball was a step up from cruder sports such as prizefighting; and among the genteel middle classes, it slowly was embraced and became a democratizing sport. Thus, in the North it provided an acceptable meeting ground for separate socioeconomic layers. In the antebellum South, the division between wealthy landowners and poor tenants was too wide for any sport to bridge.

Despite a long and storied history in the national pastime, Louisville had fallen victim to the minor league baseball torpor of the late 1960s and finally lost its team after the 1972 season. In 1982, the city renovated its stadium, attracted a AAA franchise, and began setting attendance records. Before the Buffalo Bisons regularly began drawing over one million fans in the late 1980s, the Louisville Redbirds were the perennial minor league attendance leader. Today, when all-time minor league attendance years are listed, Louisville holds six of the top twelve attendance years.

After seeing the petite ballparks of the southeastern class A clubs, I thought Cardinal Stadium in Louisville looked immense. The field had artificial turf and the outfield walls were painted blue with no signs. Three umpires, rather than the customary two, patrolled the field. Everything had a plastic, artificial look. The staff was formal and had bureaucratic procedures for entry and seating. This was big city baseball, at least for me. I had grown used to organizations where after a few days I knew most of the staff and people would come up and introduce themselves.

On the field, the game was played at a noticeably higher level. Dimensions were 360 feet to left, 405 feet to center, and 312 feet to right. The short right-field wall was made more difficult to reach with a barrier about sixteen feet high, which slanted backwards at eight feet and then rose vertically again. Hitters were strong enough to reach the distant walls (I saw six home runs, one over the center field fence) and many had big league experience. In the top of the third, the Redbird first baseman made a defensive marvel of a play on a ground smash to his left. He dove, backhanded the ball in midair, rolled, and released to the pitcher in one fluid, perfectly executed sequence of connected motions.

After the bottom of the sixth, Louisville had scored in every inning. Finally, in the bottom of the seventh, they were shut down, but only after a Redbird batter missed a home run by pulling it down the right field line fifteen feet foul. They eventually won 12–5.

Another difference at the triple AAA level was in entertainment; if Redbird Stadium was typical, the mascot was much more of a performer than at the class A level. Billy Bird raced out in a variety of small vehicles between innings, roaring down the foul lines and careening around the warning track. The athletic entertainer finally catapulted over the center field fence in a display of timing and daring that awed the large Friday evening crowd.

Next morning, I took out my well-used *Baseball America Direc-*

106

tory to check the minor league schedules. I could either stay in Louisville and watch balls take predictable hops on the artificial surface or drive eight hours to the southeast and then work my way back to the middle South. The choice wasn't difficult.

I took US 150 south and east to hook up with US 25, which shoots the gap at Cumberland and cuts off the eastern wedge of Tennessee. Interstates took me across the mountainous western tip of North Carolina. My luck with spring weather ran out in Greenville, South Carolina. On Sunday morning, it was hot and humid. The leaves were fully out, and summer had definitely arrived. I put a new supply of Dr. Pepper in my front seat cooler.

I drove out to Greenville Municipal Stadium before noon to see the Braves, an Atlanta AA farm club, work out before playing a Sunday afternoon game. The stadium was built in 1984 just for baseball, which is indicated by how the grandstand curves uniformly down the foul lines. As a member of the class AA Southern League in 1992, Greenville accomplished the almost impossible feat of winning one hundred games. For a modern minor league team to win this many games, it had to play at a .700 pace over 142 games (Greenville actually played 143 regular season games and ended up at .699). In addition to the usual obstacles of injuries, slumps, and probability ("you win a third and lose a third just by taking the field; it's what you do with the other third that counts"), minor league teams have to contend with call-ups. Players who get hot at bat or on the mound were often called up to the next higher level. Almost automatically, an exceptionally good team that loses a few of its dominant players regresses in the standings. The Braves had not only ruled the Southern League all season (Chattanooga had won ninety games and finished ten games out) but had won six more in postseason play.

Almost all the 1992 Greenville Braves who played regularly had been promoted to Atlanta's AAA farm club at Richmond in 1993. Yet, the 1993 Braves were at 20–10 going into the Sunday afternoon game and were being subjected to the inevitable comparisons with last year's powerhouse. I talked briefly with Bruce Kimm, Greenville's first-year manager, before he picked up a bat to go to

work. The coaches were working on situational hitting that afternoon. For example, runners were stationed on first and began moving toward second before the pitch. Batters practiced hitting the
hole when the infielders shifted to cover bases. Other situations
were called out by the batting practice pitcher—infield back, infield
in, squeeze on, runner on third, one out, run and hit—and batters
altered stances and hand positions on the bat accordingly.

Bruce, a forty-one-year-old former major league catcher, began
hitting line drives to outfielders playing shallow. I was fascinated
to hear him use an infinite number of inflections and four-letter
words to convey different meanings. Often the exclamation would
be accompanied by a wave of the bat or an arm to further accentu-
ate the message. Remarkably, outfielders would nod to assure him
that the terse point had been decoded.

"Bleep!" (Sorry, I meant to hit that one more to your left.)

"Bleep!" (You're right, I shouldn't have short-hopped you when
we were working on your throw to third.)

"Bleep!" (I don't know why, but I got under that one too much
and sent it over your head.)

The Sunday afternoon crowd was sparse, perhaps because it was
hot and there was no shade. Anyone who builds a baseball park
without a roof should have to spend eternity sitting in the sun in
hazy, humid, hot weather. Many fans put programs over their
heads to shield themselves from the sun. On the field, Greenville
looked like a very mortal baseball team. The Birmingham Barons
beat them 8–2.

The first night in Greenville, I stayed in a state park outside of
town. Next day I drove into town to do some chores and see how a
night in an air-conditioned motel would feel. Before leaving on the
trip, one my most irrational and useless worries concerned getting
my laundry done. Because I had never used laundromats, I had no
knowledge of how they operated. My fears had me believing that
these were dangerous places where a variety of crimes occurred
regularly. I supposed that drug deals were made there routinely,
that rapes occurred in them a few times each week, and that almost
daily a gunman would drop by to rob the attendant of change from

the machines. Like other images I concocted about places I had never seen, my fantasies were way off the mark.

I found instead that they were clean, well-managed places which were frequented by congenial people. Laundromats have several social functions beyond simply being places to wash and dry clothes. Patrons socialize, share information, and even share problems in what becomes an impromptu emotional support group. Men hit on women and women on men while their clothes are agitated; and everyone cheerfully dispenses advice to novices on working the machines.

Once I was waiting for a dryer to finish its cycle, watching the big glass fronted cylinder rotate and tumble my clothes, and overheard an exchange between two women who were folding laundry behind me. "You can always tell people who don't come here much," one said. "They watch their clothes go around."

Washing my clothes in a laundromat in Greenville, I made friends with the attendant. James Edward Brown was a trim, dapper, middle-aged black man. We spent an hour in conversation, and I told him about my trip and a little of my background. When the subject of race relations in the South came up, he was willing and even eager to discuss the issues. This was a departure from the usual; most southerners, black and white, dodged the topic when I tried to include it in conversation. James, I learned, was a former civil rights activist. He graduated from South Carolina State College in 1959 and went through the period of sit-ins, freedom rides, and other protests when the movement was dangerous, exciting, and optimistic. His complaint today isn't that things are headed in the wrong direction, just that nothing is happening. "CORE, SNCC, even the Black Panthers, are just names today, they don't do anything," he said.

As I was preparing to leave, James presented me a novel that he had written. A story about civil rights activists, it is called *The Plan*. Drafted while he was a junior in college, it was published a few years later by Vantage Press. On the back dustcover a young James Brown, dressed in an open shirt with its collar spilling onto a leisure suit jacket, looks out sensitively at the reader. James told me that he and others had tried to put some of the principles of

The Plan into practice in Greenville, but that reality had been more complicated than fiction.

After watching Greenville lose two games, I drove back into North Carolina to visit my niece in Brevard. After dinner, we drove over to her father's house. Buddy, my sister's former husband, lives in a house surrounded by huge trees on a quiet street. We all sat in the back yard, drank beer and watched my grand-nephew and grand-nieces play.

Buddy and his family typify small-town southern life. He lives, and will die, a few blocks from where he was born. His mother lives in a house across the back yard fence, and while we sat talking, other relatives came and went during the evening. Buddy works in a plant that makes machines for the textile industry, and has a ten-minute drive to work with no traffic. He fishes the lakes and rivers around Brevard on the weekends with his fishing partner, a man called Turkey. Their center of social life is the American Legion in Brevard, which until recently was the only place in town where you could drink alcohol on the premises. Buddy told me about a wild river near Brevard, and promised to take me there if I would stay until the weekend. It was so isolated, he said, that some of the holes may never have been fished.

I was tempted but passed up Buddy's offers to spend the night and stay longer and drove north, into the Pisgah Forest, parking Sweetspot a few feet from a trout stream. At first light, I got down to business, fishing a half mile of the stream before walking back down the road to make coffee.

When Crash Davis was cut from the Durham Bulls in the film *Bull Durham*, he hooked up with the Asheville Tourists in the South Atlantic League. There, Crash hit his minor league record-breaking home run and retired from baseball. A small part of the film was shot at famous old McCormick Field. Those who want to see the place now would be advised to pick up a copy of that film, because the old park is no more. I arrived in Asheville two years too late.

McCormick Field's formal opening was on April 3, 1924, and Ty

Cobb played in an exhibition game for the Detroit Tigers that day. The field had been named for Dr. Lewis M. McCormick, an early bacteriologist in Asheville, who sent flyswatter sales soaring by inaugurating the "Swat That Fly" movement in 1905.

The original McCormick had been one of the last wooden grandstand parks still in use. Many of baseball's hallowed names appeared there as minor leaguers or in exhibition games, including Babe Ruth. In 1931, the Babe looked out at the picturesque scene of this park etched into a wooded hillside and called it the most beautiful place to play in America. The reason he hadn't said this on an earlier visit in 1925 is that he hadn't made it from the train station to the park. The Babe collapsed on the platform and was hospitalized from, officially, eating too many hot dogs.

Two years ago McCormick was razed and rebuilt on the same plot of ground. The new ballpark lacks the historical character of its predecessor, but is nonetheless a captivating structure. The facade is red brick with a postmodern design, and seating takes the shape of an L, with the shank running from home plate down the right field line. A three-foot-high red brick wall surrounds the playing field. The sizeable grandstand roof is cantilevered with a small concrete press box, shaped something like a New England diner, perched on top of the stands. Dimensions are 328 feet to left, 406 feet to center, and a short 300 feet to right. In right field, a thirty-five-foot-high fence towers over the playing area. Fenway's green monster is only two feet higher.

"It's the highest fence in the minors," Ron McKee, the Tourists' general manager told me, "but that shows you how smart I am. If I had gone just three feet higher, I'd have had the highest fence in baseball."

Ron was beginning his fourteenth season as general manager in Asheville. Rotund and energetic, he is known for a personal approach to baseball management where fans are treated like family. It had been raining the afternoon I arrived in Asheville, and Ron was debating whether to leave the tarp on the field or take it off. He was wearing shorts, an old tee shirt, and sneakers. Four of the staff were discussing the situation, and collectively had three different opinions, including one strange proposal to roll it up halfway.

111

Ron decided to leave it on for the present. "Stay close," he said to me. "We might need some help with the tarp in a little while." I had known him less than five minutes at the time. After we talked awhile, it became apparent that batting practice had to be canceled.

I asked Ron if there were any good barbecue establishments nearby, and he recommended a place called the Little Pig. I ordered a sandwich and cole slaw. When the waitress brought it, the cole slaw was in the sandwich, on top of the barbecued pork. That's how they serve it in North Carolina.

The drizzle stopped and by game time weather was almost perfect. The sweet smell of honeysuckle permeated the ballpark, floating in against the odor of hot dogs and chili from the concession stands. After dark, the white blossoms from the black locust trees that crowd the surrounding hill picked up the glow from the five hundred watt park lights and appeared phosphorescent. The shrouded trees stood silently in appraisal of the nightly games, like ghostly ball players whose eternal heaven or hell is to witness forever what they used to take part in.

At eight wins, twenty-four losses, the Asheville Tourists were off to the worst start in organized baseball. "They're struggling," I suggested to Ron. "Well aren't you the diplomat?" he replied.

Ron worked the crowd while the game was in progress. A small group of youngsters followed us around for awhile, nagging him for jobs. "Stop pestering me," he told them. "I'm trying to talk to this man here." There was no malice or threat in his tone, so they continued to point out how it would be to his benefit to hire them. When they finally drifted away, he said, "They're from a housing development near here. I wish I could give them all jobs, but all we can do is let them in the park at night and hope it helps."

The baseball law of averages gods were at work in McCormick that night. Fresh off a 1–7 road trip and five straight losses, the Tourists scored three runs in the first two innings. Excellent defense killed Spartanburg rallies, though Tourist pitchers stayed in trouble all evening. I watched the Spartanburg manager pass a broken bat to a young fan, and roll a ball quietly down the aisle to another one later in the game.

At games' end, Ron stationed himself at the exit gates. He stayed until the last of the crowd had departed, saying goodnight to people, most of whom he seemed to know on a first-name basis.

If I ever move to a southern city, Asheville will be my home. People dress stylishly and drink white wine with lunch, and the mountains are beautiful. Trout are thick in even the smallest streams, and the Tourists occasionally win a ball game. Old McCormick Field is gone, but the Asheville institution carrying the spirit of minor league baseball is Ron McKee, and he's still there.

I hated to leave the little parks of the southeast, but as I pulled out of Asheville I was heading for the big time. The rest of my season would be in double A ball.

8

Achy-Breaky Baseball

BASEBALL AND MUSIC HAVE ALWAYS enjoyed a close relationship. Back in the nineteenth century, amateur clubs sang what today would be called "fight" songs on the way to games, and victory songs afterwards if they won. In this century, Hollywood has produced enough films about baseball to constitute a genre, and enough musical baseball films to form a subgenre. Two of the most notable are *Take Me Out to the Ball Game* and *Damn Yankees*.

Everyone knows songs whose lyrics call up feelings of nostalgia or whose music makes them feel like adolescents in love. In my case, "Oklahoma!" evokes those passions for a past boyhood, and "Dixie," perhaps, for my ancestral heritage.

I had wondered if southern baseball parks featured "Dixie" as background music, but at ninety games I never heard it played. Perhaps the reason is that for "Dixie" to have maximum impact, it must be played mournfully; and you can't fire up a crowd to cheer for the home team with sad, nostalgic music. More likely, it is because nowadays political implications accompany the playing of this traditional southern song, even though it was written by a Yankee. Daniel Decatur Emmett, who wrote songs to be performed in his blackface minstrel shows, listed a new tune in an 1859 showbill as a "Plantation Song and Dance, Dixie's Land." In 1860 the song appeared in New Orleans, performed by a group called Bryant's Minstrels, and its popularity led to its becoming their theme song. Within two years, the song had made the term "Dixie" synonymous with the South. The tune was played at the inauguration of Jeffer-

115

son Davis as president of the Confederacy, much to the chagrin of its Union sympathizer author.

For a baseball fan, "Take Me Out to the Ball Game" can cause the same sensations as "Dixie" does for a southerner or "Oklahoma!" to a native of that state. The version of "Take Me Out to the Ball Game" played at most parks during the seventh inning stretch generally lacks this impact, however. The usual shortened version contains only the chorus. The full song, the one that became the central melody of baseball, begins slowly, sets a context, introduces a story line, and finally builds to a rousing crescendo. Oddly, Jack Norworth had never seen a baseball game when he wrote that song. He was an early New York vaudeville star who wrote much of his own material. He was looking for a simple, rhythmic tune on a popular subject, which he could teach his audience as a sing-along in a short time. In 1908, while riding a train downtown to the theater district, he was inspired by an advertisement for a ball game at the Polo Grounds, and he began quickly to transcribe words and music on a scrap of paper. Today, baseball fans can see that original piece of paper in the Baseball Hall of Fame in Cooperstown, New York. Norworth wasn't a one-song phenomenon, though. With his wife, he wrote "Shine on Harvest Moon" in the same year. Eventually, Norworth saw a ball game. In 1942 he went to Ebbets Field in Brooklyn to watch the Dodgers and the New York Giants, and became a chronic, incurable fan. He had probably been a latent fan all along, and was just late in coming out.

I had driven across Tennessee to Nashville to meet my wife Zena for a weekend, hear some country music, and check out the Music City version of baseball. Zena is a country music fan, though she grew up in London at a time when country wasn't cool, even in this country. Nonetheless, she arrived in Nashville with tickets to the Grand Ole Opry and plans to call in at Gilley's and the South Fork Saloon.

Several country music stars played minor league baseball before making it big on stage. Conway Twitty was offered a contract by the Phillies, and in an earlier generation, Roy Acuff played baseball at the professional level. Charlie Pride was good enough to be given tryouts with both the California Angels and the New York Mets. The best of the ballplaying singers, however, was Jim Reeves.

In 1944, Jim signed a contract with the St. Louis Cardinals and was assigned to its class B team in Lynchburg, Virginia, in the Piedmont League. After pitching in Virginia, Jim moved over to the Evangeline League in Louisiana, a fast class D circuit, and went 10–8 for the Alexandria Aces in 1946. His ERA was over 7.00 that year, so he must have enjoyed some very strong batting and fielding support. After Louisiana, Jim went farther west to the East Texas League in 1947 and 1948, playing for the small towns of Marshall and Henderson. When baseball cut him loose, he hung around east Texas as a disc jockey, occasionally broadcasting baseball games for the radio station that employed him.

His Lynchburg uniform is now on display at the Jim Reeves Museum in Nashville. The museum is in a house owned and run by Mary Reeves, who was Jim's wife during his singing career. Mary is a pleasant, down-home woman who had remarried since Jim's accidental death in 1964. As she showed us through, Mary related the tragic details. Jim was killed in an airplane crash when the single engine plane he was piloting went down in a heavy storm, just eight miles from the runway. His breakthrough in music had come in 1953, so he had a brief but productive career as a singer. If his fastball had been a few miles an hour faster, the music industry might never have had Jim at all.

Downtown Nashville has an interesting seedy quality. The music industry, its central identity over the past thirty years, is slowly moving away. Top performers are increasingly booking into halls in Branson, Missouri, and the Opry, which was located in Ryman Auditorim on Fifth Street, has long since moved up the Cumberland River to Music Valley, out in the suburbs. While driving down Commerce Street on Saturday at midday heading toward the waterfront, we saw an interesting enterprise in a vacant lot next to a night club featuring an all-nude girlie revue. The exotic dancers had set up a car wash. For $7.00 the bikini-clad performers would splash soap and water and generally cavort around patrons' cars. I weakly suggested that Sweetspot had gotten a little dirty, received a frown from Zena, and kept on driving.

Two institutions in the heart of Nashville endeared me to the place. Across the plaza at the foot of Broadway on the river sat a square, unimpressive building that looked like an overgrown hot dog stand. The type of place usually hidden from tourists and known to locals only through word of mouth, Jack's Bar-B-Que was square in our path. Jack's sold mainly beer and food to go, but had a few tables with umbrellas on the sidewalk for "patio dining." While Tennessee pork shoulder is the traditional barbecue meat, Jack's also serves barbecued beef brisket Texas style. The story is that when Tennessean Sam Houston and his followers went to Texas to help out at the Alamo, they found that there were more cattle in Texas than hogs, and invented barbecued beef.

Jack dug a pit in 1976 and has been cooking on location and serving from pit to plate ever since. I had never been a booster of barbecued beef, but after trying both, found that Jack's beef was superior to his barbecued pork. And at Jack's, I learned about the Bohannon Brewery.

Brown bottles of Bohannon's Market Street Beer stood upright in a barrel of ice at Jack's. The taste was distinctive, mellow, and prominent enough to challenge the barbecue sauce. Before leaving Nashville on Monday morning, I walked to the brewery on Second Street (formerly Market Street). Although the business has only been open for a couple of years, the building dates from 1888 and is built on the site of Nashville's first brewery. The walls are bare brick, and visitors can look down on the beer-making process through windows. Inside the fermenting tanks barley, hops, yeast, and water combine to do their work. The high-ceiling interior is dim and the place smells, appropriately, like a brewery. I left carrying two mixed cases containing pilsner, golden ale, and the flavorful wheat beer, bucking them up Market Street to where Sweetspot was parked.

On Sunday, I convinced Zena that she should accompany me to a baseball game and see how I was spending my summer. In Nashville, baseball is played at Greer Stadium, away from downtown just off an interstate highway. The park occupies the site of the last great battle of the Civil War, at Fort Negley. Built in 1978, the park is symmetrical (330 feet to the lines, 405 feet to center) and has a seating capacity of sixteen thousand. Greer is home to the Nashville Sounds, a AAA club in the American Association, and in 1993, also hosted the Nashville Xpress, a AA team in the Southern League. Seating is in a circular, single-deck configuration with higher seats located a long distance from the field, as minor league parks go. A row of skyboxes sits atop the grandstand's back wall, and are in turn topped by a large press box. The most unusual feature of the park is a scoreboard in the shape of a guitar, paying homage to "Music City."

Nashville has gone from having one of the most absurd baseball parks in history to having one of the most ordinary. Sulpher Dell, where baseball was played from 1885 through 1963, was located downtown just 440 yards off the Cumberland River. The site was named for a sulphur spring and salt lick that had lured buffalo, then buffalo hunters, and finally white settlers. Teams played down below a bluff in a hole that was neither level nor big enough. No matter how it was configured, a short fence had to exist somewhere. For most of its history, left field was 334 feet, center field 421 feet, and right, a snug 262 feet. Right field was not only close in, but had an incline that began behind first base gradually, increased to a forty-five degree angle in shallow left, leveled off to a shelf about a third of the way up, and then continued at a forty-five degree angle to the fence. Right fielders played on the terrace and had to catch balls running uphill, downhill, and crosshill. Even putting a thirty-foot screen on top of the sixteen foot wooden fence in right didn't stop left-handed batters from dropping cheap home runs over the barrier.

Sulpher Dell was near the city dump and when the river overflowed in the spring, it carried odors into the ballpark. Outfielders, nearest to the dump, called the park "suffer hell." In 1954, Bob Lennon, a left-hander, hit sixty-four home runs for the Southern Association Nashville Volunteers. In a seventeen-year-long minor league career played almost entirely in other parks, Bob's second highest total was thirty-one home runs. In Southern Association history (Nashville belonged to this league during most of Sulpher Dell's existence), there were eight players who hit forty or more home runs in a season. Every one of them was a left-handed batter

119

playing for Nashville. The miracle is that Nashville batters don't have all the minor league, single-season home run records before 1963, when the old park was last used.

Today's Southern League is a double A coalition with ten teams. The eastern division consists of the Carolina Mudcats in Zebulon, North Carolina, two Florida entries—Orlando and Jacksonville—Greenville, South Carolina, and Knoxville, Tennessee. In the western division, Alabama has two entries (Birmingham and Huntsville) and Tennessee has three (Memphis, Chattanooga, and Nashville). The league goes back to 1885 with an erratic beginning that stabilized in 1902. In its best-known incarnation it was called the Southern Association and included most of the larger southern cities. Atlanta, Little Rock, Mobile, and New Orleans were traditional members.

Transition from the Southern Association to the current Southern League was roundabout. In the early 1960s, the times caught up with baseball in Dixie. All the usual forces were at work—television kept fans at home, air-conditioning made hot southern nights at the ballpark less appealing, and interest in professional football was increasing—but the Southern Association had additional problems. The National League had taken Atlanta in 1962, and that city had been one of the league's mainstays. A more deep-rooted concern was the racial unrest of the period. The lunch room sit-ins had begun in 1961. Freedom rides and the civil rights efforts of Martin Luther King, Jr., created turmoil in southern cities, and ballparks were potential centers of racial confrontation. Baseball integrated after Jackie Robinson, and by the early sixties, only the class D Alabama-Florida League remained all white. Teams still had difficulty finding housing for black players, however, and chaotic events in the larger southern society funneled down into the diamonds of Dixie.

Under these conditions, the old Southern Association folded after 1961. In 1964, the South Atlantic League changed its name to the Southern League. Over the next three decades, the league slowly slipped many of the traditional old cities of the South back into the fold. Today, Birmingham, Nashville, Chattanooga, and Memphis once again form the backbone of Dixieball.

Zena left Nashville late Sunday night after we made plans to meet in New Orleans in a few weeks. "Maybe we can catch a ballgame there," I suggested, and got a noncommittal smile in return.

Monday morning I set up an appointment with the owner of the Nashville Sounds. No one could poke around minor league baseball for long without hearing about Larry Schmittou. He is the primary owner of the Nashville Sounds (American Association), the Huntsville Stars (Southern League), and the class A Winston-Salem Spirits (Carolina League). Lists of almost all National Association committees contain his name, and in 1993, he undertook an unusual experiment in operating a class AA Southern League team (the Nashville Xpress) in the same city and ballpark as his AAA team, the Sounds.

I was eager to find out how the novel situation was developing. Larry, who insisted on making our meeting a standard interview, had obviously answered the same questions many times before and seemed a little defensive.

"How did the Nashville Xpress get its name?" I asked.

"My son Ron came up with it. All the minor league ballparks used to have railroad tracks running just outside and many still do. It evokes that past, and we already had one team tying into the city's music industry [the Nashville Sounds]."

Larry told me that his ownership group had signed a contract to manage and operate the AA team that had been in Charlotte, North Carolina, the year before. Charlotte had received an expansion AAA franchise and the league wasn't able to place the AA team in a suitable southern city. The arrangement put two teams in one ballpark, with one staff, under Schmittou's control for a season.

"Problems?" I asked. Larry minimized the problems, saying that the field naturally required a little extra maintenance and of course the staff had to work harder to keep the place clean and dispense concessions with only seven days off during the season.

Sensing that the interview was almost over, I sprung my most abrasive questions last. "Has anyone suggested that there may be a conflict of interest in the situation, considering that you own the Huntsville team in the same league?"

Larry, sitting behind his large desk, folded his arms across his chest. "There is no conflict of interest," he replied, "because we are operating the Xpress as a management service and do not own it. What most people realize is that unless I did what I'm doing the league would have to play an unbalanced schedule and every team in the league would suffer. There is no other alternative."

Figuring that I hadn't made myself quite unpopular enough, I asked a question about attendance. "Based on the per game figures in the media notes," I began, "it looks like attendance for the Xpress projects to about 175,000, assuming the same number of rainouts as last year. Do you think having two teams in the same city hurts attendance for the lower level team?"

"I don't agree with your method of projecting at all," Larry said. "Rainouts and bad weather in April and May always hold down the average at this time of year. A more informed projection shows that we'll clearly draw over 200,000 for the year."

According to *Baseball America* the Nashville Xpress drew 178,737 for the 1993 season. They were second from the bottom in the ten-team Southern League, outdrawing only Knoxville. My estimate in May was a little low, but was much closer than Larry's. Fortunately, I'm not the kind of person to say "I told you so."

Before leaving, I talked with Larry's son Ron, who directed concessions for the two teams. "It seems like a nightmare sometimes," he said, referring to the problems of sorting out work schedules for 120 employees and food orders for two teams. The groundskeeper, Dave Nasypany, had to deal with what amounted to a season-long homestand, with only seven off days. "It's me and five assistants. True summer will get the field dry and hard and we can't ever flood it. It's more watering but only in short spurts because of the playing schedule, resodding where we need to. We just have to give up everything else to keep it in playing condition."

Larry's employees did not downplay the problems involved in having two teams in one park. Ron was quoted later in *Baseball America* as saying, "I don't want to have a heart attack before I'm thirty. Things would probably go better next year [if the Xpress stayed in Nashville] but I don't much care to find out."

Larry Schmittou had insisted that owning the Huntsville Stars and managing the Nashville Xpress, both in the Southern League, did not pose a conflict of interest. At the major league level, if, say, George Steinbrenner maintained ownership of the New York Yankees but was hired to operate the Minnesota Twins for a season, would it fly? Not likely. But the minor and major leagues are not the same species. The minors have always been an environment for experimentation and have encouraged novel solutions to the ever-present fluid changes of climate. The Nashville experiment held to the letter of league by-laws, even if it seemed to breach the spirit of conflict of interest. My concern wasn't so much with the one-time solution to a minor league baseball problem, but with one ownership group penetrating minor league baseball at so many different levels and ultimately having the potential for undue influence on how the game is run. Monopolies and minor league baseball just don't seem to be a good mix.

Any competent travel agent who examined my route across the South during the summer of 1993 would have probably concluded that I was either drunk or running a high fever most of the time. Having detoured to do some sight-seeing in Kentucky, I was now back in Tennessee. About thirty-five miles west of Nashville, I turned toward Memphis, knowing that I would later return east to Knoxville and Chattanooga. The Memphis Chicks were playing at home that week, and the other Tennessee Southern League teams weren't.

The nickname of the Memphis Chicks derived from the Chickasaw Indians, one of the five "civilized" tribes, as I was taught in high school. High bluffs rising above the Mississippi River where Memphis now lies had been a major settlement of the Chickasaw Nation before the appearance of the Europeans. Later, when nineteenth-century river commerce prospered, the location offered good harbor where the Wolf River emptied into the Mississippi and Memphis became a major slave-trading market for the South. During the Civil War, the city fell to Union troops and was in northern hands during most of the conflict. Reconstruction and yellow fever epidemics after the war further demoralized and decimated the city's population. Eventually fortunes changed and Memphis was reestablished as a cotton market.

Early in the twentieth century, the blues emerged from ballads sung by African slaves and W. C. Handy made Beale Street famous. In the 1950s, Elvis Presley added rhythm to the blues and moved into Graceland, a mansion that was then on the outskirts of the city. The assassination of Martin Luther King, Jr., on a balcony at the Lorraine Motel added a sadder note to the city's history in 1968. That was also, coincidentally, the year minor league baseball returned to the river city after an eight-year hiatus.

Until 1960, the Southern Association Memphis Chicks played at Russwood Park. Russwood had a lopsided playing field that at one time measured 424 feet to left field, 366 feet to dead center and only 301 feet to right. One-armed Pete Gray had one of his best seasons there in 1944, hitting .333 and stealing sixty-eight bases. On April 17, 1960, the Chicago White Sox and Cleveland Indians played an afternoon exhibition game at the park, and that evening a fire broke out, threatening the midtown area and reducing most of the ballpark facilities to rubble.

While I was in Memphis, John Guinozzo, the Chicks' longtime official scorer, brought in pictures of Russwood during its heyday and in the aftermath of the fire. As with many southern baseball parks, segregated seating had been the rule. Black fans had traditionally been limited to the left field bleachers. This detached section of the ballpark was so far removed from the main grandstand that it was the only section of stands left intact after the horrendous fire.

The current field in Memphis, Tim McCarver Stadium, began as an American Legion field in the 1960s and has been expanded over the years. My first visit occurred simultaneous with the arrival of a late afternoon thunderstorm. I sat in the back of Sweetspot listening to local radio while waiting for the deluge to stop. The stadium had a fresh coat of blue and white paint and its parking lot was lined with trees. After the storm was over, I went into the club offices. They sat up against the left field wall and their windows— covered with screening—faced onto the playing field. When right-handers pulled the long ball, home runs bounced off the roof of the office. The left-field fence took an interesting jog around the club offices and ran in front of aluminum outfield bleachers, which carried across left center. Distances ran 323 feet to left, 398 feet to dead center, 325 feet to right and about 370 feet in the power alleys. The seating was single deck and a roof canopy extended past first and third bases. The most recent renovation included a skybox facility behind home plate, and new, if somewhat tight, press box facilities.

In 1993, Memphis was one of eight cities chosen to experiment with a new computer program for scoring. John Guinozzo ran through the system with me before a game one evening. It was called the Automated Scorebook and allowed keying in every play that could be scored manually. I tried to think up situations that would confuse a computer but the system handled every problem I proposed. It even double checked against unusual scoring decisions ("Are you sure you want to credit an RBI in this case?").

One of McCarver Stadium's more unusual features is the artificial turf infield. It fits tightly against the outfield grass but the potential for unusual bounces is there at the lip. The outfield turf is a lighter shade of green because the infield was cut away and replaced with fresh plastic for the 1993 season.

The earlier thunderstorm had left the field playable but wet. When players walked across the sliding pits and onto the artificial turf, they left footprints. By game time, the infield had a patterned appearance, suggestive of abstract art, when viewed from above. The rain held down the crowd to just over two thousand and the Chicks beat Greenville 9–5. Rain fell intermittently throughout the game and to reward those fans still in the park in the seventh inning, the staff passed out free tickets to a future game at the exit gate.

Next day I called Bruce Kimm, the Greenville Braves' manager, and arranged a meeting with him in the visiting dugout after batting practice. At forty-one, Bruce looked to be in good enough shape to catch a few innings. While growing up in Iowa, he had set a state high school basketball scoring record of forty-six points in a game. The Atlanta Braves hired Kimm to manage at Greenville following nine seasons coaching in the National League with Cincinnati, Pittsburgh, and San Diego. Despite last night's loss, his

125

Greenville Braves were in first place in the Southern League's eastern division by five games.

Before coaching, Bruce spent four years in the major leagues as a catcher, playing with the Tigers, Cubs, and White Sox. The height of his playing career occurred in 1976 when he caught all of Mark "The Bird" Fidrych's twenty-nine starts in the pitcher's highly publicized rookie season. Bruce had caught Fidrych the year before in AAA Evansville and had grown accustomed to his unusual demeanor when pitching.

"Did Fidrych affect your concentration when he would wander around talking to himself on the mound?" I asked.

"Not at all. That was his way of staying focused. It made the players 'up' to play. In twenty-nine starts, 970,000 fans came to see him pitch that year. Each game was like a playoff."

Statistics support Bruce's assessment of the year. He ended up hitting .263 overall, but hit .303 in the games Fidrych pitched. Bruce was optioned to Rochester in 1978 and after coming back for two more major league seasons, he was forced out of baseball by a shoulder injury. He hadn't stayed in touch with Fidrych over the years since they were teamates.

"How are you finding the bus rides this season?" I asked.

"They aren't bothering me that much. I was out of baseball for a year in 1981. Sold insurance, drove a bread truck . . ."

"You drove a bread truck?"

"Yeah. That's why bus rides don't bother me too much."

Greenville won the next two games. Bruce had them playing like demons in the field; each game featured an outstanding shoestring catch by Greenville outfielders at crucial points. They were winning two of three games but were still far below the pace of last year's one hundred-win Greenville club. I asked Bruce if he felt any pressure to match the 1992 club success.

"Hell no," he replied. I'm too busy trying to get the players to forget about it."

Being in Memphis reminded me of an earlier trip I had made through the South, when I was twelve years old. My father, grandfather, and I loaded up a 1949 Ford and left Oklahoma for a two-week family-visiting vacation through Georgia and Florida. My grandfather was then in his seventies and no longer drove. It would be his last visit to see siblings and other kin he had left behind when he moved to Oklahoma forty years earlier. My father was returning, for the first time, to where he had lived as a small boy. I had never been out of Oklahoma before, and was seeing the South as part of a huge adventure.

My father chewed tobacco and instead of using a cup, would open the car door while driving and spit tobacco juice in the general direction of the highway. Updrafts would flick the juice on the inside of the car door while the side stream would coat the exterior with black streaks. It took a pretty strong stomach to get in on the driver's side of one of my father's cars. While he was spitting, the car would drift towards the center line. I would get ready to grab for the wheel while my grandfather, helpless in the back seat, braced himself and looked resigned to calamity.

When we weren't about to have a head-on tobacco juice collision, my father relieved the boredom of long miles with a game, which he thought to be educational. Passing a green crop in the field, he would ask: "I wonder if that's oats or rye growing there?"

I never knew and wasn't very interested, but my grandfather, even knowing that it was a game, couldn't stay out of it.

"Oats this time of year!" he would say sarcastically. He had been a farmer all his life.

In those days, there were no interstates and few bypasses. When a large city lay on the route, you followed the highway signs through it. We left Oklahoma in the morning, drove across Arkansas during the day, and crossed the Mississippi River into Memphis late at night. I was dazzled by a neon American flag atop a city building. The colored lights on an intermittent cycle made the flag appear to wave. The flag may have been on the Peabody Hotel, then one of the most prominent features of the skyline.

Now, forty years later, I walked down to the Peabody Hotel in the center of Memphis to see if any old pictures of the hotel were on display. Downtown Memphis had been given an economic booster shot with restoration of the landmark, first opened in 1925. Rather ordinary structurally, the building was made distinct by attaching Spanish ornamentation. When I walked into the lobby, I was surprised to find a large crowd of people lining a carpeted path between the elevators and lobby's fountain. They said they were waiting for the ducks to arrive.

It seems that in 1932 when the hotel manager brought live ducks back from a hunting trip, he put them in the hotel lobby's fountain, a beautiful piece of sculpture made from a single stone. Today four of their decendents ride down on the hotel elevator from their roost on the penthouse roof each morning, waddle across a red carpet to the fountain, and ceremoniously leave the lobby the same way in late afternoon. The ritual now draws a daily gaggle of tourists who jostle each other for space to photograph the ducks.

I went up to the mezzanine for a better view, but that area was lined with spectators too. A woman behind me peered over my shoulder. "You can move up to the railing," I said. "There's room."

"I don't want to get in your way," she said, nodding toward my camera.

"Ha! I'm not going to take a picture. I feel silly enough just standing here to watch ducks walk in."

The four ducks made their entrance to a march by John Philip Sousa, strutted along the narrow path left by tourists, and plunged into the fountain as the crowd applauded.

As soon as the woman left, I took a picture. My original aim, to find a historic picture of the Peabody Hotel, was unsuccessful, but I have a good, distinct image of four ducks paddling in the clear water of the hotel lobby's baroque fountain.

Return Baseball to the Inner Cities (RBI) is a new Memphis baseball program. The general consensus in baseball is that nonwhite, ethnic, inner-city youth are no more interested in baseball than they are in polo. Tom Stocker, the Chicks' director of broadcasting, explained what he thought were the main reasons inner-city youngsters weren't playing baseball much any more in Memphis. He cited space (few parks in the inner cities); economics (high costs for bats and gloves); and difficulties in rounding up the large number of participants needed compared to basketball. The fact that previous generations hadn't been deterred by the same obstacles didn't figure into his explanations.

128

The RBI program was started by the major leagues but many minor league organizations have become involved. Buffalo, New York, has been one of the most prominently committed cities since 1989. The intent was to teach baseball skills to inner-city youth, in the hopes that the learning experience would carry over to attendance at professional games as they got older. A pitching machine was used so young batters wouldn't be overpowered by a strong pitcher. Games were scheduled to teach the responsibility of coming on time and to experience competition. Schools and churches were the contact organizations and local parks were used for diamonds. The Memphis program hoped to involve twelve hundred children in the 1993 program, which hadn't yet started when I was there.

Lack of minority representation in baseball employment and attendance was also noticeable. According to Tom, in 1992 four hundred applicants showed up to apply for the small number of jobs available at the baseball winter meetings. Only twenty-five of those applicants were from ethnic or racial minority groups. I had seen a dearth of minority employees in baseball, and the higher up the management scale the fewer there were. The proportion of black and other minority fans at Memphis baseball games was actually higher than I had seen in other southern cities, but still constituted less than 5 percent of all fans on a given night, and may have been closer to 1 percent on the average. Thirty-five percent of the greater Memphis area was populated by African Americans, the largest minority group, and the percentage within the city limits was even higher. Like other baseball organizations, the Memphis Chicks club was grappling with the lack of interest in baseball exhibited by minorities. Although the RBI program was a recognition that this lack of interest existed, and was an attempt to entice the next generation of inner-city youngsters into baseball's sphere, club officials really had no explanation for the overall phenomenon.

I had discussed the problem of low attendance by the black community with every organization I had visited. At each club, officials seemed genuinely concerned and perplexed. Even when efforts had been made to specifically market to the black community, results were poor. General managers were frustrated over their collective inability to attract these fans.

In perhaps twenty baseball parks, I asked black fans what they thought about the situation. They cited the high cost of attending and other reasons Tom Stocker had listed. What they didn't explain is why entertainment money went into other recreational activities and baseball was neglected by the black community.

Before professional basketball and football became serious alternatives for participation and watching by sports fans, baseball was the only athletic institution on national center stage. Baseball was segregated, and despite the eventual collapse of racial barriers that began with the hiring of Jackie Robinson, its leaders fought to have baseball remain a white male dominated sport at the major and minor league levels. Baseball was historically a white man's game in ways that basketball and football never were, and the sport generated decades of frustration and ill feeling for black athletes and the black community in general. When alternative sports became available, little wonder that blacks would embrace them in preference to a game in which they had not been welcome except in their own low status leagues or as fans who entered through a special gate and sat away from the action in the bleachers.

In his *Stolen Season* (1991), David Lamb set out one of the most reasoned discussions of the lack of black fan interest now available in print. While he has no definitive answers, his point is that baseball should start seriously asking who is coming and not coming to the park. The drift toward baseball as an all-white sport and business is not a desirable trend.

I stayed in Memphis for four days and wanted to stay longer. The Chicks' press box was a lively place on game nights. John Guinozzo kept up a stream of stories about teams of the past and players like Bo Jackson who had come through Memphis on the way up. Bo, he said, hit the ball harder than any player he had ever seen. Phil Stukenborg, sportswriter for *The Commercial Appeal*, could write his nightly coverage and talk baseball at the same time.

During one game, the pitcher threw one in the dirt. The ball skipped underneath the catcher's glove and rolled to the backstop. A club employee, running the scoreboard pad from an adjoining booth, flashed the words PASS BALL on the scoreboard.

"That's the correct decision," Eric McCool, media relations

head, called through the open door, "but next time make it past tense."

The same thing happened the next inning, and the young staff member flashed the words PAST BALL on the screen. Eric shook his head slightly and went next door to conduct a grammar lesson.

Memphis is also a city that takes its barbecue seriously. I found a place called the Interstate, which was smokey, small, dingy, and not on the interstate highway. The meat was succulent and the portions were large. In Memphis, you could only use the word barbecue intelligently as a noun. (In the northeast, people say things like "I'm gonna barbecue a chicken." "I'm gonna barbecue a duck." In Memphis, everyone understood that the word referred to pork. While I was in town, Memphis hosted a barbecue festival where original recipes were cooked and judged. Beef was banned at the festival.

The best game of the Greenville-Memphis series was on my last night. It was a tightly played match, but rocked along routinely for several innings. During the lull, John Guinozzo told the story of a substitute organist seven years before who played "Three Blind Mice" after a controversial call. The umpire pointed up to the press box and threw the organist out of the game. Earlier in the 1993 season, he said, the mascot (a man in a Chickasaw Indian brave costume) was ejected for fake-mooning an umpire after a close call.

In the sixth inning, the Chicks' held their nightly car giveaway. These cars, donated by local used car dealers, occasionally approached respectability in appearance but this evening's offering was twelve years old.

"Ever have anyone refuse these things when they win?" I asked Eric.

"All the time," he said.

While the game was slow, I left the press box to look up David Hersh, the Chicks' owner. The Chicks are actually owned by a group including nationally prominent names—Ron Howard, Tim McCarver, for whom the stadium is named, and television journalist Maury Povich—but Hersh is the decision maker. He had been receiving a blitz of media attention all week because of a newspaper article in which he was highly critical of local coverage of the

131

Chicks. "More time," Hersh commented, "is spent discussing Memphis State's recruitment success [for their basketball team] than the Chicks get in any day, even in the summer."

Hersh contended that sports talk show hosts didn't come to Chicks games and couldn't name four roster players after a month into the season. Announcers countered that the club advertised promotions and not players. Fans called in to radio stations saying that it was hard to generate interest in transitional players. Other fans defended the club, talking about the great atmosphere at the ballpark. This week, anyway, the Chicks were in the news. Keeping them there was Hersh's job.

The game went into the tenth inning and the Braves scored two in the top half. Memphis came back with one in the bottom, and with two on and two out, a batter scorched one toward the gap in left center. The Braves' center fielder ended the game with a shoe-string catch going to his right, finishing with a graceful, bent-leg slide while cradling the ball gingerly in his outstretched glove.

I stopped off to say goodbye to Phil Stukenborg in the parking lot. He was standing outside the Braves' bus interviewing the player who had just saved the game.

"I'm following the Braves over to Knoxville," I told him, "for the weekend series."

"Call me if anything interesting happens," he said. Good newspaperman that he was, he would make a stringer out of anybody.

9

The Far Out Lookouts

IN THE MIDDLE OF THE NIGHT about an hour out of Memphis, heading east on an interstate, the Greenville Braves' bus swung past me, making good time on the nearly empty road. I tucked in behind the team for a few hours and when I was very tired, pulled off at a commercial campground to sleep and finish the trip in daylight the next day. The Braves' bus, driven by Bob Elliott, pushed on into the night. The team had played hard, gone into extra innings to pull off a dramatic win, and its reward was a night of fitful sleep on a bus bouncing through the Tennessee countryside.

Late the next afternoon, as I approached Bill Meyer Stadium in Knoxville, I saw the Braves' bus parked outside in the parking lot. They had left after a late meal and had driven the four-hundred mile trip straight through, arriving at midmorning.

I wondered why they hadn't just spent the night at the halfway point in Nashville and driven in today. Their uniforms had to be cleaned, the driver told me. So he'd rushed to get them here early enough. The players went to the motel and the bus driver took the clothes to the cleaners.

Bob had pushed his limit as a driver, which was ten hours. Over that, a relief driver had to be on board. He showed me the bus—a standard, forty-six passenger vehicle with few amenities. The Braves traveled everywhere by bus and didn't pay for extras like video equipment, a standard feature on many modern buses.

Bob liked baseball, but had few romantic illusions about the game or the players. "They're overgrown kids. Won't pick up a

133

thing after themselves. All of them chew tobacco and knock the cups over." Bob lit a cigarette. "No smokers on the team though. Not one. Not even the coaches."

Within the month, one of Bob's problems was solved. In 1993, minor league baseball banned tobacco in any form, even the smokeless products, snuff and chewing tobacco.

The Knoxville Smokies played at Bill Meyer Stadium which, oddly, was also called Neal Ridley Field. Finding the place by whatever name hadn't been easy. Construction on freeway off-ramps in the center of town made a map almost useless because streets no longer ran where the map indicated. The directions in my *Baseball America* directory said to exit on Summit Hill Drive and follow the signs to the ballpark. Few signs existed, and the ones that did had been twisted and turned in wrong directions to confuse visitors.

Bill Meyer was an old stadium sitting on a site where baseball had been played since 1921. Steel girders and well-aged concrete gave the place atmosphere, and blue paint everywhere signified the Toronto Blue Jays affiliation. A warehouse with several broken windows peeped over the left field fence. Fans sat close to the action in Knoxville. Fences ran 330 feet down the lines, and 400 feet to dead center.

As the Friday evening game began, the sky was dark and threatening, and the weather was cold. After an inning and a half, the rain came down in torrents. Fans ran for shelter under the grandstand and slogged about in ankle-deep water. I drank a cup of coffee and waited for the inevitable announcement. The game was suspended after about twenty minutes, to be picked up the following evening. The Greenville Braves had driven all night to get to Knoxville, and were rained out after being on the field for less than half an hour.

Knoxville would seem to have the credentials to be a first-class minor league baseball city. They landed a position in the Southern Association in 1930 and have maintained teams in most seasons since then. In 1992, however, the Knoxville team drew 90,387 fans, not only the lowest total in the Southern League but the lowest of any AA team in the country.

I never had a chance to discuss this figure with the Knoxville staff. In visiting thirty cities and baseball organizations, Knoxville was the only club where I didn't meet with someone on the staff to talk about the current baseball situation. I called twice, was told both times that everyone on the staff was too busy to see me, and when I suggested an alternate meeting time, was told to call back then to see if time was available. They were overwhelmed, I guess, by taking care of those 1,287 fans per night.

One reason for low attendance may lie in a statement in the 1993 souvenir program. Garth Iorg, the 1993 manager, was quoted as saying, "Toronto's philosophy at the minor league level is to develop the players without paying too much attention to team records." Good thing, because the 1992 Knoxville Blue Jays lost a Southern League record-tying fifteen games in a row. Fan response should send a signal that they don't come to the park just to see player development.

Before 1993, the team had been called the Knoxville Blue Jays. Apparently realizing that something had to be done to nourish local identification with the club, the name was changed to the Knoxville Smokies, a return to the name of teams of the 1930s and early 1940s. A new logo, containing both the Knoxville skyline and an outline of the Smoky Mountains, provided a modern, tasteful patch of color on the team uniforms.

Later in the trip, in the press box at Tulsa, I heard a good story about Knoxville baseball. A reliable source—the host of a Tulsa radio sports talk show—said that he had attended minor league games at Bill Meyer Stadium in 1963. One night a couple had sex in the right field bleachers, about ten rows down from the top. He thought it was during the sixth inning. They were part of a rowdy crowd from the University of Tennessee, and were clearly visible from the press box even though several other students sort of surrounded them. "I know this isn't the kind of story you would want to write about," he told me, "but it really happened."

Next evening, before the makeshift doubleheader, I walked around with Garry Griffith, the Smokies' radio play-by-play announcer, as he did pregame interviews. Gary was in his first year with the club, having broadcast games of the South Atlantic League for four years in Fayetteville, North Carolina. He seemed

135

eager and excited about his new job, and could be a big help in attracting fans to Knoxville games in the future.

We walked over to the visitor's dugout to say hello to Bruce Kimm. He was trying to get a right fielder to recognize his hand signals from in front of the dugout for proper positioning in the outfield. He gave us a look that meant, I think, "Should this stuff really have to be taught?"

Greenville took both ends of the doubleheader. In the first game they were outhit 14 to 9 but played perfect defense while the Smokies committed two costly errors. After winning the second game 4–3, the Braves' record was 29–14, for a .674 percentage. Apparently the players didn't know they weren't supposed to be competing with last year's one-hundred-win team.

Not long out of Knoxville, I saw the first sign. Thereafter they appeared every ten miles or so, usually on a barn roof or the side of a large building. "SEE RUBY FALLS." "LOOKOUT MOUN-TAIN—RIDE THE INCLINE." "SEE SEVEN STATES FROM LOVER'S LEAP." "SEE ROCK CITY GARDENS." Forty years earlier, the same messages had fired my youthful imagination. My father, worn down by the long drive from Oklahoma and my constant nagging, finally agreed to take me to see the sights near Chattanooga. We descended into the mountain to see Ruby Falls, an underground waterfall lighted by colorful beams, which made the clear water gleam with red, blue, and green tones. A tour guide led us through the cavern, passing a rocky formation that had been worn smooth and round by the thousands of tourists who rubbed it as they passed by.

"Nine hundred and ninety-nine out of every thousand people who pass by here rub that rock," the guide announced, and I eagerly added to its shininess with all the pressure a twelve-year-old palm could bring to bear. I looked back at my father as he strode by the stone with touching it. The expression on his face was bemused, half way between "Like hell I'll rub a rock!" and "I'm embarrassed by this silliness." Ruby Falls wouldn't be on my itinerary this trip. Some memories are just too good to mess with.

My destination was Chattanooga, but first I had a detour just across the Tennessee border in Dalton, Georgia. On that long-ago trip across the South with my father and grandfather, our first stop had been in Dalton. We stayed with one of my father's cousins and saw an assortment of family members who lived in and around the small city. Though it has since been removed, I remembered well the house we stayed in. It was a shotgun house, a type of dwelling one room wide and two rooms deep. A porch ran across the gable-ended street front and we sat on a porch swing in the evening as people dropped by to see the three generations of Oklahoma visitors. Most of the Georgia branch of the family had been mill workers in the 1950s, employed in the textile and carpet mills for which Dalton had become famous.

My father had developed the unusual habit of referring to his father by his last name when he was talking with someone else, as in: "Green thought it would take us two days to get here, but we made it in one and a half." I decided that this was a highly sophisticated form of address and began trying it myself. This led to such idiotic utterances as: "I heard Green tell Green we would probably be leaving in the morning." My father overheard me and put an end to it, right here in Dalton.

Although I had yet to reach the deepest South on my current trip, I had seen fewer shotgun houses than ever before. The obviously declining house type was humble but functional. It originated in Haiti by blending a traditional Haitian house type with a form brought from Africa by slaves. Many free black Haitians lived in shotgun houses and some who immigrated to New Orleans early in the nineteenth century brought the shotgun with them. From there it spread across the South and became common housing for poor blacks and poor whites. Elvis Presley was born in one and before Elvis another blues man, W. C. Handy, also had his beginnings in a shotgun dwelling.

One of the reasons I had come to Dalton was to find out where my great-grandfather, Isham Jackson Green, and his wife Rebecca were buried. I searched through burial records of all the listed cemeteries in Murray and Whitfield counties, but their names never appeared. I had one last, slim possibility. In Atlanta, a folder in the state archives had contained a note from a researcher saying that she had walked through an old cemetery in Dalton and had seen the Green family name on several tombstones. The note was a quarter-century old, but I drove to the corners of Stone and Happy Streets to check out the markers. The small cemetery covered about half a city block in an old section of Dalton. It was filled with oak trees. About half of the ground was mowed and the other half was overgrown. Many of the grave stones had tumbled over and were scattered around. Some had been nudged from below by roots of trees. A majority of the stones were marble and had been eroded beyond the point where names could be recognized. I saw a groundhog scurry under one headstone, which was lying flat on the ground, into a hole it had dug there.

I realized that I wasn't going to find out where Isham and Rebecca were buried, and in all likelihood I would be the last person to ever try. I knew all I ever would about my great-grandparents. I knew that marble tombstones and shotgun houses don't last forever, and that young boys should listen more carefully when a grandparent tells war stories.

JoLynn Drake, public relations manager for the Chattanooga Lookouts AA Southern League team, took me up to the roof of Joe Engel Stadium so I could take some panoramic pictures of the old ballpark. A recent graduate of the University of Florida in sport science, she had been with the team since the previous October. As usual in minor league baseball administration jobs, her work ranged over a diverse set of duties, including the production of publications and media relations. JoLynn was pretty in the way that only young southern women sometimes are, with a wholesome smile and an athlete's movements. She had played baseball on organized teams with boys and was totally devoted to the game. Her goal, she told me, was to be the first female general manager in the majors. If staying focused can accomplish that aim, JoLynn should have a good shot at it. A few nights later in the press box, a staff member was talking about another of his hard-working colleagues with disbelief:

"He didn't have to work! He could have been out on this really hot date! He'd rather be here at the park!"

"Who wouldn't?" asked JoLynn.

JoLynn didn't seem to be in a big hurry so we stayed on the roof and talked about baseball in Chattanooga. Joe Engel Stadium had all the credentials of a great ballpark. In 1930, Babe Ruth christened the park with its first home run in an exhibition game, one of many the Babe opened with a blast. The park and the neighborhood surrounding it had both grown old. Outside the right-field fence, railroad tracks held train boxcars sitting on sidings. Railyard sounds and clanging bells floated in on the warm afternoon breeze. Beyond right center, I could see a rusting steel bridge superstructure. After dark a stream of automobile headlights and taillights traced patterns of illumination across the bridge.

To the southwest, a neighborhood of older homes hinted that once a middle-class population had surrounded the old park, but economic decline was now evident. Across the street, outside the left-field fence, a fast-food restaurant had become a target for batting practice home runs. Its green plastic mansard roof sported several noticeable dents from balls that carried the street.

Despite its age, Joe Engel was exceptionally clean and modern looking. The exterior was pinkish brick with muted green roofing. Steel girders supported the roof canopy, which ran from first to third base. A modern press box sat atop the roof and offered an excellent view of the field. One of the few minuses in this fine park was that the grandstand was inclined at a very shallow angle, so fans behind the box seats were a long way from the action for a minor league park.

The groundskeeper told me that the field had been recently redone by a firm called Southern Turf. This company had been getting major contracts lately, surfacing fields and offering supervision for maintenance of its work afterward. It had taken the infield down two feet, and installed three miles of pipe under the playing surface. In 1990 and 1991, twenty-four rainouts had been called at Engel. In 1992, after installation of the new drainage system, that number had been reduced to one. The field looked a little ragged now in late May because the rye grass was dying and the bermuda hadn't fully taken hold.

When Engel opened in 1930, left field was 368 feet, left center

139

383 feet, and center field a whopping 471 feet, with right a more manageable 324 feet. The cinderblock walls had never been moved and were covered with colorful doubledecked advertising signs. An inner chain-link fence had been built to modify the home run distances, and had been moved several times. At present, left ran 355 feet, left center curved out from 368 to 395 feet, center was a still-solid 415 feet, and right was now 318 feet. Just to the left of dead center a grassy incline rose sharply six or eight feet to a bright red Coca-Cola sign. The team name Lookouts was painted in red on the incline. Before 1987, the hill was in play, and outfielders in pursuit of long flies ran the risk of falling off the steep shoulders of the mound.

Many of the great ones have played at Engel. While neither were members of the segregated Lookouts, Willie Mays played for the Chattanooga Choo Choo and Satchel Paige played for an earlier professional black team in Chattanooga in the 1920s. A spirit of craziness has consistently permeated professional baseball in this city along the Tennessee River. Joe Engel, the legendary owner for whom the stadium is named, once traded a ballplayer for a turkey. He ran bizarre promotions and once, in anticipation of an overflow crowd, stored the baseballs to be used in a freezer overnight so few could be hit into the fans who stood in roped-off areas inside the outfield fences.

Joe Charbonneau was a player made for Chattanooga baseball. Larry Fleming, the *Chattanooga Times'* writer covering the Lookouts, pointed out to me the spots where he had seen Charbonneau, a right-hander, hit three out in one night over the distant left field wall. In 1979, Joe blazed through league pitching with a .352 average. He named his dog "Diarrhea" and his daughter "Dannon," after the yogurt company. After games, he would frequent Chattanooga bars and was quick to take offense and precipitate bar brawls. When he wasn't fighting, Joe would open bottles of beer with his eye socket, eat lit cigarettes, and drink beer through a hole in his nose. Charbonneau had an impressive rookie year with Cleveland in 1980, but lasted only a few more years in baseball. He had a bad back to go along with his mental eccentricities.

Even fans joined in the giddiness at Engel. Larry Fleming

pointed out a longtime Lookouts' fan who attended every game and always sat in the same spot. The man carried his own chair into the stadium and plunked it down in the opening between the grandstand and the right field bleachers. He wore a straw hat straight from the 1920s and carried a megaphone, with which he shouted instructions and positioned the fielders.

In a stadium with this history, you have every right to expect a weird ball game. Baseball people use the term "ugly" to describe a badly played game, and along with 3,207 other fans, I saw the essence of ugly on my first night at Engel. The first seven innings were routine and decently played, then things became increasingly improbable. Orlando struck for five runs in the top of the eighth, including a home run lifted over the right field wall. The Lookouts came back with two in the bottom of the eighth. Orlando added six in the top of the ninth. An Orlando player hit one off the Marlboro man, four straight left-handers hit the ball hard, and another home run went out in right center, very well hit. No one on either team came close to the left-field wall all game, but Orlando had flooded the lineup with left-handed batters and the short right-field fence couldn't hold them. After six runs, the Lookout second baseman booted a routine chance. Everyone on the field appeared to be a bit edgy, probably assuming that this meant another half dozen runs. The Cubs could manage only one more run, however, making the score fourteen to four.

Instead of slinking off quietly in disgrace, the Lookouts unexpectedly came back with fire in their bats. Orlando's pitcher Ernie Johnson gave up nine hits and seven runs in the bottom of the ninth. Most of the runs were technically earned, and the Cubs ended the game with only two errors compared to the Lookouts' three. These figures were misleading, however. Outfielders consistently broke late and infielders couldn't get their gloves down. In the bottom of the ninth, the Orlando third baseman didn't make a play that would have been routine, preferring instead to argue that the ball was foul. Lookout runners darted from base to base while the argument ensued.

After the Cubs' manager finally removed the traumatized Johnson, the Lookouts could manage only one more run and ended up

141

on the losing end of a 14–12 score. This led to the predictable jokes in the press box about extra points being blocked. Twenty-two runs had been scored in the last two innings, from twenty-seven hits. At least one-third of the hits had been tainted, and perhaps more. Neither team was having a particularly bad year, but for two innings a kind of collective incompetence settled over the playing field of Engel Stadium.

One Orlando player was quoted as saying "The last time I saw a game like this I was playing American Legion ball." The Cubs' manager told *Times*' writer Larry Fleming after the final out, "That was so ugly it doesn't feel like a win."

JoLynn had told me about the Chattanooga Regional History Museum in downtown Chattanooga. David Esterbrook, a museum director, had organized a display on Lookout baseball and was known as the local authority on the history of professional baseball in the city. "Don't miss the film on Jackie Mitchell," JoLynn said.

In 1931, the Yankees came through Chattanooga for an exhibition game. Ruth was on his way north to a big season where he would hit .373 with 46 home runs and 163 runs batted in. Gehrig would equal Ruth's home run output that season, hit .341, and batting cleanup, drive in 184 runs. On April 2, Joe Engel had signed seventeen-year-old Jackie Mitchell, a female left-hander, to a contract for the 1931 Southern Association season. In the first inning of the exhibition game, the Yankees opened the inning by hitting the Chattanooga starter hard. Lookouts' manager Bert Niehoff yanked the starter and called Mitchell in from the bullpen. Ruth was caught looking at a third strike, Gehrig went down swinging at a curve ball, and Tony Lazzeri worked the side-arming left-hander for a walk. The manager then removed Mitchell and called in another pitcher. That may have been a mistake, because the Yankees battered Chattanooga pitching the rest of the afternoon and won, 14–4.

When baseball commissioner Kenesaw Mountain Landis was alerted to the happenings, he ruled Mitchell's contract void, thus ending the participation of women in professional baseball for many years. The story, now a standard chapter in baseball lore,

142

was usually told as another Engel publicity stunt with which the Yankees magnanimously cooperated.

David Esterbrook showed me how to operate the machine that ran film clips. The short segment, captured by newsreel photographers trailing the Yankees around the South, showed a different story than I expected. Babe Ruth didn't appear to be fooling around, and his strikeout was not a gentlemanly gesture at all. He took at least one swing at a Mitchell pitch, and complained seriously when a third strike was called. Gehrig's strikeout sequence isn't shown, but Lou was reportedly more gracious about his failure to connect. Jackie Mitchell was shown discussing the events later in her life, a middle-aged woman with a marvelous moment to remember, a moment that layers of mythmaking and sexist assumptions hadn't been able to erase. If you go to Chattanooga, you can look it up.

Back at Engel, batting practice was rained out, so I sat and watched the ground crew work on the field. When it removed the tarp, which had a leak, a large puddle had formed around third base. Amidst much cursing and hand-waving, the crew began shoveling mud into a tractor-drawn carrier and throwing Diamond Dry onto the worst spots. A worker dropped a bag of the powdery dust, which exploded when it struck the ground. He inhaled some of the product and staggered off the field to seek medical aid. Another typical day was underway at Engel Stadium.

10

Deep in Dixie

LARRY FLEMING HAD RECOMMENDED Interstate 59 as a little-traveled and attractive line to Birmingham, Alabama. Before driving into Birmingham, I intended to stop in the small town of Trussville, Alabama, about twenty miles to the northeast, to talk with Jimmy Bragan, president of the Southern League. When I telephoned from the main street of the small town, Jimmy's wife Sarah told me that he had been held up in a meeting in Birmingham and wouldn't be available for awhile. Chancing upon a familiar candystriped revolving symbol, I used the time to visit a southern institution that I hadn't frequented in many years, the village barbershop.

The barber, who told me his name was Cecil, had the Chicago Cubs game on in the empty shop. Cecil obviously didn't keep an appointment book; a sign warned customers, "If you leave the shop, you lose your place in line." The Cubs game was a slow affair, so Cecil began filling me in on local color. Jimmy Bragan was a customer of his, and Jimmy, he said, knew the difference between barbering and what they do at salons.

"What," I asked, "is the difference?"

"They don't know anything about barbering, is the difference. Oh, they can cut your hair, make you look good, but that's not barbering. That's not barbering at all."

One difference was the way Cecil shaved my neck, using a hot cloth and shaving lather. Another was that I left with practically no hair at all. His haircut took care of me for the rest of the trip, and then some. The real difference, however, was gender. Cecil's

145

shop had the feel of maleness. Everything from the tattered fishing magazines that were thrown haphazardly about to the Cubs game on television to the brightly colored, sweet-smelling skin-bracer that Cecil slapped on my freshly shaved neck would have been foreign in a salon.

My first-ever paying job had been in a small-town barbershop in Oklahoma. I was a shoeshine boy (ten cents for shoes; a quarter for cowboy boots) and in exchange for space and supplies, swept the floor, cleaned windows, and ran errands. I whiled away the slack hours by poring over the batting averages of the Tulsa Oilers, and got free haircuts that looked very much like the job Cecil had just done on me. The salons may have cut into the number and promi-nence of small town barbershops, but if Cecil's place was typical, little had changed in those that remained. William Faulkner would have felt at home in the barber shop at Trussville, Alabama.

The official office of the Southern League was around the corner and up the street about a block from Cecil's. Sarah showed me into the two-room office. Both rooms were filled with baseball memora-bilia and pictures, and stuffed pheasants crouched on the walls. Jimmy Bragan, the Southern League president since 1979, was a hearty man with a large stomach. He pointed to an old picture of himself—a few pounds lighter—in a minor league baseball uni-form. Jimmy had been to see Cecil recently. His graying hair was cropped as short as mine, and we sat there talking, looking like two marine drill sergeants.

Jimmy was a member of a large, baseball-connected family that included his brothers Bobby, a former major leaguer with the Na-tional League Phillies and Dodgers in the 1940s, and Peter Bragan, Jr., the present general manager of the Jacksonville Suns in the Southern League. Jimmy played minor league ball into the 1950s. One year he out hit Frank Robinson when they were teammates on a club in the lower minors. "Frank was hurt a lot that year," he explained, "but I've never let him forget it."

A minor league president's duties include overseeing the playing schedule, making out the umpire schedule, imposing fines and an-swering a trough full of correspondence. The job was heavily weighted toward public relations and trying to balance the interests of diverse groups, including team owners. Jimmy was on the road a lot. He attended about one hundred games per year, and tried to swing through each of the league cities at least twice. Sarah and Jimmy ran the office together, and their long years of experience in baseball had put them on a first name basis with almost everyone in the profession.

"I'm going to call you prof," said Jimmy, on finding out my occupation. Sarah looked slightly uncomfortable with that. "Can't you call him doctor?" she asked. Jimmy agreed that was a good idea, then almost immediately reverted to "prof."

I made a pitch for resurrecting the old Dixie Series, a season-ending playoff between the winners of the Southern League and the Texas League. This had been a standard series for decades, including the years when I was an adolescent, and had aroused almost as much interest in parts of the South in September as had the World Series in October. I didn't have to convince Jimmy.

"When the Texas League got a new president last year," he said, "one of the first things I did was to call him and suggest the same thing. He didn't want any part of it. He said 'Sure as hell Orlando and El Paso would win the leagues, and we'd spend more money on plane fare than the series brought in.' We'll probably never see the Dixie Series again."

I spent a delightful hour and a half talking baseball with the Bragans. As I started to leave, Jimmy began opening drawers and giving me things. He gave me a Southern League media guide, a baseball cap, and an official league baseball. When he found out I was going to a game in Birmingham that night, he insisted that I use his box seat tickets. I left before Jimmy could continue the potlatch, but he was still glancing around for souvenirs to dispense as I walked out the door.

Before the 1993 season ended, Jimmy Bragan announced his retirement as Southern League president. He was quoted in *Baseball America* with this epitaph for minor league baseball of bygone times: "When I inherited this job in 1979, the emphasis was on baseball. Now the emphasis is on marketing and legalism and that sort of thing. Maybe it's age, but some of the fun has been drained out of it for me."

Birmingham baseball was first played in a park called the Slag Pile down by the Great Southern Railroad tracks. The unattractive name was fitting—overflow crowds sat on a pile of slag that rose above and beyond the outfield fences. The city's most famous park, however, was Rickwood Field. It opened in 1910 and is now the oldest standing ballpark in the United States. Named after Rick Woodward, who owned the Barons in the first part of the twentieth century, the stylish old structure had recently been listed in the National Register of Historic Places.

The Birmingham Barons played their last game at Rickwood Field in September of 1987. The park still stands in Birmingham's west side, maintained after a fashion by the city's recreation department, as a shrine to the game's past. I drove Sweetspot through an entrance in a chain link fence and parked next to a wall painted with white pennants listing the championship years of Baron baseball.

Rickwood was the first concrete and steel structure built for minor league baseball. Its facade is a two-story brick elevation. The lower level consists of an arcade whose arches with iron gates open as fan entrances, and the upper level resembles a building front on a city street, with plentiful windows and brick ornamentation. Inside, the old wooden press boxes sit rotting atop the roof canopy, and the backstop screen dangles from its anchors on the roof's edge. The field is mowed and the basepaths are raked, however, and high school and summer league teams still tread the grass, which is laced with clover.

Rickwood mirrored the changing fashions of baseball in the twentieth century. Originally, left field was a long 405 feet from home plate, center field was 470 feet, and right field, restrained by railroad tracks that bordered the property on that side, was only 334 feet. When the home run came into vogue in the 1920s, wooden fences were built inside the old concrete barriers at 325–393–335. The old outside concrete walls are still in place, and I walked through an opening in the center field fence to see them. Someone was maintaining a large vegetable garden between the two walls, about ten feet wide and fifty yards long. The corn was a

148

healthy green color and already about two feet high in late May. I was deep into Dixie now.

Following the fashion of the days, Rickwood was segregated for the first half century of its existence. When the white team was on the road, Rickwood became home to the Birmingham Black Barons. Here, Negro League pitcher Satchel Paige began the disconcerting habit of placing a gum wrapper on home plate, announcing to the opposition that he would pitch with that as his base, and then doing what he had bragged he could. Before becoming infamous as the commissioner of public safety who turned dogs loose on black protestors in the 1960s, Bull Connor had been a baseball broadcaster for the white Birmingham Barons of the Southern Association. White and black ballplayers were not allowed to intermingle, and when the white team played at Rickwood, black fans had to sit in unsheltered bleachers 355 feet from home plate. Even in 1966, the white Barons had to play a season in Mobile, Alabama, because of an archaic city ordinance prohibiting interracial mixing of ballplayers.

Finally, Rickwood succumbed to the shifting of baseball fans to the suburbs. The west end of Birmingham had spiraled downward economically and the team's owner had started lobbying for a new park in the 1980s. Because of political and economic infighting, a new park was not built anywhere in Birmingham. Instead, the municipality of Hoover, seventeen miles to the south, raised funds for a multipurpose stadium and the Barons relocated. Hoover Metropolitan Stadium sat in a typical suburban area, far from downtown Birmingham and not even near the downtown center of Hoover. Before the stadium, Hoover's main claim to fame was as the site of the largest enclosed shopping mall in the South. The Riverchase Galleria contains the longest skylight in the Western Hemisphere. Driving onto the stadium grounds, I had the feeling of entering a shopping mall. Acres of concrete and forests of light poles greeted me.

I opened the Barons' 1993 souvenir program and the first pictures I saw were not baseball players, but the Barons' front office staff. The "President and CEO," before entering athletics had been product manager for Van de Kamp's Frozen Foods. Beans or baseball, small matter to the marketing specialist. Access to the sky suite and press box level was by elevator. An attendant checked tickets and passes and turned away the unauthorized. The impersonality of the stadium's name was carried throughout the team's entire approach to baseball. Even the fact that concessions served the tasty Red Mountain Wheat Beer on draft couldn't endear me to the Hoover Met.

The Barons were drawing well, nonetheless. In twenty-four 1993 home dates, they had averaged over 3,500 fans per game, and had been second and third in Southern League attendance figures over the past two years. The evening's crowd was close to the average, but the stadium seated ten thousand and at one third that number, people seemed to rattle around in the park.

I watched Knoxville pitcher Paul Spoljaric, who was being touted as a certain major leaguer within two seasons, shut down the Barons on a two-hitter through six. He threw fast balls, a hard slider, and a hard curve, nothing that dropped or broke very much. The young left-hander was reminiscent of Ron Guidry on the mound. He had jumped from low A (Myrtle Beach, South Carolina) last year to AA, and needed seasoning and maturity. After being hit hard by three straight batters in the bottom of the seventh, he was taken out. He slammed his glove on the bench and began storming up and down the dugout. Often managers not only permit but tacitly encourage these childish displays in players. "Intensity," they call it, as if intensity and good manners were mutually exclusive.

I must have been in a hurry to leave Hoover after the game because I did two unusual things. First, I began driving south late at night, toward New Orleans. I tried to never travel at night, for the simple reason that I had come to *see* the South, not just drive blindly through it. Second, I took the wrong interstate. Instead of exiting on I-59, which slants across southern Alabama and slices off a corner of Mississippi before dipping down into New Orleans, I took I-65. This highway veers back southeast into Montgomery before sloping southwest to Mobile. Sometime after midnight, I pulled off the highway, parked Sweetspot in a motel lot, and went to sleep in the back. The next morning I discovered the mistake but it was too late to rectify it by turning around. Thus were Montgomery and Mobile added to my itinerary.

After having breakfast in Montgomery, I drove around to see some of the sites associated with the civil rights movement. Montgomery was the first capital of the Confederacy for a few months before the government moved to Richmond, Virginia. Today the building that housed the Confederate government is Alabama's state capitol. In Tennessee, I had talked with an Alabaman who was fishing in a river near where I had camped. He had told me, with some disgust, that Alabama governor Jim Folsom had successfully had the Confederate flag banned from flying over the state capitol. Formerly, the Confederate flag had flown between the stars and stripes and Alabama's state flag, but surely enough, it wasn't up there today.

In one of those ironic juxtapositions that saturated the South, the Dexter Avenue Baptist Church sat only a block from the former headquarters of the Confederacy. The plain brick building with gothic windows displayed little ornamentation except for a wooden belvedere above the gable over the front door. A young woman ushered me through the historic structure, pointing proudly to a large mural depicting the history of the church and other scenes from the civil rights movement. The mural began with Rosa Parks boarding a city bus where, after a hard day's work on December 1, 1955, she refused to give up her seat to a white man. On December 2, 1955, a historic meeting took place in the basement of the church. Dr. Martin Luther King, Jr., pastor of Dexter Avenue Baptist from 1954 to 1960, presided and before the evening was over, the Montgomery bus boycott was underway. The prominence of the little church in the civil rights movement was underscored on January 30, 1956, when foes bombed its parsonage. Coretta Scott King, Martin's daughter Yolanda, and another church member escaped unharmed.

The traditional symbols of the South were under fire everywhere I traveled in the summer of 1993. In Memphis, I had followed the story of a band that was prohibited from playing on a local television station unless it agreed to play without Confederate uniforms. The band, which made music with common instruments such as

151

washboards, cowbells, and spoons, billed itself as a Confederate band, and refused to go on without the uniforms. A month earlier, it had broken tradition and agreed to do a performance without playing "Dixie," staying instead with the traditional favorites "Oh! Susanna," "Sewanee River," and "When Johnnie Comes Marching Home."

In Mississippi, the NAACP had filed a lawsuit attacking the state flag as unconstitutional. As in Georgia, the state flag had an image of the "stars and bars" symbol of the Confederacy embedded in it, so both states faced a somewhat different dilemma than did Alabama. In talking with residents of all the Deep South states about the issue of Confederacy symbolism, whether in the form of flags, uniforms, or song, I could see an argument that was becoming increasingly heated.

Those who defended the display of Confederate symbols evoked the issue of pride. Ancestors had fought and died for the principles they believed in. The symbols represented history, warts and all. Freedom of expression gave everyone the right to display the Confederate symbols. "Besides," one man told me, rather weakly, " 'Dixie' was wrote by a Yankee anyway." Opponents countered that the symbols represented slavery. They felt they could deprive people of civil rights because, when displayed in public places, the symbols had the chilling effect of inhibiting the expression of real feelings. The symbols taunted blacks and were a divisive force in race relations.

After the official tour of the Dexter Avenue Baptist Church was over, I talked for awhile with the young woman who had shown me through. Gradually she dropped the formal tone she had been using and became more forthcoming. When I asked her about the decision to remove the flag from the state capitol, she said, "Personally, I'm glad the thing isn't up there anymore."

Alexandria, Virginia, a city near where I live, has taken an interesting position on public display of the Confederate flag. This was the boyhood hometown of Robert E. Lee, lying across the Potomac River from Washington, D.C., which has had a majority black population for many years. In a compromise reached in 1970, the flag was removed from public buildings and was flown on only two days—January 19, Lee's birthday, and May 24, Confederate Memorial Day. The city adopted, as part of the compromise, a policy of not asking African-American employees to raise or lower the flag. For over two decades, the city's position had been workable and still, though it was born in the intensity of the civil rights movement, seemed imminently fair.

Few persons I spoke to in the South in the summer of 1993 were interested in compromise, however. Feelings seemed to grow more heated as the southern summer descended full force upon me during the trip.

As I pulled into Mobile, the odometer turned over the ten thousandth mile I had driven since the trip began. Fewer than five minutes later, the left rear tire blew and I lurched and flapped to a stop on a busy highway. While there is no really desirable place for a blowout, the flat tire gods must have been planning this one for weeks. I was on a railroad overpass, with no shoulder. Construction had narrowed the lanes from three to two immediately in front of me, and just to my rear was an entrance ramp. Continuing, even at the risk of damaging the wheel, was impossible because the road narrowed just ahead to two crowded lanes edged with concrete Jersey walls on each side. My only choice was to change the tire where I was.

I turned on the flashers and began emptying my living quarters onto the highway to get at the spare tire. When I began working on the wheel nuts, the danger of the situation became apparent. Cars would hurtle up the on ramp, see me, careen crazily into the adjacent lane of traffic, nearly be hit by cars driving at speed down that lane, swerve back to avoid them and miss me by inches. I ducked a few times, then gave up and stopped looking, trusting to the reflexes and luck of the drivers behind me. I'm not sure how quickly I changed that tire, but I know that it was a new personal record.

I found a store that sold new tires near the waterfront and ordered two to replace the one that had blown out and its partner on the rear, which was also showing signs of wear. While the tires were being installed, I had lunch and a stiff drink to calm my nerves. Mobile is Alabama's only port. It is located on the west side of the dredged Mobile River, not far from where the river empties into the

153

bay. On the waterfront, horse-drawn buggies lined the street to show tourists the sites of the old southern city. I approached a man, dressed in a buccaneer costume, whose name, he hold me, was Tony.

"Do you know where Hartwell Field was?" I asked him.

"Hartwell? Hell yes. I used to go to games there when I was young. It isn't far."

"If I take the tour, can you drive me by there?"

"Hartwell isn't there. They tore it down."

"I'd still like to see where it was."

"Hartwell? Well. What the hell. I'll drive you by there. I'll show you where I used to live when I was young."

Mobile had fielded teams in the Southern Association, at two different time periods, for over forty years. Its last professional baseball team had been a Southern League entry in 1970. The baseball park had been partially destroyed by a hurricane in the midseventies, and then apparently demolished by the city. Three persons, Larry Schmittou, Jimmy Bragan, and now Tony had assured me that nothing remained of the park, but I didn't see how such an important site could simply be obliterated, and had to see for myself.

The space that Hartwell occupied was still open land, used now by the city fire department for training exercises. It was a prime, downtown area bordered by large, imposing houses and trees draped with Spanish moss. For classic southern beauty, the approach rivaled that leading to the park in Savannah. City officials would be advised to get busy on a ballpark. Even if they missed the current Southern League vacancy, another was certain to appear in the fluid minor league system soon, and a facility would complement the downtown area in much the same way that Camden Yards has become a partner to Baltimore's inner harbor.

Tony and the others were right, of course. Nothing was left. Tony oriented me to the park's former layout. A chain link fence now ran down a line formerly occupied by the wooden right-field wall. Just outside the wall was a water-filled ditch.

"I used to catch crawfish in that ditch," Tony said.

Beyond the ditch, a brick building that housed a pulley factory provided a target for left-handed batters, who used to regularly bounce home runs off its wall.

The scene was surreal. I was sitting in a horse-drawn buggy, driven by a man dressed as a buccaneer, excitedly discussing a ballpark that wasn't even there. By then, Tony was as enthusiastic about the stop as I was. He took a picture of me with my camera, saying:

"No, no, stand farther over to your left, or I won't be able to get where the right field fence used to be in the background."

Named after owner Rick Woodward, Rickwood Field (Birmingham, AL) hosted baseball for the first time in 1911.

Big Dave Nitz, play-by-play announcer for the Shreveport Captains.

Spar Stadium, Shreveport, LA, "like a huge rotting insect whose tissue had eroded, leaving only the membrane."

Shotgun houses in Mississippi.

Ray Winder Field, Little Rock, AR, before Wilbur Mills Parkway was built just outside the right field fence.
(Courtesy of Bill Valentine, Arkansas Travelers Baseball Club)

In 1976, pinch-hitter Roscoe Steadman of the Little Rock Travelers "calls his shot."
(Courtesy of Arkansas Travelers Baseball Club)

Signing autographs before the game at Ray Winder Field, Little Rock, AR.

*Proposed tribute to
The Mick outside
his hometown of
Commerce, OK.*

The vacant Will Rogers Hotel, Claremore, OK.

Cotton-Eyed Joe's. From the front porch you can see Route 66, hear the train whistles blow, and smell the hickory burning. (Courtesy of Michael D. Green, Potomac, MD)

The Warehouse Market, Elgin Street, Tulsa, OK. Built over McNulty Field, it has class even in disrepair.

Lawrence Dumont Stadium, Wichita, KS.

Joe Bauman, at home in Roswell, NM.

The author, taking a well-deserved break from the toil of attending baseball games.

11

In Evangeline Country

IF I HAD TO PICK A SINGLE baseball situation to epitomize minor league baseball in the south, it would be the Evangeline League. Except for Natchez, Mississippi, and two Texas border towns, the teams were all Louisiana based and within a one-day drive of each other. From 1934 to 1948 (excluding the war years), it ran as a class D league, and moved up to class C in 1949. Its demise came in 1957.

At Nicholls State University in Thibodaux, Louisiana, a history professor has organized a permanent display dedicated to the memory of a vanished minor league. Paul Leslie is codirector of the Evangeline Baseball History Project at Nicholls. Teaching and research are his livelihood. His full-time work is baseball *aficionado*.

Nicholls State is an unlikely looking place for a baseball museum, or any other kind of museum. It is almost treeless and except for the heat layered across the campus, the southern Louisiana flatlands might be the northern tundra. I met Paul Leslie inside the library and we spent a couple of hours looking at the exhibits he had arranged and talking about the Evangeline League.

The 'Vangy was always a fast league for its classification and had remarkable players and teams. In 1948, Ray Sanner of the Houma Indians turned in what was perhaps the most exceptional one-season performance in minor league baseball history. He topped the Evangeline League batting statistics in average, doubles, homeruns, RBIs, and total bases.

Impressive, you say, but not singular? Sanner also won twenty-one games and lost two as a pitcher, for a .913 average that year. In one stretch, he won seventeen games in a row. Sanner's season, documented carefully by Professor Leslie in the baseball journal *Nine*, might have been even *more* impressive except that he suffered from what a teammate called "migrating headaches" and missed several pitching starts, and he left the team in late August after a dispute over sale of his contract.

As players competed in the steamy, oppressive southern Louisiana heat, fans of the Evangeline League teams poured adoration on their favorites. Slot machines carried players' names and pictures. Civic pride in teams was so great that umpires sometimes had to be escorted out of town after a close game. Leslie had over one hundred names on a mailing list of former Evangeline players, and told me that each year the college sponsored a reunion in the springtime. The exhibit contained the usual baseball memorabilia and a collection of letters describing extraordinary events in the league's history. Sturdy-looking woolen home and road uniforms graced the exhibit with team names forming a litany of Cajun sounds—Abbeville, Baton Rouge, Jeanerette, Lafayette, New Iberia, Opelousas.

Paul Leslie had written several articles about the league and, I hoped, would one day set down its colorful history in a book. Another of his interests was Huey Long, a not dissimilar subject, given Huey's involvement in the seamier side of Louisiana politics and the eventual scandal that marked the Evangeline League. In 1946, Houma won the pennant handily with a 92–38 record. The team continued the carnage by routing Alexandria four games to one in the first round of the intraleague play-offs, and finished its season by beating Abbeville in the finals, again four games to one. Its star pitcher, Bill Thomas, had won thirty-five games in 1946 and was a perfect 5–0 in the playoffs. Nonetheless, four Houma players and one Abbeville player were accused of having been in contact with gamblers who had offered them money to throw games during the season. Thomas had apparently refused, but failed to report the incident. Eventually all five players were found guilty by a National Association judge and were suspended from baseball. Two of the five, including Thomas, were reinstated two years later, but the scandal shook fans' faith in their teams. Houma's attendance, which had been over 100,000 in 1947, dropped to just over 43,000 in 1950 and in that same year, Abbeville drew only 22,811 through the gates. The league struggled on through most of the 1950s but never again with the same passion and intensity as before there were five men out.

I thanked Paul for showing me around and drove back to Houma, where only an open field and a mulberry tree marked the home field of the Houma Indians when they tore through the Evangeline League at a .708 pace in 1946.

I had arranged with three friends to travel together across southern Louisiana. Our plan was to take a three-car caravan across US 90, and beyond that things were a little vague. Given three cars, four people with diverse interests, and the spontaneous approach to life that both my friend Lee and his army buddy Jaybo embraced, the week promised to be unpredictable at best and with a little luck, downright chaotic. I met the others at the motel in Houma and for the next several days we split up, got back together, left muddled messages for each other ("I'll meet you at the first bar on Route 90 after the swamp boat place"), and after three days had progressed only ninety miles from New Orleans.

Jaybo, a wiry, young-looking sixty or so with a perpetual look of mischief on his face, had an atlaslike knowledge of Louisiana. He told me about a man in Alexandria I "had to meet" because he was knowledgeable about Louisiana baseball. Jaybo started looking through his billfold, a bulging piece of leather full of business cards, laundry slips, and cocktail napkins with telephone numbers on them. The search became an autobiography: "I knew him in the army." "I did some work with him over in Texas." One number he viewed somberly and said, "He died several years ago."

"Why do you keep the number?" I asked.

Jaybo grinned. "His wife is still alive."

US 90 became a tether line for us, and I became accustomed to driving along it slowly and looking for one or both of the familiar two other cars at roadside restaurants or bars. Every evening we met for dinner. The number at dinner varied considerably because Lee picked up locals the way other people collect souvenirs.

159

For the first time since leaving home, I had the feeling of being in a foreign country. The scenery was exotic and different. Above ground cemeteries, necessitated by the high water level under the sandy soil, looked like miniature villages. Sugarcane plantings ran next to Route 90, with the tough-looking plants sitting high atop long, narrow mounds. Everywhere conversations were carried on in French, but even English sounded like a foreign language because of the Cajun cadence.

Not all the inroads of the twentieth century had managed to obliterate the Cajun culture. In Saint Martinville, a picturesque town on the Bayou Teche, a small park hosted the Evangeline Oak. This stately old oak, rising from the banks of the bayou, marked the legendary meeting place of Emmeline Labiche and Louis Arceneaux, the real-life counterparts of Longfellow's Evangeline and Gabrielle. Like the Cajun culture, the oak has withstood time and even the destruction of hurricanes. In early June of 1993, I saw its small bright green leaves appearing on schedule for at least the 225th time.

On Thursday, the four of us met for a farewell dinner at Mulate's, a well-known Cajun restaurant in Breaux Bridge. We ate catfish smothered in jambayala and drank icy, metallic *fume blanc*. A live band played "Blues a Bebe-Beausoleil" and the "Bosco Stomp" with the traditional fiddle, accordion and banjo. Mulate's was a place for dancing. Older couples glided around the floor, while younger ones whirled and cavorted in the center. Often three generations of the same family were on the floor at the same time, stepping time to the twang of the Cajun band.

I said my goodbyes and headed north toward Alexandria, leaving Route 90 in favor of an interstate. I hadn't seen a ball game in a week, and it was time to get back to work. Traveling with friends had left its mark, though, and the way north was lonely. The highway seemed desolate and isolated, and when I pulled over to sleep even Sweetspot's usually cozy confines seemed almost inhospitable.

Route 1 led north to Shreveport. The midafternoon sun bounced off the highway in shimmering waves, making me think I saw pools of water to navigate in the road ahead. Louisiana was really three

160

distinctive regions: the Cajun and Creole south I was leaving; the northern half, which was more typical of the Deep South; and the western border, which looked more toward Texas and the West for lifestyle. Shreveport stood in the northwest corner of the state, and appropriately, the Shreveport Captains Professional Baseball Team belongs to the Texas League, and has, off and on, since 1895.

Texas League players first took the field in April 1888, in a time when fielders still didn't wear gloves. The usual sporadic collapses occurred in the first few decades, but by 1902, the league was generally stable. At first, all the teams were based in Texas but gradual expansion into Louisiana and Oklahoma loosened the Lone Star State's grip on the league. The league was originally given a class D placement, and steadily moved up to C in 1907, B in 1911, and A in 1921. Anchored by large cities such as Dallas, Fort Worth, Houston, Oklahoma City, Tulsa, and Shreveport, the league was designated AA in 1946 and enjoyed its heyday from then until the late 1950s. After some experimentation with interlocking schedules with the Mexican League from 1959 to 1961 (as the Pan-American Alliance) and with the Southern League in 1971 (the two leagues formed the Dixie Association), the Texas League returned to independence and had continued to prosper despite losing Dallas and Houston to the majors. The current makeup of the league had a four-team eastern division with Arkansas (at Little Rock), Jackson, Mississippi, Shreveport, and Tulsa. The western half featured three Texas teams—El Paso, Midland, San Antonio—together with Wichita, Kansas. These geographically dispersed cities spanned six large states and, as the crow flew, 1,008 miles separated the western-most team, El Paso, from Jackson, the one farthest east.

Shreveport is laid out along the south bank of the Red River and named in honor of Captain Henry Miller Shreve, a steamboat builder and a veteran of the Battle of New Orleans. Before Shreve arrived in 1832, the Red River was unnavigable above Natchitoches because of a centuries-old log jam that stretched for over 160 miles. The Great Raft, as it was called, made it possible to walk across the Red River in spots without getting wet. Using powerful steamboats designed especially for the job, Shreve worked for five years to clear the river. Because of his success, the town (originally

161

called Shreve Town but renamed Shreve Port to acknowledge the navigability of the river) prospered.

Henry must have been a hell of an engineer. In 1837, a rival town sprung up three miles downriver on Coates Bluff. Shreve cut through a bend in the Red River and left Coates Bluff sitting on a shallow backwater, and that was the end of the competition.

Now called the Captains after Shreve, the Shreveport clubs of my youth were known as the Sports, and in the early part of the century as the Gassers. Today the Captains play at Fair Grounds Field, just off I-20, in a shiny new park that replaced decaying Spar Stadium in 1986. At first, the concrete and plastic structure reminded me of Birmingham's Hoover Met, but once inside I could see that it was built to human dimensions, seating 6,200. Attendance was good throughout the series I saw there, and with 4,000 to 5,000 fans the park seemed to pulse with excitement.

Bill James, writing in *Baseball Abstract*, called this the most difficult hitting park in professional baseball. Power alleys are deep (385 feet), each line runs 330 feet, and center is 400 feet away with a twenty-four-foot blue wall to provide background for the hitters. High humidity and an altitude of only 206 feet keeps the balls from carrying. In the first game I saw, no one hit a home run despite fourteen runs. The media notes credited Shreveport with only twenty home runs after fifty-three games to date. By comparison, Arkansas, the visiting team, had thirty-nine home runs and they were last in the Texas League in hitting.

Baseball's collision with the changing customs of late twentieth-century society is far from over. The traditional American individualism has taken a turn toward isolationism. Americans sit in their homes watching videos, experiencing "virtual communities" on their computers, and making their cars solitary cocoons with electronic inputs and outputs. Earlier in the century, people spent their leisure time in the company of others—at the theater, the amusement park, the community celebration of patriotic holidays, and the sports event.

More than other public amusements, baseball has always been a total sensory experience. That first sight of the green field is accompanied by the smell of hot dogs and roasted peanuts. Vendors bark out the names of their products and the crack of bat and pop of ball into the glove echo through the stands. Baseball on television is not the baseball experience, but a different breed of reality. The sounds of the crowd microphone are not the sounds of the crowd, because you are not helping to make them.

As I moved away from the small, simple fields of the Southeast to the larger and newer baseball parks of the Deep South, the press boxes became increasingly cut off from the field. At Shreveport, the facilities were first rate. The press had a pregame buffet every evening, access to a full bar throughout the game, and a glass-enclosed, air-conditioned box with excellent vision. The club officials were congenial and I envied the working conditions of the writers who made their living by coming to the park for every home game. With all its comforts, however, seeing the game from the press box was something like sitting in a living room and watching the game electronically. Big Dave Nitz, the Captains' play-by-play announcer, obviously felt the same because he had moved his equipment outside the booth to an open concrete perch which put him in the noise, the weather, and the excitement of the crowd.

Taylor Moore, president of the Captains, had an interesting approach to the dilemma of new technology and baseball. Instead of fighting against the inroads television had made in fan involvement, he embraced the medium. A few years before, he had taken a rather typical minor league television operation (a few games were taped; videos were made on request to aid in coaching) and formed Moore Video Productions, Inc. Now, over twenty games per year were telecast on cable, and three had been picked up by the local CBS affiliate.

A television studio that housed a local sports show was located underneath the stands of Fair Grounds Field on the first base side. Every game was taped and the tapes were made available to coaches. One camera shot the batter head to toe for hitting analysis, and a large video library was available for both hitters and coaches.

I was invited to watch a game from the perspective of the television control room, while the game was being televised. The small room was a maze of monitors and machinery. Four technicians controlled the input from five cameras around the field, and a production manager coordinated their efforts while he explained to me what was happening.

"We use numbers to designate the different cameras instead of locations like third base ground, high home, center field. The usual configuration is five cameras and the numbers were assigned as they were added historically."

The technicians were college interns majoring in television production. Somehow, everyone seemed to be able to talk, laugh, engage in horseplay and yet accomplish what seemed to me to be an overwhelming job of coordination. Each camera had responsibilities. One followed the ball, one shot the pitcher, one picked up the defensive play. A home run, when watched on television, seemed to be a simple unified activity. Yet the sequence was produced by a formula in which the producer cut from one camera following the ball over the fence, to another catching a reaction shot of the pitcher, to another showing the runner rounding second, and so forth. Watching the monitor that contained the images being broadcast, I could see how the sequence was always similar on television, and how much of the real scene was missing.

Television production wasn't only technical. The producer had to know enough baseball, for example, to understand that a manager's second trip to the mound meant a new pitcher, or which pitching counts are favorable for steals so that a camera could be directed to the bullpen or to the basepath, as necessary. A few feet over our heads, oblivious fans crunched peanuts, spilled beer, and yelled the usual epithets at the umpires.

The Captains' fascination with technology also showed on the outfield fence. Pitching speeds, picked up on a radar gun behind home plate, were flashed below a sign "SPEED ON OVER—RED RIVER CHEVROLET" for all the fans to see. The experience was educational. Fastballs came in at speeds in the high eighties, curves in the midseventies, and change-ups as low as fifty-four miles per hour. Fans could appreciate, perhaps for the first time, that batters must contend with speeds varying up to thirty-five miles per hour, in addition to constant changes in location and movement. The star hitter's failure to succeed seven out of ten times was more understandable when one saw the Red River speed board.

On my last day in Shreveport, I set out looking for old Spar Stadium, home of the Captains until 1986. Following a map was impossible: construction on an interstate through the city had made even a recent map useless. Neighborhoods had been bisected and streets simply stopped at the edges of the dirt and concrete. I finally pulled into a used car lot to ask for help.

"You want to sell that pickup?" a salesman asked. "I been looking for a '72 Chevy."

"No, I'm looking for Spar Stadium, the Captains' old ball park. I can't get there following the map."

The salesman helped me plot a way around the highway construction. The park was within half a mile of where we sat, but I was forced to take a four-mile detour. A second salesman, overhearing our conservation, said "That's in the Allendale section. Do you have to go there?" as a third salesman, standing nearby, shook his head gravely. Old ballparks always seem to be in "bad" neighborhoods, according to local people who live in the suburbs. This wasn't the first time I had been implicitly warned against going into a high-crime, poorer, usually all-black district just to see a ballpark.

"I want to take some pictures of it," I said, "before they tear it down."

All three salesman shook their heads in unison.

"I sure wish you'd sell me that truck," one said as I left.

"I can't," I said. "It has to get me to El Paso."

I looked back and saw them all talking together as I walked back to Sweetspot, probably taking bets on whether I would ever make it out of Allendale alive.

Spar had been abandoned because of general deterioration, lack of parking, and the unsavory reputation of the neighborhood surrounding it.

"Fans wouldn't come," Dave Nitz had told me in the press box the night before. "They didn't feel safe."

"Neither did the press," said a writer. The writer's car had been broken into during a game. Others I talked with said that despite the general perception that Spar was unsafe, neither crime nor vandalism had really been a serious problem. Taylor Moore told me that a new highway had been the real problem, as construction severed major arteries to the stadium and driving there became inconvenient. To his, and other club officials' credit, they seemed to take no pleasure in having abandoned the old park. It had just become inevitable for a combination of reasons.

The used car salesman sent me along Texas Street to Spar, and not far from the park, I drove through an inner-city ghost town. A three-block-long strip of shops and businesses had ceased to exist; every single store on both sides of the street was deserted. Freeway construction wasn't to blame here; the small stores had just ceased to be viable. Most weren't even boarded up, just empty.

Spar sat there in the hot sun looking like a huge rotting insect whose membrane had disintegrated, leaving only the skeletal rods. The roof had blown off the grandstand cover and had never been replaced, although the Captains kept using the exceedingly odd-looking field afterwards. I shot a picture through a gaping hole in the left-field wall and then walked through the opening. The base paths were all grass now. The city still mowed the field but the grass was heavily laced with clover. The rest of the park, like Texas Street, had just been left to weather and erode. Faded signs on the outfield walls were barely legible. Seats were cracked and paint was peeling everywhere.

The old park had seen some action. In 1956, right fielder Ken Guettler hit sixty-two home runs for the Shreveport Sports, a Texas League record that still stands. The right-handed batter hit thirty-nine of them through the muggy Louisiana air over the twenty-foot-high left-field wall through which I had just walked. He wore eyeglasses with thick, coke bottle lenses but at 5'11" and 190 pounds had a compact, powerful build. Guettler played in only 140 games in 1956, and that was his last good year. He struggled along for three more years, playing for five different teams but never hitting more than five home runs or batting higher than .232. Guettler retired at age thirty-two, never having registered one major league at bat, and died at age fifty.

One of the most famous denizens of Spar was not a ballplayer, but its longtime groundskeeper, Al Gaedke. When the new park opened in the 1930s, Gaedke moved into a small house in the far right-field corner where he lived alone year round. During the off season, he made the outfield into a small golf course. The owners put a flock of sheep in the park in the 1938–39 winter to keep the grass trimmed, but the experiment ended badly. Dogs got into the ball park and wiped out the sheep, proving, I guess, that humans make more practical groundskeepers than sheep. During Al's tenure, the park was known unofficially as "Gaedke's Gardens."

No one bothered me as I roamed around the old park. In fact, the seats, concession stands, and dugouts disclosed few signs of vandalism, just general decay. Perhaps the wear of time had eroded things to the point where vandalism was superfluous. The old gathering place wasn't going gently, however. Even now, as I looked her over from every angle, there was no doubt that this was a site where people had come to celebrate baseball.

By noon it was already over ninety degrees and I was on my third Dr. Pepper. The hot breeze of the last two days had died; now it was just hot without a breeze. I had been in the South for two months, and had experienced ninety-degree-plus days in Florida but nothing like the bone-wilting, juice-sucking, head-pounding heat of Shreveport.

Not far from Fair Grounds Park, I found some shade under a large oak tree at the edge of a church parking lot and got out a lawn chair. It was too hot to do anything but sit and wait for time to go to the new ballpark with its air-conditioned press box and icy drinks. The church marquee read

ASSEMBLY OF GOD

2000 YEARS UNDER
THE SAME MANAGEMENT

About fifteen feet up in the oak tree a mockingbird sat nervously on her nest, very suspicious of my motives.

167

12

The Land of Cotton

AFTER TWO MONTHS, TWENTY-PLUS cities, and twelve thousand miles, I thought that I knew what made a good baseball town. I would have bet that a sizeable city in the land of cotton, where major league teams offered no nearby competition, university football and basketball weren't big, and working-class people were in the majority, would be baseball heaven. Then I went to Jackson, Mississippi, home of the Jackson Generals, a AA team in the Texas League, and had to change my mind.

The Generals play in Smith-Wills Stadium, a baseball-only park built in 1975 when the Victoria, Texas, team relocated to Jackson. The park was ideally stationed in an attractive, upper-middle class residential and shopping area, just off Interstate 55. It had plenty of parking and was surprisingly modern looking and comfortable for an eighteen-year-old ballpark. Fans sat close to the action, and looked over a well-manicured field to see nothing but trees and other foliage over the outfield walls. After dark, the Marlboro man seemed to be walking right out of the woods, saddle slung over his shoulder.

During my visit, the Generals started the week at 36–21, the best record in the Texas League at that point. Sportswriters were touting several players as sure future major leaguers. Weather conditions were ideal for baseball—no rain was forecast for that week, and though it felt hot to me, Jacksonians kept saying that it was still unseasonably comfortable.

Jackson had 196,637 residents in 1993. At almost the exact size,

Shreveport (198,526) had drawn 207,925 fans through the turnstiles the previous season. Yet Jackson, last in the Texas League in attendance for 1992, attracted only 140,040 that year, the worst of all the southern AA teams except for Knoxville, with its hopeless 90,387. Jackson's attendance was actually up over 1991, when the club hosted only 114,660 fans, but as of June 6, 1993, the Generals were dead last in Texas League attendance with an average of 2,536 fans per game.

Jackson had never been exactly a bubbling cauldron of baseball activity. Before joining the Texas League in 1975, the city hadn't had a professional baseball team since 1953, when it had an entry in the Cotton States League. In fact, Jackson had been without professional baseball for thirty-eight seasons during the twentieth century, an unusually high figure for a town of its size. A good team playing in a fine park with an excellent location hadn't been able to overcome the lack of a baseball tradition in Jackson, demonstrating that the former ingredients are not the only ones necessary for a successful franchise.

My second night in Jackson I saw one of the most dominating pitching performances of the trip. Alvin Morman, a hard-throwing strikeout pitcher, went six innings with eleven strikeouts, one base on balls, and one unearned run. His fastball was consistently in the low 90s with movement and his hard curve came in at almost slider speed, but with more break. After Morman was removed, I walked down to the bullpen to talk about his performance with some of the other pitchers on the bench. One said that Morman had been taken out because he had thrown a lot of pitches, it was a hot night, and Jackson had pretty well won the first half of the season. I asked if Morman had known that he was in reach of a Texas League record for strikeouts in a single game. (Actually, the Texas League media guide doesn't list the single-game strikeout record for a single pitcher. The team record is twenty-one, and at Morman's six-inning pace, he could have expected only fifteen, as the bottom of the ninth would be unnecessary.)

"Sal [Sal Butera, the manager] says, 'What's the big deal about a AA record, when he's going to the majors?' He may have a major league record ahead of him," said one of the relief pitchers.

The handling of pitchers has been one of the most controversial areas in player development in recent years. Even with careers extended by superior conditioning techniques, modern pitchers can never hope to approach such feats as Cy Young's 511 victories. In the dead ball era, when Cy pitched, pitchers could ease off and lob the ball in, knowing that it wasn't going far. A complete game before 1920 saw, on average, forty fewer pitches than a complete game today. And today, the relentless radar gun exerts pressure to make each throw light up a high number. How much work is enough for a developing pitcher, and how much is too much, is one of the crucial decisions a minor league manager makes.

I saw Morman make one more impressive start, in Arkansas against the Travelers, and then an injury shortened his season. Despite a final 7–1 record and a 2.64 ERA, he didn't pitch the 109 innings required to be listed among *Baseball America's* league leaders at season's end. However, of the eleven pitchers who threw for the Generals in 1993, no one pitched 109 innings, and only one pitcher exceeded one hundred. Jackson ended up with the second highest win total in the Texas League in 1993 with 73 (in a 134-game schedule), but no pitcher recorded even 10 wins for the Generals. The student of minor league baseball who has been grounded in major league reasoning and conditions must constantly adjust his or her expectations.

My four-day stay in Jackson was the most restful period of the trip. The city of Jackson was originally known as LeFleur's Bluff, after a French-Canadian fur trader who founded a trading post on the Pearl River shortly before the arrival of the nineteenth century. LeFleur's Bluff State Park, across the street from Smith-Wills Stadium, now honors this founder. The park's quarter-acre campsites are shaded by huge oak trees and back up to Mayes Lake. Every morning I got up early, walked ten yards to the lake, and caught pan-sized bream on a popping bug with my fly rod. Nothing else worked. I tried a variety of lures and plugs, dry flies, streamers, and spinners and never got a strike, but the bream were absolute fools for the popping bug. I sat in the shade, read, wrote a little, and rested up for the long, hot drives to come in Oklahoma and

171

Texas. Temperatures stayed in the nineties, which the locals kept telling me was very reasonable.

In the evenings, I walked over to see the Generals manhandle the Shreveport Captains. The matchups didn't produce outstanding games, but gave the press fodder for wordplay ("Gens make Captains salute 7–1"). I was late for one game at Smith-Wills because I stopped at a field in the state park to watch a summer league game between seven-year-olds. Parents beamed at the frantic efforts of their offspring, as the little players wandered around the field looking bewildered that a game was going on and that they were in it. The players seemed more interested in how good they looked in their new uniforms than in where the baseball was.

On Tuesday, Big Dave Nitz and I had lunch at a restaurant near where the Shreveport Captains were staying in Jackson. I had met Dave the previous week in Shreveport where, in addition to acting as director of media operations, he did the play-by-play radio broadcasts. Dave was a mellow-voiced broadcaster who had a direct, professional delivery with no gimmicks and no sensationalism. He had thirty years of experience and a sound, thorough knowledge of baseball and sports in general. He described his own style of delivery as choppy, with bursts of description, but I had been impressed with his ability to paint a verbal picture of the game while avoiding the intrusive personality quirks that interrupted the flow of other broadcasts I had heard. I had made it a point to listen to at least part of one broadcast at every stop where radio coverage was provided, and had heard many ploys used to generate fan interest. One announcer tried to provoke controversy by being sarcastic about everything, including his employer; another had a guest commentator on to talk about football while the baseball game was being broadcast!

Dave was born in West Virginia in 1942 and took his first broadcasting test for Tom T. Hall, the songwriter, who was then a station manager in a small West Virginia town.

"My background was in journalism but I didn't get a degree until I had been in the business for years. I began covering Appalachian League games and have been fooling them ever since," he said.

172

The Appalachian League in those years was a cluster of small mountain towns along the West Virginia, Ohio, and Kentucky borders. "I can remember doing Sunday out-of-town games, traveling at my own expense, for $15 in those days," Dave said. "Once in Harlan, Kentucky, there was a coal miner's strike and things were pretty hot. While I was broadcasting, a man in the stands was shot. I said, on the air, 'Apparently someone in the stands has been shot.' They didn't stop the game, so I just kept broadcasting."

"Since you travel with the team all season, you probably know the players better than anyone not on the field. Does that ever give you problems with objectivity?" I asked.

"No, if they screw up, I say so. That's my job."

I knew that he did it with consideration and tact, however. In Shreveport I had heard him feed the local sportswriters an item about one of the players becoming a father the day before. The player had been passing out cigars in the clubhouse, but wasn't married. Dave suggested using some wording along the lines of "the mother is doing fine," to avoid a direct reference to a situation that is still somewhat delicate according to the chivalrous code of the South.

Dave, like many of us in and around the baseball enterprise, had wanted to play professionally. He was a pitcher, good enough for semipro teams in West Virginia but without the velocity to make it as a professional. "I had a good curve and a workable knuckleball, but no one wanted a twenty-one-year-old soft-throwing knuckleballer."

After lunch, as we were sitting and talking, I told Dave about the outfielder I'd met in Macon, in the Sally League, who was playing both baseball and football professionally. "He's playing for Macon until June 21 and then going to summer camp with the Green Bay Packers."

"Terrell Buckley?" Dave asked. "He quit baseball yesterday. There's an article in *USA Today*."

The paper said that Terrell walked away from the $850 per month Macon Braves paycheck to concentrate on preparing for a season as the Packers starting left cornerback. Terrell had taken the Packers' $6.8 million contract and said goodbye to cheap motels and long bus rides, and baseball had lost a gifted athlete.

I was standing in the pop-up chicken line at Smith-Wills Stadium on my last night in Jackson when the episode with William and Ink began. Pop-up chicken had resulted from a promotion the previous night, which specified that if an opposing batter hit a pop-up during the top of the eighth inning, every fan would receive a coupon for a marinated, grilled chicken sandwich the following evening. Sure enough, the first batter hit one straight up, the catcher caught it, so: pop-up chicken. About the third inning I wandered down to the open grill where the marinated chicken was sizzling, and was standing in line next to a young man, probably in his thirties, with short, curly, dark hair and a perpetual smile. He said his name was Ink.

We began talking about baseball but soon the conversation drifted over to fishing. I told him that I had been catching small bream in the state park lake across the street.

"You should meet William," he said. "He knows the best fishing spot in Mis'sippi. It's near here too."

We collected our chicken sandwiches and, at Ink's invitation, I went back to the bleachers to meet William. William was an ordinary-looking man, probably in his forties, and seemed a little grumpy that Ink had brought me back. He glowered when Ink mentioned telling me about "the best fishing spot in Mis'sippi," but softened somewhat when he found out that I had bought the beer to go with the chicken sandwiches, and we began talking.

I told them a little about my trip, Ink bought a round of beer, and William began to reveal a few details about a "lost" or hidden lake where largemouth bass grew to such a mammoth size it made your arms tired to land them. William bought a round, I bought another round, and in the seventh inning, the beer vendors disappeared and Ink came back from the concourse to reveal that the concession stands had stopped selling beer. William immediately decided that the game was over anyway, and suggested we leave to stop by a bar between the stadium and where he lived. His assessment of the game wasn't exactly accurate since Jackson trailed only

174

3–1, and had two runners on in the bottom of the seventh. By this time, however, I was intrigued by the story about the lost lake and the bass that cruised its depths, looking like submarines under the water and leaving a wake when they swirled around near the top. Off we went to the bar.

Eventually, with Ink's urging, William agreed to an expedition to the lost lake the next morning. We would leave at sunup, fish for a few hours, and get back before the heat struck. I had planned to leave for Little Rock the next day but a few hours delay to fish in what had taken on the dimensions of an Edenic paradise was little matter.

When we left the bar, William suggested that I come to his house then so that I would be where he lived and we could leave early. "You can park in the yard," he said. "No need to go back to any goddam state park to park." He gave Ink the keys to his pickup and rode with me to make sure that I didn't get lost. Judging from the equipment in back of William's cluttered pickup he was a painter by trade, though there was no mention of going to work the next day, or having been at work on previous days. Any mention of work, in fact, made William defensive so I didn't make any direct inquiries.

We drove for what seemed a long time, circling around Jackson to the southwest side. William lived in a small white house with a dirt front yard, most of which was under a huge elm tree. A rope and tire hung from the elm, and I parked under the tree, at William's direction. They arranged for Ink to take William's truck home, and return in the morning for the fishing trip. "Sunup, right?" I said. They both mumbled and left me in the yard. William went inside and every light in the house seemed to come on. Voices punctuated the still night. Angry voices.

I slept through my alarm the next morning and didn't wake up until after 8 A.M. I hurriedly dressed and knocked on William's door. No answer. And there was no sign of Ink or of William's pickup.

I made coffee, had breakfast, and assembled my fishing gear. Still there was no sign of either Ink or William. The next time I knocked, about an hour later, a woman opened the door and with-

175

out saying anything, turned and went back into the living room. I followed her in and she said, by way of introduction, "You one of the ones he was drinking with last night?"

"Ah, we left the ball game early and stopped by a bar for a couple of drinks on the way home."

"Couple my ass," she said. "I could smell him before he walked in the door."

She and William must have had some delightful conversations when they really got wound up. "Well, is he up?" I asked.

At that point William walked in, hair uncombed, still more asleep than awake.

"We're running a little late," I observed.

"Got to have some goddam breakfast," William said. "Come in the kitchen."

"I wonder why Ink isn't here?" I asked.

"Don't worry about that goddam Ink," he said. "We'll find him."

After William finished breakfast, collected his fishing equipment, and got into an argument with his wife, I went outside to wait. This approach to fishing was totally foreign to me. I was accustomed to setting a time and leaving, and the delay was getting on my nerves. Finally, about 10:30 A.M. we went in search of Ink. He wasn't at the house where William said he rented a room, and neither was William's truck.

"Anyway," said William, "I got to get a goddam check cashed before we go. It's at my sister's house."

I drove William to his sister's house in another neighborhood in Jackson, and waited in the pickup while he went inside. He was in his sister's house for about twenty minutes, and once again I could hear loud voices. William's sister was badgering him about something he should have done, and hadn't.

When he came back, he announced: "She ain't got the goddam check. My niece is got it."

It was nearly noon. I sighed. "Where does *she* live?"

"Sandhill."

"How far is that?"

"We'll take the goddam backroads," he said, evasively.

"How far?"

"I know a goddam shortcut. About twenty-five miles."

"Listen, I think I better call this fishing trip off. I'd planned to be in Little Rock tonight, and I want to stop in the Delta on the way."

William looked hurt and didn't reply for a minute. "You said you wanted to see the goddam South," he said slowly. "I wanted to show you what fishing could really be like in the goddam South. I can go fishing here anytime. I wanted to make this goddam trip for you."

I hesitated.

"Ernie," he said, "last year I hauled a fish out of this same goddam lake, held him up, had to hook thumbs in both gills to get him up, he came up to my waist before his tail cleared the ground. You ask Ink if I'm a goddam liar!"

Off we went to Sandhill.

The distance was closer to thirty-five miles, and this time I went in with him to speed things up, if possible. William's niece said hello, surprisingly, but then completely ignored me and began haranguing William about something he had said he would do for her and hadn't. William's life seemed to be filled with unkept promises and hostile women. She did, however, have the check and we collected it and left after about only fifteen minutes.

Back in Jackson, I asked William: "Where is the bank you use?"

"Bank? I'll show you the goddam liquor store. That's where my checks is cashed at. That's probably where Ink is at, too."

Ink wasn't at the liquor store but had called there to leave a message for us. He had taken one of their mutual friends, a man called Henry, to retrieve his truck, which had broken down outside of Jackson somewhere the night before. We sat on the fenders of Sweetspot outside the liquor store, getting a little shade from the building, to wait for Ink. William suggested we have a beer while we waited, and wanted to know if I had any in the cooler. I pointed to a sign on the building that read:

"NO DRINKING ON THESE PREMISES"

"Goddam, you worry a lot. That don't mean nothin'. It means you cain't drink inside the store, is all."

After telling him I knew the meaning of the word premises, I took a couple of beers out of the cooler. William seemed to be a good customer at the liquor store, using it as a combination message center and bank as well as for its intended purpose. "Right," he said, taking the beer. "I forgot I was talking to a goddam perfesser."

While we were waiting, he showed me his fishing tackle. He had a large box the size of a suitcase, with twenty or more smaller boxes inside. Each, he explained, was outfitted for a different kind of fishing and was a complete setup in itself. The best fishermen I had fished with, my regular fishing partner Doyle, and Grover, my stepfather, were meticulous about their gear, but I had never seen anything like William's organizational system for comprehensiveness and neatness. It was all the more remarkable because his pickup looked like a rolling junkyard and his house had been chaotic.

I took out my small traveling supply of lures and showed them to him.

"You've caught fish with them goddam thangs?" he wanted to know.

About midafternoon Ink showed up with Henry, a black man somewhere around William's age. They were both covered in grease and hadn't been able to get Henry's truck running. Their arrival naturally called for beers all around to talk things over. As we talked, it became clear that both Ink and William had other black friends, and they seemed to be entirely without prejudice or any hint of a patronizing attitude. I wasn't surprised that this was true of Ink, who seemed to like everyone, but I hadn't expected William to be so open-minded.

While we lounged in the shade, I asked Ink about his name. Was it a nickname?

William laughed loudly when he heard the question. "Tell him your goddam name, Ink!" Without waiting for Ink, he shouted "IN-KILL-LEES!" He repeated the name three times, laughing so hard that he was doubled over, clutching his stomach with one hand and balancing his beer with the other. Ink looked embarrassed. I couldn't understand what William found so hilarious about the name Inkeles, while the shortened version Ink didn't even provoke a smile from him. After he regained some control, he tried to say the name again but just the thought of repeating it caused him to laugh uproariously. Afterwards, I realized that in the day I had spent with him, this was the only time I saw William laugh, or even smile.

We invited Henry on the fishing expedition but he had to get some parts for his stalled pickup. When he left, William and Ink began discussing the purchase of liquor supplies for the fishing trip.

"I have plenty of beer," I offered.

"How much you got?" Ink asked.

"A couple of six packs in the cooler."

They looked at each other in amazement and, without saying a word, turned and walked into the liquor store. They came back in a few minutes with a case of beer and a large sack containing a fifth of bourbon, a pint of vodka, a large bag of Doritos, and an assortment of mixes. Another brief consultation followed, and they went back into the liquor store. I followed them in, unable to imagine what else they could buy. They walked around, pointing at the shelves and discussing various options, finally buying a bottle of brandy and another case of beer. Feeling a little left out, I bought a bottle of white wine to have with the fish at dinner.

"How long are you guys planning to stay at the lake?" I asked as we loaded the liquor.

"We're fixing to stay a couple of days," said Ink.

By the time we left it was late in the afternoon. I had long since forgotten about leaving for Little Rock that day and just hoped we would get to the lost lake before dark. William rode with me again, and Ink led the way in William's truck. On the way, William began to worry about the possibility of my revealing the location of the lake.

"Don't be putting where this goddam place is at in no goddam book," he warned me.

I said I wouldn't.

"You're lucky to be going because the onliest ones that knows about it is me and Ink and Henry and (he named about six other persons)."

179

"I'm not going to tell anyone where it is. You want to blindfold me and drive in yourself?"

He gave the possibility some thought.

"Come on," I said. "I won't tell anyone how to get there."

"Ah hell, you couldn't find the goddam place again anyway."

This sounded more like a comment on my navigational ability than on the remoteness of the lake, but I let it pass. We went from a main highway to a side road, then a gravel road, eventually turning onto a dirt track running through some piney woods, finally emerging into a field overgrown with head-high patches of blackberries and other brambles, where we drove alongside a small creek lined with trees and came to an earthen dam.

The "lake" was disappointingly small, covering less than a couple of acres, and the banks were so choked with undergrowth that access was limited to only a few spots. Reeds growing several yards out into the water promised to make fishing even more difficult. William peeled out of the pickup and by the time I had opened the back of Sweetspot, he was established at the most open fishing spot and had already hooked a medium-sized bass. He caught another one as I was assembling my telescoping rod, and another as Ink and I walked over to the pond. After landing each fish, William threw it about ten feet up on the bank and cast again.

"William's a good fisherman," said Ink, needlessly.

"Why is he throwing the fish up here?" I asked Ink.

"Waiting for me to string 'em."

"Aren't you going to fish?" I asked him.

"Some," he said.

I looked at him. "I guess you and William are pretty good friends."

"William's a good guy, really. He's bad to drink, though." Ink was carrying a beer and pulling at it between sentences.

I walked around the small pond and began casting toward one end. The fish were there, and they were easy to catch, though none of us hooked any of the behemoths that William insisted were plentiful. I watched William while he fished. He hadn't seemed particularly athletic in movement or even graceful in general, but with a fishing rod in his hand, he was transformed. Watching him play a two-pound largemouth bass was like listening to the rhythm of a piece of classical music. Once I heard him tell Ink that there was a large bass behind a stump, and when Ink cast he said: "Not *that* goddam stump." With that, his arm tensed and he unleashed the longest cast I have ever seen, sailing over the dark distant mark, then flicking his wrist to make the topwater lure change directions and angle around the surface obstacle. A fish struck, William set the hook, and when the bass broke the water it was seen to be the biggest catch of the day.

This "lost lake" must have been a former farm pond, probably stocked with bass and bream at one time, and now lying unused because the farm had gone under. We had passed an old barn on the way in, and I had seen other ruins at the end of the overgrown field. The pond was undoubtedly on private property, and we were obviously trespassing. I began to suspect that some of the day's procrastination was deliberately timed to get us here late in the day to minimize the chance of discovery.

In less than an hour we stopped fishing and sorted through the catch, keeping a few for dinner and releasing the others. I fileted four bass weighing between one and two pounds, and took out my camping utensils. My one-burner stove would have taken too long to cook the fish, so William rigged up a grill from part of a bed frame he had in the back of the pickup, overlaying it with pieces of corrugated metal used in reinforcement of concrete. In the confusion of getting the trip underway, none of us had thought about dishes to accompany the fish. I produced a few pieces of fruit from the cooler, and offered William and Ink each a container of yogurt. They both looked at the yogurt tubs suspiciously and refused to even consider them.

After a dinner of crisply fried fish, Doritos, and peaches, the mosquitoes came in earnest and I climbed into the back of Sweetspot to go to sleep. William and Ink, apparently impervious to the insect attacks, stayed up by the fire, drinking and talking. At one point, I heard Ink say, "Ernie's a pretty good guy, isn't he? I mean for a perfesser and everything?"

"I guess," said William, "but he worries about every goddam thang. He'll be a nervous wreck time he gets to El Paso."

181

The next morning I took US 49 out of Jackson for a leisurely drive north through the Mississippi Delta country. The Delta region was bounded on the west by the Mississippi River and on the east by the hills of central Mississippi. The soil, planted in cotton and soybeans, was fertile, the land was flat, and the air was sultry. At Yazoo City, I took 49 west through the heart of the Delta. Yazoo City was a member of the short-lived Delta League of 1904, a class D six-team minor league. Only two of the teams, Clarksdale and Yazoo City, were in the Delta region, but the shaky little league folded after only one season anyway, before anyone could demand a more appropriate name.

I pulled off the road just north of where state road 14 comes into US 49W to watch a crop dusting plane at work. The small yellow biplane flew close to the ground, releasing spray over the crops and giving a section of highway 14 a dose of the insecticide before banking sharply and going back for another run.

The little town of Midnight, Mississippi, sat north of the fields being sprayed, about twenty buildings hunched together against the late morning sun. The town was surrounded on all four sides by crops, planted in straight lines across the flat terrain. At the one-room post office, a woman was swatting flies, squashing them against the front window that looked out on the street. She told me that this office was the only "Midnight" listed in the U.S. Postal Service *Zip Code Directory*. The name, she said, derived from a poker game played many years ago among several wealthy plantation owners on the Delta. It was a high stakes game and one player lost a large parcel of land. The winner, noting the time when he won the hand, announced to the others that he would call his new acquisition "Midnight," and when a small town was later established, it bore the same name. I wrote out a postcard to some friends in Maryland and gave it to the woman. She postmarked the card with the town name and went back to her fly swatter.

The Mississippi Delta country came closest to any place I had been to the South of my imagination. Rows of green crops stretched across the flat, rich soil; weathered shotgun shacks lined the hot, sleepy little streets; and people moved slowly in the steamy heat. Narrow, muddy rivers seemed barely to flow. White farmers in rough pickup trucks raised an index finger slowly in greeting, and black people averted their eyes. US 49W was a concrete ribbon through the land of cotton, the heart of Dixie's land.

At Indianola I took a small country road marked SR 448 over to US 61, and turned directly north. A sun devil kicked up in an unplanted field to my left, and I drove along wishing I had someone along to share the South with me.

I took US 61 north through Clarksdale and looked at the map. Memphis was only forty miles or so to the north. I thought about spending the night there, even though the Chicks weren't in town, to see what Phil Stukenborg was writing and see if anyone else I knew was around. Then I envisioned trying to explain to Eric McCool how I had left three weeks earlier to work my way west, and was now back in the same place. I turned into the sun on US 49 and crossed the big river into Arkansas at Helena, my third crossing of the trip.

Walking through the turnstiles at Ray Winder Field in Little Rock, Arkansas, tripped a magic wire somewhere, and I was back in the 1940s. Alfreda Wilson, the longtime Arkansas Travelers' organist, was pounding out a patriotic tune, and all the concession stands were human scale and humanely priced. By the time I had walked down to a seat behind home plate, I was trying to think of a way to convince Zena to move to Little Rock.

From the first row of seats behind home plate, I could see the right fielder only from the knees up, and the center fielder's feet were missing. The field had a pronounced hump, with the infield forming the apex. The right field situation was in fact a considerable improvement this year; formerly, the right fielder wasn't visible at all from the third base dugout. Visiting managers had to walk almost to the foul line to position their right fielders. Just off both base paths and behind home plate, a noticeable slope, dropping a couple of feet, provided an interesting sensation for fielders chasing foul balls. Runners taking a wide turn around third had to puff back up hill to get home. The broadleaf grass had a liberal sprinkling of clover, which was blooming brightly in June, making the field resemble a close-cut version of a suburban lawn.

In the first inning, a batter on the visiting Jackson Generals team

183

hit a pop foul behind home plate and it drifted back toward the screen. The catcher took it inches from the screen, and just a few feet from where I was sitting.

"Nice catch," I said.

"Thanks," he replied. I mentally chalked up another tally mark favoring minor league baseball over the distant action in the big leagues.

During the game I walked around to see the field from different angles. Beer flowed freely in the left field stands, home of the "Hooters Trav Rooters," who ranked with the rowdiest in baseball. On the third base side, ground level fans were literally on the field. Seats had been built out into foul territory past the third base dugout. This may be the only park in baseball where some fans had a closer view of the action than managers and players. Children could lean into the end of the dugout and bother the players full time during the game.

I reached the pressbox, suspended from the grandstand roof, by a catwalk. Inside the cramped quarters, revolving ceiling fans tried to cool the corps of writers and club officials, pressed together in the tiny space. Late in the game, an invasion of moths, flying around by the thousands, descended on the playing field and added to the general din that was Ray Winder Field on a warm summer night.

The park, opened in 1932, was of steel and concrete construction with a roof canopy over the grandstand. Left field was 325 feet, center 405 feet, and right field, a short 300 feet away. Wilbur Mills Freeway now runs immediately outside right field, so a 55-foot right-field screen has been erected to protect motorists. A home run launched over the screen usually clears the parkway as well.

Ray Winder is one of the few sports stadiums owned by its baseball club. The Arkansas Travelers, in turn, are owned, technically, by fans, 1,200 stockholders who hold varied amounts of interest in the club. Realistically, the Travelers belong to Bill Valentine, their general manager since 1976 and one of the longest tenured general managers in minor league baseball.

Bill is a former major league umpire who, together with Al Salerno, formed an umpire's union in 1968. They were fired, ostensibly for incompetence, and never umpired again. Bill wasn't incompetent, but unionizing was a few years ahead of its time. He returned to his home town of Little Rock and did radio and then television reporting and announcing for two years. A stint as assistant director, and then director, of the Arkansas Republican party followed. In December of 1975, Valentine was offered the job of general manager of the Arkansas Travelers. He saw the neglected condition of the ballpark, went over the low attendance figures and generally unpromising picture of the club's account books, and told them flatly: "You can't afford me." They met his terms, though, and the alliance was formed.

In 1975, the year before Bill Valentine took over, the season's attendance was 64,000. In his first year as general manager, the total jumped to over 90,000. By 1978, that figure had doubled to 184,000, and in five of the past seven years, Arkansas, with the second smallest market of any Texas League city, has led the league in attendance. Recently, only Tulsa, with its larger, more modern stadium and bigger population base, had consistently outdrawn the Travelers.

I met Bill on a hot June afternoon in the business office at Ray Winder. Usually Bill didn't arrive at the ballpark until after noon, but on game days this still meant that he put in an eleven-hour day. The meager club office housed one of the smallest staffs in double A baseball, smaller in fact than many at the class A level.

"We have to operate differently from clubs who have rich owners," Bill explained. "The Travelers don't fly anywhere. Anywhere we go, we go by bus."

The general rule in the Texas League is that most clubs go by bus to games with clubs in their division, and fly to cities in the other division. "We have a sleeper bus with a VCR and a refrigerator, and we're centrally located. We don't fly anywhere," Bill told me. "We don't fly anywhere."

Bill repeated sentences in a sharp, staccato delivery whenever he wanted to emphasize his point.

"Come with me," he said. "You have to walk your property. You have to walk your property."

We were off on an inspection tour that lasted for two hours. In

185

appearance, Valentine fit exactly the general image of a baseball umpire. Broad and compact, with a crew-cut, he had a stern and usually unsmiling face, and a firm, definite manner. His demeanor was suggestive of a drill sergeant in the army. He noticed the most minute details as we walked around the park, such as a clock hanging crookedly, and barked orders to the next employee he saw to get it fixed.

We walked out to the stands. "Look down that aisle," Bill directed. "What do you see? What do you see?"

"Nothing. Nothing." I was getting into the rhythm of the conversation.

"No gum, no stickiness from cokes, no trash. This is every day. Every game. The whole park is the same way. Let's go into the johns."

We walked into an immaculately clean rest room. "The most important reason women won't come to the ballpark is dirty rest rooms. See that?" He gestured to a container fastened to the wall. "Hand lotion. What other ballpark has hand lotion? You ever see another woman's rest room in a ball park with hand lotion?"

I admitted that I hadn't, then added that I had never been in another woman's rest room, period.

The men's room was equally clean. "See this," he said, pointing to an elevated area in front of a urinal. It had the appearance of a ceramic tile pitcher's mound. "For boys. They're too short to reach big urinals." He stood on the mound with his back to me as he delivered the explanation. Thinking he was just demonstrating the mound, I walked around to look, then saw that he was using the facility, never missing a beat in the running commentary.

Next we inspected the concession stands, tucked traditionally under the grandstand. The taco stand had $18,000 worth of stainless steel formed into shelves Bill had designed to expedite taco service. I was impressed. Five hours before game time and the park was spotless. None of the newer parks I had seen could match it; most of the older ones were ill kept by comparison.

Back in the club offices, I talked to Bill about the franchise's success. When he arrived in 1976, minor league clubs were being sold for almost nothing; sometimes all a buyer had to do was to take over the debts. The Travelers' amazing increase in attendance ran counter to the period's general decline in baseball attendance. How did he do it?

"Promotions," Bill said. "I started a midget on opening day 1976. Sent out the word I was looking for one and one day in late winter, sitting where I am now, the door opens and I don't see anybody." (A four-foot counter ran at a right angle from the club office's door.) "Then Roscoe Steadman comes around the corner and says, 'I hear you're looking for a little person. I'm your man.' He was three inches shorter than Bill Veeck's midget. That's how tall he was."

Unlike the 3'7", sixty-five-pound Eddie Gaedel whom Veeck put in to pinch hit for the St. Louis Browns in 1951, Roscoe didn't take four balls and trot down to first. He grounded out, then was "ejected" for arguing the call at first. A woman, about Roscoe's height and posing as his wife, ran onto the field and hit the umpire with her purse. The fans loved it, and the promotions frenzy was on.

By promotions, Bill didn't mean on-field contests between innings. There were none of those. Promotions really meant giving away tickets. Businesses would sponsor a night, paying the club a fee and issuing free tickets to get customers to come to their establishments and pick them up.

"I can make more money by letting people in free than I can by charging," Bill said.

"How can you make money doing that?" I asked.

"Concessions! Concessions!" From a desk drawer, Bill pulled records that showed, he said, that you could make more money by giving away tickets than by charging for them. "The bottom line is how much money you make, not how many people pay for a ticket. You promote your product, and when people come they'll buy your concessions."

Bill told me that he had coined the slogan, "The Greatest Show on Dirt" to use in the Travelers' promotional literature. "The circus people heard about it and sent word that they'd sue us if we didn't quit using it. I changed the programs and pamphlets to 'The Greatest Game on Dirt' and that satisfied them."

187

Bill took me to his private office under the stands, a cozy, well-furnished room that was windowless except for a small, one-foot-square opening filled with thick glass. This peephole provided a tunnel of vision through the stands to the scoreboard. When the crowd roared, Bill could check the board to see what had happened.

Soon he began defending his philosophy of promotions again. "We aren't selling baseball," he said. "We're selling entertainment. G-rated family entertainment. Little kids can run around the park unsupervised, completely safe. Nowhere else in town can they do that, not the shopping malls, not the streets, not the parks, nowhere." I had heard this chilling sentiment expressed elsewhere on the trip.

"You saw the stands emptied about 9:30 last night?" he asked me. "The second perfect game in Arkansas history was thrown here a few years ago. In the seventh inning, people began filing out! Leaving! Lots of them!"

Bill offered me a challenge. "Ask ten people at the game tonight where Arkansas is in the standings. Not two out of ten will know. Not two out of ten."

We'll see about this, I thought. This isn't the Florida State League.

Before the evening game, I wanted to see one of Little Rock's most reluctant shrines. Thirty-six years earlier in September, local and national media attention hadn't been devoted to the Travelers' seventh-place finish in the Southern Association. Hometown future hall-of-famer Brooks Robinson wasn't getting much press, either. Struggling to catch on and stay in the big leagues, Brooks was finishing the 1957 season, his third partial season with the Orioles, with a batting average in the .230s. The headline stories that September, in Little Rock and the rest of the nation, focused on an inner-city high school trying to cope with forced integration.

The first thing I noticed on driving up to Little Rock's Central High School was how imposing the building appeared. It was a massive structure formed from brown bricks and white concrete. The art deco style emphasized the vertical, with elongated windows and a stepped, Mayan temple effect in the center. The flat roofline was broken by squared columns, which extended up like battlements. To the nine black students who integrated Little Rock public schools in 1957, the building must have seemed an impenetrable fortress.

Arkansas national guardsmen, called to duty by Governor Orville Faubus, had lined the street in front of the high school. On the first day, a lone black girl was turned away while students and angry parents spat and hurled vicious racial epithets at her. Next day, the black students arrived *en masse*, accompanied by clergymen, and were turned away. The immediate crisis was resolved when President Dwight Eisenhower federalized the National Guard of Arkansas and issued orders to escort the students to class. Their year of trauma, however, was just beginning.

One of the black students had the same name as I. Because I was white, my senior year in high school, which started that same September, was not turbulent. My school, in the next state over to the west, was in an all-white small town and was not directly touched by the turmoil of integration. I was free to concentrate on baseball and girls while a black Ernest Green tried to get an education under conditions of unbelievable tension and stress. I felt the collective guilt of all white southerners pressing heavily upon me as I looked across the empty summer lawn of Central High School.

That evening I stood on Ray Winder's concourse as fans filed into the park before game time stopping, more or less by chance, five fans. The question: Do you know where the Travelers are in the Texas League standings? The correct answer: Second in the four-team Eastern Division.

Fan #1: "No."

Fan #2: "Oh, they aren't doing well at all. I read, or heard somewhere, that they're way down, maybe tenth." (The entire Texas League has eight teams.)

Fan #3: "Second or third. It doesn't really matter because Jackson has won the first half." (I scored this as correct; he obviously followed the team's fortunes.)

Fan #4: "By Texas League, do you mean like, are you saying

189

that they're in the Texas League; that's like the league they're in?"
(Fan #4 was a teenager.)

Fan #5: "I think it's in the newspaper. I haven't checked it for years, but that's where you can find out if you want to know, in the newspaper."

I concluded my survey at that point. Four of five, or 80 percent of my small sample, did not know where the Travelers were in the standings. The old umpire had made the right call again.

13

Return to T-Town

ALMOST IMMEDIATELY AFTER I crossed the state line between Arkansas and Oklahoma, a car whizzed around the pickup and three young men inside extended their arms outside the car windows with "thumbs up" signs, good natured smiles on their faces. Sweetspot had personalized license plates that read, "SOONERS." The plates were a double tribute to the pickup's state of residence for its first seventeen years and to the mighty University of Oklahoma football team. I drove along, basking in my new-found popularity, troubled only a little by thinking about the reception the plates would get later in Texas.

I had left Arkansas on a small highway to pick up what was left of old Route 66. The "Mother Road," as John Steinbeck dubbed it in *The Grapes of Wrath*, ran 2,448 twisting, snaky miles from Chicago to Los Angeles in its heyday. First authorized in 1926, it was finished by the midthirties. From Joplin, Missouri, the route jogged straight west and made a half loop through only thirteen miles of Kansas before dipping down into Oklahoma. In 1984, the fabled byway was declassified. Today it either lies under interstates, bears different road numbers, or sits unused with grass sprouting up through the old road bed. In little more than half a century, the highway was born, became a main thoroughfare, lapsed into obsolescence, and finally became a nostalgia piece. In the past few years, historic preservation societies have sprung up along the old road; and the familiar US 66 markers have reappeared to guide the curious through the small and large towns it once enlivened.

191

I hooked up with the old highway in the little town of Commerce, Oklahoma, and stopped for awhile to visit the former haunts of the Commerce Comet. The northeast quadrant of Oklahoma has given birth to a surprising number of remarkable people—Will Rogers, Jim Thorpe, Woody Guthrie—but Mickey Mantle has been the only Oklahoman from this area to hit a baseball 565 feet. At the police station where I asked for directions, the officer on duty told me a few Mantle stories and sent me to the last place Mickey had lived in Commerce before moving to Dallas. The red brick bungalow on Maple Street, just a couple of blocks off Route 66, was small but well kept and had a swimming pool in the yard. Mickey had lived in several houses in Commerce and in other little towns in northeastern Oklahoma, most of them meager, battered places weathered to the same color as the piles of gray chat they were tucked among. Mounds of chat, the dead-looking residue from the lead and zinc mines that ran underground everywhere in this corner of the state, still swell out of the prairie around Commerce today, now sprouting green undergrowth.

Mickey was taught the art of switch-hitting by his father, Mutt Mantle, who had been a semipro ballplayer in the tristate area of Oklahoma, Kansas, and Missouri. Mutt worked by day in the dangerous zinc mines of the Eagle-Picher company, whose underground caverns stretched all the way to Joplin, twenty miles away in Missouri. Under his father's guidance, Mickey developed into a high school three-sport legend in northeastern Oklahoma. When Yankee scout Tom Greenwade signed him in 1949, he was assigned to Independence, Kansas, in the class D Kansas-Oklahoma-Missouri (K-O-M) League. Ancient buses carried his team along Route 66 and smaller two-lane blacktops to Bartlesville, Carthage, Chanute, Pittsburg, and Miami, and to a league championship. Mickey hit .313 in eighty-nine games but as a shortstop recorded forty-seven errors. The following season he moved up to class C ball with the Jopin Miners in the Western Association. In towns like Topeka, Kansas, and Muskogee, Oklahoma, Mantle blistered the ball. He topped the league with a .383 batting average, 141 runs scored, and 199 hits. Although he didn't win the home run title, word began to spread about the distance he was getting when he connected. Also, Yankee officials were beginning to speculate that Mickey might be more comfortable in the outfield. His erratic play at shortstop continued and he made four errors in the All-Star game in Muskogee. At season's end, the eighteen-year-old Mickey was called up by the Yankees, his apprenticeship in the lower minors over.

I saw him once in the early years. In 1953 or early 1954, when I was a high school freshman, he came to a winter basketball game in Claremore to watch his younger twin brothers, Roy and Ray, play in a tournament. He sat quietly, even then staring straight ahead as if disconnected from his surroundings, hesitant to make eye contact lest strangers attempt to strike up a conversation. As I remember, no one approached him. He had played through two solid seasons with the Yankees by then, and the media were forecasting great things for him, but he hadn't yet acquired mythic proportions. Late in his career, when I lived in Washington, D.C., I was always trying to see him play when the Yankees visited the Senators. He had trouble registering four hundred at bats in those seasons, and invariably would be out of the starting lineup for one injury or another when I went to a game. Mickey seemed to lose interest in baseball as his physical skills deteriorated. Sometime in the late 1960s, he put together a five for five game against the Senators. After the game, reporters asked him if he had ever done that before. No, Mantle said, that was his first time going five for five. Someone checked and learned that he actually had done it before, and had forgotten.

Roy and Ray Mantle, four years younger than Mickey, were outstanding high school athletes. The Yankees signed them to contracts and both played a season in the class D Sooner State League, each hitting over .300. They were also fast, and in spring training with the Yankees the following year, they outran everyone except Mickey, who could fly in those days. Oklahoma sports reporters confidently began predicting an all-Mantle Yankee outfield within a few years, but it wasn't to be. Roy suffered a career-ending leg injury while running out a base hit, and Ray lost two years to the army after being drafted. He never went back to baseball.

On the Oklahoma prairie outside Commerce where Mickey used

to play, the Sooner Pride Committee has raised a large sign. It proclaims an intent to put up a sixteen-foot monument to the Commerce Comet. A thermometer measured donated funds. One hundred twenty-five thousand dollars are needed for the monument, and the red mercury was only at the $30,000 mark when I saw it. If all the funds have to come from the little town of Commerce, which appears to be anything but prosperous, Mickey's monument might never materialize.

I followed Route 66 where it was still possible, working my way roughly southwest through the small towns down deeper into Oklahoma. In some stretches, the fabled road bisects stretches of vacant prairie, under a huge blue sky full of brilliant white cloud formations stretching from horizon to horizon, and I saw the same scene that Ma Barker and Bonnie and Clyde had sped through sixty years earlier, flying hell-bent away from their latest bank robberies. In Foyil, I drove over the original pale pink Route 66 concrete, which hadn't been resurfaced since it was first laid.

Route 66 runs through one end of Claremore, my birthplace. The town is better known for the Will Rogers Memorial, located on a ridge on the west side. Willie, as he was called in his youth, was actually born on a ranch about twelve miles to the north, near what became the small town of Oologah. "No one but an Indian could pronounce Oologah," said the part Cherokee Rogers, "so I just say I'm from Claremore."

I intended to sleep in a real bed at my mother's house for a week and commute down to watch the Tulsa Drillers play. My first stop in Claremore, though, was the city cemetery. The quiet graveyard sits on a gentle hill sloping down to a cow pasture. In the distance, trucks roll by on the Will Rogers Turnpike. Flowers, many now brown and brittle in the Oklahoma heat, sat uncollected on graves where they'd been laid on Memorial Day, a few weeks earlier. I walked around in the still air, pausing at each family grave to remember something about the resident: an uncle; a cousin who had died within the past year; two sets of grandparents; the same cousin's father; my father; my stepmother; two half brothers who died in infancy before I was born; an aunt and uncle on my father's side; another cousin; and a great-grandmother whom I had never

194

known. Some sort of turning point in a person's life is reached when more members of his or her family lie inside the cemetery than walk around outside.

T-Town was my father's name for Tulsa. I'm not sure how much of its history he knew, but the nickname was a natural. The Locha-pokas, a band of Creeks in Alabama, were uprooted and force-marched along the deadly Trail of Tears in 1836. They brought with them ashes from the sacred fire at their *tulsey*, their old town, and started a new council fire, hoping that a reborn life would rise from the ashes like the phoenix. The oak underneath which the council fire was started still stands at Eighteenth Street and Chey-enne Avenue in Tulsey Town, fenced in and surrounded by the white man's buildings.

Professional baseball in T-Town is played at Fifteenth and Yale, on a corner of the State Fairgrounds, in Driller Stadium. The park opened in 1981 as Sutton Stadium, named after oilman Robert Sutton, who donated most of the funds for its construction. In 1983, when Sutton was allegedly involved in an illegal oil-pricing scheme, the name was quietly changed to Tulsa County Stadium. Tulsa has long been one of the mainstays in the Texas League. For years the team was known as the Oilers, until the more suggestive and macho name Drillers was adopted. A mock oil derrick standing just to the right of center field outside the fence reminded fans of Tulsa's former image as the "Oil Capital of the World." Tulsa long ago ceased to be a dominant oil producer, and when I visited the park, the wooden edifice was under wraps, with an uncertain fu-ture.

Driller Stadium's grandstand seating was originally built as three distinct structures, with a smallish, red grandstand behind home plate and two larger stands running down the baselines. Over the years, builders have filled in the space between the stands, re-placed the original artificial turf, and added new offices and a styl-ish press box. Today Driller Stadium hosts what is really a AAA operation with a AA classification. The organization was one of five finalists for a AAA franchise in the early 1990s, and obtaining one seems merely a matter of time.

Dimensions of the field have remained unchanged since it was built. Before batting practice, I walked around the outfield walls. The grass was a deep green, perfectly manicured, and kept fresh in the Oklahoma sun with gallons of water and a ryegrass mixture. The infield looked as if no foot had ever scarred its surface. Left field, which butted up against Fifteenth Street, was 335 feet down the line and a short 349 feet to the left field power alley. Home runs fell into the street, but so far drivers had been lucky. Once, I was told, a home run hit the street and bounced into the open window of a car, causing no damage and pleasantly surprising the driver. Dead center was marked at 390 feet, while right field ran 340 feet to the foul pole with a 368-foot power alley, making it a little harder for left-handed batters to spray Yale Avenue with home runs.

The park had the largest seating capacity in the Texas League, with 10,722 seats, and the team consistently drew enough fans to justify its size. Formerly a multiuse stadium, it was now used only for baseball. And it drew real baseball fans. On my first night in the park, I discovered that Tulsa spectators, unlike those in most other minor league parks, still booed home town players as well as visitors when they performed poorly.

A month earlier, a killer tornado had wiped out part of the small town of Catoosa, just east of Tulsa. The previous day's game had been canceled because of more tornado threats. The stands were constructed of frail-looking aluminum; and practically the only things made of concrete were the rest rooms, which sat on the con-course like cinder block, wartime bunkers. Signs at each restroom entrance read "Designated Storm Shelter."

The canceled game had added more misery to Tulsa's scheduling problems. The team was in the midst of a "home stand from hell": thirteen home games in twelve days, a stretch that would now in-clude two doubleheaders, if no more cancellations occurred. I had been running into trouble with Texas League scheduling myself. Trying to plot an itinerary across the southwest was difficult be-cause teams would typically come in for a five- or six-day stay instead of the usual three or four game series. This year's schedule

was the brainchild of league president Tom Kayser, who was forever explaining its necessity.

I met Tom on my first evening in Tulsa, where he had stopped
on a swing through all the cities in the league. He was a young,
energetic man who looked like a recent MBA graduate from a Big
East Ivy League school. The contrast between Tom Kayser and
Southern League president Jimmy Bragan was like that between a
modern computer and a manual Remington. The only similarity I
saw, and the only one that really needed to exist, was a commitment to the well-being of baseball. Tom came into the press box
before the game and began making suggestions to the newspaper
writers for stories about umpires and other ideas he had been
thinking about. When he introduced himself, I had an inkling that
I should recognize the name. Even his face was familiar, from pictures, I realized later, on all the Texas League publications. "Are
you with the Drillers?" I asked, thinking maybe he was one of General Manager Joe Preseren's assistants.

"No, no!" he said with conviction. "I'm the league president!"

One of Tom's projects for 1993 was to reduce average game
time. He instructed umpires to have hitters ready when warmup
pitches were finished and told coaches to jog to the mound for conferences with pitchers. The latter directive wasn't particularly successful, especially when a relief pitcher needed additional time to
warm up, but by year's end, the league game average was two
hours, thirty-five minutes, ten minutes less than in 1992. His goal
for the following year (1994) was two hours, twenty minutes.

Tom's emphasis on efficiency might seem to run counter to the
relaxed tradition of baseball, but things have gone too far in the
other direction in recent years. I like to watch baseball played, but
waiting while a self-absorbed batter adjusts every reachable piece
of uniform between every pitch is merely irritating. Besides, Tom
Kayser approached things with a good-natured ebullience. During
one game, he joined me behind home plate and pulled out a stop-
watch. He didn't really time anything while we sat there, preferring
to talk baseball. The umpires and players saw the watch, however,
as he intended.

Umpires are the direct responsibility of a minor league president, and Tom naturally felt a little protective toward them. Once, while I watched from the press box, a Tulsa batter tattooed one that seemed to split the third base bag as it sailed over. "Foul ball!" cried the umpire. A chorus of moans went up in the press box, but Tom said: "The umpire was right. It was clearly foul." Headshakes and mutterings of disagreement ensued. "You can't see it from here, you don't have the angle. That's why you think it was fair," Tom added, not bothering to explain why, with the same angle, he was so sure that the umpire was right.

In the first inning of the first game I saw in Tulsa, powerfully built right-hander Trey McCoy hit a three-run homer, his club-leading fourteenth. McCoy was having a solid season at the plate, hitting .286 with forty-four runs batted in. Even considering he could take advantage of the short Tulsa left-field power alley, his power was impressive. At twenty-six, however, he was in an un-usual status for AA ball. Texas Rangers' minor league director Marty Scott had recently said bluntly that it was the last chance for McCoy. Trey had "retired" and left teams three years in a row as a consequence of being homesick and unable to cope with slumps. While on-field play is all fans see from the stands, the successful development of a baseball player requires a synchronization of physical, emotional, and social development. Until this year, home runs just hadn't been as important for McCoy as going home.

Trey was selected for the Texas League All-Star team at midsea-son. He continued to hit; at season's end, he led the club in most offensive categories. Twenty-nine home runs and a new attitude earned him a promotion for 1994; he would play a hundred miles down the Turner Turnpike in AAA Oklahoma City. Some players just settle in sooner than others.

I had traveled through many a lifeless town across the South, and invariably on the outskirts would pass an enormous Wal-Mart serving as the nerve center of an octopuslike clutter. Entire towns had been vacated, their economic and social life's blood sucked out and spewed pell-mell along poorly planned, land-gobbling, auto-mobile-driven stretches that spread relentlessly throughout the South. Still, some southerners use the word "growth" to describe this wasteland.

Nowhere was this process more dramatically demonstrated than in Claremore. The town's beginnings were in the early nineteenth century when a band of Osage Indians settled near a large mound that punched up out of the prairie next to the Verdigris River. When Cherokees began to settle in the area, trouble was inevitable. Believing that the Osages had stolen horses and cattle from them, the Cherokees under Chief Too-an-tuh (Spring Frog) attacked the Osages, whose chief was probably named Clermont. The Osages tried to defend Claremore Mound with bows and arrows but were no match for the rifle-wielding Cherokees. After their defeat, the Osages were moved north and west, where much later, they had the last word. Oil was discovered on Osage land and the tribe became wealthy.

In 1874, the village of Clermont moved east several miles to settle adjacent to the new Frisco railroad. The post office was mislabeled Claremore that year, and the name stuck, since some old-timers recalled the original Osage chief's name as Clah-Mo anyway.

Years ago, the little town and the surrounding countryside inspired homeboy Lynn Riggs to write *Green Grow the Lilacs*, which became the Rodgers and Hammerstein musical *Oklahoma!* In 1903, while drilling a test hole for oil or gas in Claremore, drillers struck an underground pool of foul-smelling water that corroded any metal it touched. Though it contained no radium, it was extolled as "radium water" and was thought to cure everything from rheumatism to pimples. Will Rogers, mocking the water's supposed medicinal powers, wrote that a legless man had made the mistake of sitting in the baths too long and had gone away a centipede. A health industry grew up around the waters, and the small town within a town offered baths, hotel rooms, and other amenities. In my youth, Radium Town, as the few blocks were called, had declined into a dark, mysterious place where prostitution, bootleg liquor, and sometimes murder had replaced radium water. Some of the old bath houses and motor courts are still there, lying vacant or serving as living quarters for the luckless.

As an infrequent visitor over the past thirty-five years, I had seen the town's alteration more clearly than its residents, who had experienced it as a day-by-day, gradual transformation. First, a Wal-Mart store sprung up on Route 66 in the Tulsa direction and the downtown stores I knew as a boy began to close. Within the last few years, the first Wal-Mart had closed, only to be replaced with an even larger one, lying even farther away from the town center.

Two grand old hotels had anchored the northern end of Claremore, lying a block off the Frisco railroad tracks across Route 66 and forming twin pillars leading into the main business district. The Mason Hotel, which housed the world's largest gun collection before a museum was built for that purpose, was torn down and replaced with a low, flat building unrelated architecturally to the early twentieth-century style of other buildings on the main street, so that the town now looked lopsided. I went into the chamber of commerce offices to see what the fate of the remaining landmark, the Will Rogers Hotel, would be.

The Will Rogers is a six-story building made of light brown brick. The arched street floor windows are boarded up, and it lies vacant. I was told that the building is for sale and that the local historical society is attempting to buy it, so far unsuccessfully. As of June 1993, its owner had no plans to tear it down; demolition costs were estimated at $175,000. The upper two floors had housed radium baths and the plumbing had generally become unusable over the years. Before closing, the Will Rogers had gradually become a residential hotel for the transient or the elderly.

Austin Ben Tincup had died at the Will Rogers Hotel on July 5, 1980, at the age of 86. Ben was a Cherokee and the first Oklahoma Indian to play baseball in the major leagues. A curve-balling pitcher, he was also the first Oklahoman to throw a perfect game in professional baseball. On June 18, 1917, Ben Tincup set down twenty-seven Birmingham Barons in a row while pitching for the Little Rock Travelers of the Southern Association. In 1971, he was inducted into the Oklahoma Hall of Fame.

I stopped by the offices of the *Claremore Progress*, the century-old town newspaper, to read his obituary. Several dates, including his birth date, had been inconsistently reported in baseball records. For more information, I paid a visit to Tincup's grand-niece,

Frankie, who lives in Claremore. Frankie had a copy of the Cherokee Nation's Roll Sheet, which listed Austin Tincup, son of James
and Lucinda, as "half blood." "He was almost full blood," said
Frankie. "You couldn't sell Cherokee land if you were over half
blood, so people tried to get on the rolls that way. Besides, being
full blood Cherokee wasn't something to brag about in those days."

Ben had been born in Adair, Oklahoma, a small town about
twenty-five miles northeast of Claremore. Even early on, northeast
Oklahoma was a delivery ground for baseball players. In addition
to Ben, the tiny town produced Ray "Rabbit" Powell, who played
in the big leagues for nine years and hit over .300 twice for the
Boston Braves, and Jim Bluejacket, another curve-balling Cherokee
who might have lasted longer than three big league years had he
not jumped to the Brooklyn Federals in 1914. Ben Tincup broke
into organized ball in 1913 with Muskogee, Oklahoma, and when
that franchise failed, shifted to Sherman, Texas. After he won his
last fourteen games, the Phillies called him up in September. He
roomed with Hall of Fame pitcher Eppa Rixley and mopped up
after Grover Cleveland Alexander. Actually, not much work was to
be had the way Rixley and Alexander were pitching in those years.
Ben stayed the 1914 and 1915 seasons with Philadelphia, then alternated between the minors and World War I for the next few
years. After the war, he spent twelve years with the Louisville Colo-
nels, one of the best teams in the minor leagues, and averaged sixteen wins per season. Even after each professional season was over,
Ben kept playing baseball. Back in Oklahoma, he would sign up
with a semipro team and pitch or play the outfield for a few weeks
more, supplementing his $500-a-month professional salary. After
retiring as an active player, Ben managed, coached under Leo Du-
rocher, and scouted for Casey Stengel.

Off the field, Ben's life was not as happy. He married a woman
from Kentucky, and they had two daughters. Both were killed in
separate car wrecks. In his later years, he bought a small ranch
near Claremore and referred to it as his "poor farm."

In 1971, John Ferguson of the *Tulsa World* drove down to Claremore to interview Ben Tincup on the occasion of his induction into
Oklahoma's Hall of Fame. Ben had moved into the Mason Hotel to

treat his arthritis with radium water. A picture from that time shows him standing in front of part of the famous gun collection; a solid-looking, silver-haired old Cherokee wearing a western string tie and a rattle-snake belt. Ferguson wrote, "While Tincup's tantalizing slider is gone, his keen memory is still there."

After they tore the Mason down, Ben moved across the street to the Will Rogers Hotel. When he died, his funeral was sung in Cherokee. I asked Frankie if he had been ill.

"I think he just decided to die and did. He willed himself to die. The old Cherokees could do that." Maybe so. Ben Tincup did things that few others have done. And once, in 1917, he achieved a state to which none of us are ever supposed to aspire. He was, according to the rules of baseball, perfect.

Although the Mason was gone and the Will Rogers stood on its last legs, one institution in Claremore was going strong. Cotton-Eyed Joe's Hickory Smoked Bar-b-Que Restaurant was still chopping and smoking and dishing out succulent, tasty pork ribs. My sister, Janice, who has a Ph.D. in ribs, has moved around a lot in her life. When she arrives in a new city, her job is to find the best barbecue place in the area, and then I come to visit. Based on her choices of prime places over the years, I have distilled the essential characteristics of a barbecue joint. The restaurant should be in a converted house, once fashionable but now in a less-desirable section of town, with the pit set up in the back yard so that the effluvium of wood smoke tickles your nostrils as soon as the car door opens. The house should be near a railroad track, so that the sounds of a train whistle and the taste of ribs become unconsciously intertwined over the years, and the tables inside should have plastic covers for a fast swipe with a wet rag as the customers leave. A little garish neon over the door is crucial, and a limited menu is a must. Barbecue places that offer chicken and fish and vegetables *du jour* just aren't focused enough to concentrate on their main business. Furnishings should date back at least twenty-five years, and if they do, you have some assurance that prices and selections haven't kept pace with the times either.

Cotton-Eyed Joe's has all the imperatives and wonderful ribs besides, with crunchy cole slaw and tangy baked beans. On the other side of the railroad tracks, about forty yards in front of the house-turned-restaurant, runs storied Route 66. I may be biased toward Cotton-Eyed Joe's, for the barbecue joint is part of my family history. In the late 1930s, my Aunt Dell married a young Irishman named Walker Casey. To support three children, Walker worked in the zinc mines of northeast Oklahoma, the same mines near Picher where Mutt Mantle, and later Mickey, worked. One day he tamped dynamite into a hole in the mine wall that already had explosives in it. He was killed instantly, and with part of the insurance money, Aunt Dell bought an old house next to the Frisco railroad tracks in Claremore. Later, she married a carpenter who expanded the cold, draughty house. But the house was never large and it bulged with their ten children, and hangers-on like my sister and me, who spent many mealtimes at the long dining room table, competing for the home grown vegetables and Kool Aid.

When my aunt and uncle moved across town, their daughter and son-in-law converted the old place into a barbecue restaurant. Now the business belongs to one of their offspring. People pour into Cotton-Eyed Joe's and plunk down hard cash for meals today, but the old place saw a lot of mealtimes over the years before the neon sign went up.

My mother and I had lunch at the restaurant one hot midday before I drove down to Tulsa to go to "work." We sat in what had been the living room and talked about family associations. On the wall was a large, shiny Bowie knife, hand made by my Uncle Troy, mounted on a wooden plaque. The ribs came with a dark, rich sauce created by one of my aunts, though which one is in dispute.

I told my mother that, when I was young and spent the night with my cousins, we would sneak out of a back room window and run the half mile downtown to the Yale Theater. When the ticket booth closed after the last show began, we would slip through the lobby and watch the movie already in progress. She took the news silently and looked at me uncertainly, not sure what the appropriate punishment was for a middle-aged man who confesses to a youthful transgression.

"Now you tell me," she said finally.

Barry Lewis, a Tulsa sportswriter, was temporarily filling in as scorekeeper for the Drillers. Watching him keep score one night, I asked if he had seen the new computerized systems. He looked down at his score sheet, with its complicated system of symbols and cross-checks, and said: "When I get through scoring a game, the sheet isn't just rows of numbers. It's a work of art."

One day I skipped batting practice and followed Eleventh Street, the former Highway 66, down toward the center of Tulsa. Where Eleventh Street bent and ascended a slight rise before penetrating the tall buildings of central Tulsa stood a magnificent structure called the Warehouse Market. The old building was an example of a type of art deco architecture called Pueblo Deco, and it was on the hit list. I wanted to see the landmark once again before it disappeared, or was "saved" as the facade of a chain hardware store.

The site is special for another reason. The warehouse was built over McNulty Park, home of the Western Association Class A Tulsa Oilers. McNulty was built in only twenty-two days in February 1919, and was the location of Tulsa professional baseball until 1929. It seated seven thousand but was cozy even by pre-Ruthian dead ball standards. Left field was 310 feet, center was 320 feet, leaving left center essentially without a power alley. Right field, hemmed in by the Midland Valley Railroad tracks, was only 274 feet. I could still see remnants of the rail bed and even some of the old tracks.

In the park's eleven-year existence, Tulsa led the league in hitting seven times. McNulty was also the setting of one of baseball's most curious records. From 1922 through part of the 1925 season, center fielder Lyman Lamb ignited a barrage of doubles unequaled before or after. In 1924, Lamb set the organized record for doubles in one season with an incredible 100. Playing in 168 games that season, he amassed 261 hits and an impressive .373 average. Lamb's nearest rival for doubles in a season was Paul Waner, who hit seventy-five in 1925 but was playing in the 200-game season of the Pacific Coast League. The closest any non-PCL hitter came to Lamb's record was Ervin Beck of Toledo who hit 71 in 1900, a sum equaled by Lamb himself in 1923 when he was warming up

204

for the all-time mark. In three consecutive McNulty years, Lamb reached totals of 68, 71, and 100 doubles.

At Driller Stadium later that evening, I asked Barry Lewis and fellow sportswriter John Ferguson about the doubles record. Between them existed an encyclopedic command of the game's history. Barry speculated that ground rules at McNulty had played a role, but that seemed unlikely. There was no direct record of such rules, at least that I found, and balls over the fence obviously were credited as home runs. Mule Washburn and Yank Davis of the Oilers hit forty-eight and forty-two homers, respectively, and Lamb himself chipped in with nineteen in his record year of 1924. The right-handed hitting Lamb later recalled trying to pull everything he hit over the third baseman's head, so he was trying for doubles. Even harder to understand with McNulty's configuration, however, is how the short fence in left center was conducive to doubles. Anything that stayed in the park would have been a short throw to second. Lamb had some speed, averaging fifteen stolen bases per year in his three full years at McNulty, but he never led even his own team in that department.

In 1925, Lamb was made playing manager of the Tulsa Oilers. When the team faltered, playing in seventh place at midseason, Lamb was fired and played out his career in a number of towns in the Southwest. In three and a half seasons at McNulty, Lamb averaged .349 and about seventy doubles per full season. In every other park, he hit .292. His highest non-McNulty season for doubles was forty-seven, hit for Wichita Falls in the Texas League in 1927. Rarely has a player's hitting stroke and a ballpark's layout meshed so nicely as in those few years on Elgin Avenue in Tulsa.

McNulty Park patrons saw Babe Ruth, who played in a 1929 exhibition game there when the hapless St. Louis Browns, Tulsa's major league affiliate, inexplicably beat the Yankees. Red Grange played in an exhibition there, and Jack Dempsey went a few rounds before the park was razed in 1929 to clear ground for the Warehouse Market. Eight years earlier the ballpark had been part of an unseemly spectacle when life and baseball intersected in an unusual way. Tulsa was the scene of one of the nation's bloodiest racial riots, a tragic affair that started On May 31, 1921, and left hundreds dead and Tulsa's black homes and businesses in ashes.

The riot started when a young black man named Dick Rowland was accused of trying to rape a white woman. To prevent Rowland's lynching, black men from the neighborhood known as "Deep Greenwood" after its central street armed themselves and massed around the courthouse. In retaliation, armed white Tulsans invaded the black section of town, conducting a systematic destruction of the community, and killing many of the residents who offered resistance. White mobs roamed through the black community at will, looting and burning black homes. When the initial resistance was broken, blacks were rounded up and confined in internment centers. One of the sites where armed guards detained black prisoners was McNulty Park. A photo, dated the day after the riot began, was taken from just inside the left-field fence. It showed an expanse of uneven grass in the outfield, a third base dugout at field level covered with a tin roof, and several hundred black men, women, and children, sitting in bleacher seats. About thirty white men were milling about in left field, holding rifles and shotguns.

By the following day, June 2, the four thousand or more black Tulsans who were being held at gunpoint in various sites around the city were consolidated at the fairgrounds, where Driller Park now stands. Judging from the looks of fright, determination, and mutual hatred that glared out from the pictures of the riot, baseball was not foremost in the minds of those who occupied McNulty Park on June 1, 1921.

For my last night at the Tulsa ballpark, I decided to retrace my route to games during the early 1950s. I started at the northwest edge of Collinsville, a small town seventeen miles west of Claremore where I had lived in my teens, to see what had become of Sallee Field, the combination football-baseball field of my high school days.

The field was still there, with its familiar stone entrance pillars supporting the curved metal sign with its name, and was still used for high school football. The baseball field had been at the northern end past the gridiron, whose uprights were removed in the spring from what became shallow center field. The orientation had been wrong; batters faced southwest. The skin infield had always been full of pebbles, and the playing surface had sloped upward from home plate to center field. From shortstop, I had to throw downhill to first base and balls were forever sailing over the first baseman's upstretched glove.

I played high school baseball for three years on this field, and American Legion baseball in the summers, but no day stood out more clearly than an early spring day in 1955. I was a sophomore and tryouts had been in progress for a few weeks. First cuts had already been made, and the season's opener was approaching. The school furnished sixteen uniforms, enough for an intrasquad game with coaches pitching, and that was the size of the high school team. About twenty players were left on final cut day, and I was not high on the list of probables.

Football and basketball lettermen were pretty much guaranteed roster slots because of their athletic abilities, and I had played neither sport. My fall and winter sports activities usually consisted of nagging other boys into hitting flies or grounders to me by the hour, regardless of the time of year or weather. Almost all the remaining positions were earmarked for baseball-only juniors and seniors who had been on the team in previous years, which left about five of us to compete for one uniform.

I was sent into center field in a late inning of an intrasquad game on that final day. A batter sent a hard line drive to my glove side and I caught it on the dead run, wheeled and threw to the correct base to hold an astonished runner at second. The next batter hit one to deep left center and I turned, put my head down and ran toward the ball's eventual arrival spot. It was a backhand catch, barely in the webbing, again on the dead run.

I know that my memory may have exaggerated the splendor of those fortuitous catches, but I put on that last uniform for the first game that year, and wore it for three years much the same way as a symphony conductor sports a tuxedo.

The first year, before moving to shortstop, I was used as a late inning defensive replacement for the center fielder, a tall, muscle-bound football tackle who lacked finesse. After wincing visibly while the hulking senior backpedaled and lunged sideways in the

207

general direction of fly balls, the coach would send me in, usually after an especially clumsy error. As I ran toward the outfield, the monster would see me and start in, yelling loudly: "ATTABOY GREEN, YOU'RE THE MAN, GET IN HERE BABE, YOU'RE THE ONE!" When we passed, he would snarl viciously but softly so no one else heard: "You little piss ant! You better miss everything that comes out here! You catch a fly and I'll kick your ass up between your shoulders after the game! You hear me, Green?" Even routine catches had elements of heroism that season.

Baseball is played somewhere else in Collinsville now. The old backstop is gone, the benches are gone, the few rows of bleacher seats are gone, and the basepaths and infield have gone to grass. Little is left to indicate that all the catching, throwing, batting, spitting, glory, embarrassment, and cursing each other ever happened at all.

14

A Southwestern Sultan of Swat

I STAYED IN TULSA FOR A WEEK, longer than at any other stop on the trip, and left there more reluctantly than any other place except my home in Maryland. Tulsa baseball was in good hands, though. General Manager Joe Preseren and his staff had been hospitable, and even the ballpark food had been good. Hot fajitas on the menu indicated that the Southwest was close. I had said my goodbyes, arranged to meet Tom Kayser at a future stop, and begun driving west. The trip was beginning to wind down so I tried to focus on the people and places still on the calendar.

I wasn't quite finished with Oklahoma. Forty miles west of Tulsa, the small town of Yale was one-time home to the great Sac and Fox athlete, Jim Thorpe. His plain, five-room gray clapboard bungalow was open to the public and I stopped to learn more about his life. The little place wasn't inundated with business; I was the first person to sign in two days. A solitary woman served as caretaker and guide.

"Two of Jim's daughters still live in Yale," she told me. The house had been their home as girls and had served Jim as a base of operations. He traveled a lot even after the Olympics and his professional sports careers were over. And like other famous athletes, he didn't handle retirement well. The death of his young son at age three, when Jim was thirty, exacerbated an already serious drinking problem, which continued the rest of his life. As a laborer, movie extra, lecturer, and, during World War II, a merchant marine, he wandered the country as a lost soul.

209

The little house managed to convey a good sense of Jim Thorpe's life-style even if he spent little time there. It was plain and simple, with sturdy, solid furniture. Few action films remained to show him performing at his athletic peak, and none were in the home, but a football opponent once described tackling him as "like hitting an oak tree which was doing the hundred in under ten seconds."

Jim's retirement from sports coincided with the arrival of the Great Depression and he often had a hard time finding work. In Los Angeles he toiled as a painter, then began landing low-paying jobs as a movie extra. He was usually in the background as an Indian chief or an athlete in B movies, but occasionally showed up in better pictures.

In 1953, two years after a sanitized film biography—*Jim Thorpe, All-American*—was released, Jim died of a heart attack in California. His third wife, Patricia, made an unusual decision about the disposal of his remains. While Jim's body lay in a temporary crypt, she went to Mauch Chunk, Pennsylvania, with a proposition. If the town would change its name to Jim Thorpe, Pennsylvania, she would move his body there and have a memorial constructed. Even though Jim Thorpe had no connection with Mauch Chunk and had probably been unaware of its existence, the economically depressed little town agreed. Jim's body remains there today.

This would be little more than an odd ending to an unusual life, but Sac and Fox tradition makes it more unsettling. Jim's children opposed Patricia Thorpe's plan and continue to do so, insisting that his remains must be returned to their origin and be given a traditional Indian burial. Until this happens, they believe his soul is destined to wander in death much as Jim Thorpe did in his star-crossed life.

A few miles north of Yale I picked up the Cimarron Turnpike and drove west. I stopped at a toll booth sitting in the middle of nothing, maybe ten miles north of Stillwater, home of Oklahoma State University. A pretty woman wearing a Stetson took my money.

"Can I have a receipt?"

"I don't know if I should give you one or not."

"Why?"

"This is Cowboy country." She had seen my SOONER tags as I drove up.

At midafternoon there was very little traffic on the Cimarron Turnpike. The flat prairie was almost treeless and visibility seemed to run forever. Toward the western horizon, the sky had turned dark and ugly, with flashes of lightning zig-zagging downward. I was in bright sunshine and seemed to be driving from daylight into midnight. The light had an eerie quality and made the few trees glow with the half-dark, half-light sky behind them. I turned on the car radio for a weather report. Every lightning flash sent a loud crash of static through the speakers.

Worried about the weather, I took Interstate 35 north instead of staying on smaller highways. My goal for the evening was Wichita, Kansas, to see the Texas League Wranglers play. Kansas was a little far north for a Southern trip, even by my liberal delineation of the South's boundaries. Wichita was in the Texas League, however, and I wanted to see Lawrence-Dumont Stadium. Built in 1934, it was one of the oldest still in use by professional baseball.

In Oklahoma, I had the feeling of being on the edge of a third subregion of the South. First the busy Southeast had given way to the languid Deep South, and now Tex Mex food had replaced grits and dumplings, and cowboy boots and Stetsons were *de rigueur*. There were deeper, more abstract subcultural variations, of course.

I had been in the South for almost three months, and my training as a sociologist dictated that I look for patterns, themes, and motifs. I had expected, before beginning the trip, to collect impressions, categorize them, and sort out the central meaning, but it wasn't happening. W. E. B. DuBois had warned against even trying what he called "car window sociology." Writing in *Souls of Black Folks*, he commented derisively on those who "seek to understand and know the South by devoting the few hours of a holiday trip to unravelling the snarl of centuries."

The South had always inspired feeling and handled reason harshly. I had at times felt a part of it, but the snarl of centuries had not unraveled into orderly piles as I looked out the car window.

211

My general impression was that the South was undergoing one of its periodic identity crises. Shaken by civil rights, suburbanization, and instant communication over the past thirty-five years, it had fragmented into enclaves where traditional values still held sway. Cotton fields had been covered by condominiums in places, but elsewhere I had met people and seen communities straight from a William Faulkner novel.

I had seen a lot of baseball in the South, and had viewed that institution much the same as other southern customs and rituals. Unlike the South as a region, however, southern minor league baseball had changed as a whole. Fans still supported their teams, but were not emotionally involved with them. Now I still had a few games to watch, a few more places to see, and to my west, a storm to outrun as it closed in over the plains.

I had been warned. In Tulsa, Tom Kayser had told me that Lawrence-Dumont had been through a five-million-dollar renovation in 1991 and was a very different ballpark. I had to see for myself, though, and went knowing that renovation couldn't remove the atmosphere from a ballpark that had been built in 1934. One look convinced me that I was wrong, and a second look that I was dead wrong.

From directly in front, the stadium resembles the side of a three-story, middle-price-range motel. It has been painted mauve, teal, and Shaker blue. Skyboxes line the rooftop canopy. Early patrons eat grilled chicken sandwiches at the Hard Ball Cafe, an open air eatery just past first base. When children get bored with the ballgame (about the middle of the first inning), they romp on swings and slides in the OK Corral, just beyond the Hard Ball Cafe. Parents who want to keep an eye on their little bundles of energy watch both the game and their children from the Parent's Hitchin' Post. This place is cute.

When I checked out the concessions, I found that water was selling for twenty-five cents. Young professional couples were not only buying the stuff, but were lining up for it. They were drinking the water like, well, like it was beer.

The field still had an interesting configuration. Left field ran 344 feet with a power alley of 374 feet, center was 401 feet, and right field only 312 feet away. Seating was L-shaped, with the shank running down the left field side; and right field seating was shortened by the restaurant and play area. The view over the left field wall was dominated by a church with a tall white steeple, and the city skyline was a backdrop behind the center field wall. Above everything wonderful white cloud formations hung, floating in an azure sky.

The infield was artificial turf, and in the game I saw, the first three hits were grounders past short, all possible groundouts on grass. This was on Saturday night and a crowd of over six thousand showed up to see the Famous Chicken perform. He gave his usual good show, harassing the umpires and leading his little chickens around the infield. The crowd loved him, applauded wildly, and pretty much forgot that there was a ball game in progress.

Highway 54 shot straight west out of Wichita like a bullet from a high powered rifle. Along about Greensburg, the momentum was spent and the road's trajectory tailed off toward the southwestern corner of Kansas. Highway 54 was a lonely road. Fields of grain were planted on either side of the highway, and signs announced towns—Pretty Prairie, Zenda—invisible across the flatness. West of Minneola less of the plains were planted and sagebrush appeared, signaling the beginnings of the desert Southwest.

In Liberal, Kansas, I stopped to take pictures of the home field of the Liberal Bee Jays of the Kansas Jayhawk League. In Oklahoma, Bob, a friend of my mother's, had told me about a level of baseball with which I was unfamiliar. Liberal fields a team in a summer college league. The team has a bus, charges admission to games, and publishes programs. Newspaper coverage furnishes publicity, and advertisers buy signs at the park and space in the team program. The team has had graduates who played in the major leagues, with Ron Guidry being the most famous. Managers have included professional baseball men such as former major leaguer Bob Cerv. In 1993, the Kansas Jayhawk League had ten teams, all but one in Kansas. While the field was rough by professional standards, it was maintained at least as well as many college baseball diamonds.

213

Eleven summer college leagues operated in 1993, with the Cape Cod League in Massachusetts perhaps the best known. Alaska had two leagues, and since professional baseball had never been played in the northernmost state, the college summer leagues furnished Alaska's highest level of organized baseball.

The summer leagues form one answer to the problem of how to get competitive experience for players who choose to remain in college. Liberal's summer schedule had ranged from 100 to 120 games in the past, and the competitive level was higher than in most college conferences. In the best case, a summer league allowed a player to gain meaningful playing time and still finish college before making a decision about a professional career. With the demise of semiprofessional baseball and the collapse of the lower minors, the leagues filled a gap for players and smalltown fans alike.

Highway 54, continuing to drop toward the Southwest, slices across both the Oklahoma and Texas panhandles. This was the high plains, with elevations around three thousand feet. The few small towns had huge grain elevators, which from a distance looked like the skylines of cities. From Dalhart, Texas, to Tucumcari, New Mexico, the road was lonelier still. In Dalhart, a sign warned travelers to plan ahead: "NO SERVICES FOR 46 MILES." A railroad ran alongside the highway but there were no houses. Cattle didn't even graze this high plains desert.

At Tucumcari, New Mexico, old Route 66 was buried under Interstate 40. This town of motels was a minor oasis for the Okies heading west after the arid Texas panhandle, but signaled the beginning of the long, dry stretch across New Mexico, Arizona, and southern California. Even if their ancient Model A's made the trip, the Dust Bowl refugees were likely to be met at the California border and turned back, "if you ain't got the DO-RE-MI," as Woody Guthrie put it.

I followed Interstate 40 due west for about fifty miles, and turned south on US 84. Mesas and pinon oak dominated the landscape. Miles before entering Fort Sumner I passed billboards proclaiming the "authentic" Billy the Kid burial site. I never would have doubted that if a place claimed to have Billy the Kid buried there, that they actually did. Once I began reading the signs about the "real gravesite of Billy the Kid" I naturally started wondering: Have they really got Billy in there?

Billy's probable graveyard was a walled, Spanish-style cemetery behind a museum. His tombstone had been stolen twice. Once it stayed missing for twenty-six years before it was recovered. Now the stone is shackled in iron.

I had the old cemetery to myself. Lightning was flashing to the south, and thunder was crashing and rolling the way it does only on the open high plains. After the peal, the noise rolled and seemed to crumble as it moved away.

Between Billy's likely burial site and the location of original Fort Sumner, where Billy had been shot by Pat Garrett in 1881, stood a fairly sizeable baseball field. It was overgrown, and apparently hadn't been used lately, but had an impressive bank of lights. The field had concession stands and two rows of bleachers. With darkness approaching, the lightning flashes and peals of thunder made it easy to imagine eerie goings-on at the baseball park. Maybe the ghosts of Billy the Kid and Pat Garrett, their differences mostly patched up after a century together in the nether world, met occasionally for a little pepper near where the most famous event in both their lives occurred. Or maybe Pat would hit a fly ball over Billy's head, and Billy was afraid to turn his back on it, because once someone kills you it's hard to fully trust them again.

I considered spending the night in Fort Sumner, but absolutely nothing was open on a Sunday evening, and I wanted to be in Roswell early the next morning. I picked up a two-lane road marked as State Highway 20, and as I crossed the Pecos River the rain started. Ten miles south of Fort Sumner the wind began to blow fiercely and the rain slammed down in earnest. From the northwest, the wind hit Sweetspot at an angle and moved the three-quarter ton truck from one lane to another.

The ninety miles between Fort Sumner and Roswell contained nothing—no towns, no houses, not even a hill to break the weather. Tumbleweeds were blowing around wildly, and when the wind shifted to true north, a couple of tumbleweeds raced up from behind and passed the pickup even though I was driving fifty miles per hour. Visibility dropped to almost nothing between lightning

215

flashes, and I pulled over beside a cattle guard to wait out the storm.

I turned the truck into the wind to provide a little protection while I climbed into the back. Tumbleweeds were hitting the truck with a loud WHOOSH. I made a cup of coffee on the camp stove and watched the coffee slop out as the truck rocked violently. I began speculating about how high the wind would have to be to send Sweetspot airborne. The wind shifted a few degrees, driving water through what had been, up to now, a tight-fitting camper window.

The lightning explosions seemed to be getting closer. I tried to count the seconds between the glare and the sound of thunder, but they were occurring on all sides and it was impossible to relate which crash accompanied which flash. The display was spectacular. Chains of light were sometimes vertical, sometimes horizontal. Some were horseshoe shaped, one looked like a fishhook, another resembled a chicken's wishbone. A sudden sharp electrical discharge took the appearance of two ropes woven together. Sometimes the bright streaks seemed to vibrate as they flickered before disappearing. After about forty-five minutes the wind subsided, the rain tapered off to a drizzle, and the electrical storm was over. I drove toward Roswell, noting that New Mexico State Highway 20 had my vote for the most desolate road in America. Four miles out of Roswell, I finally passed another car.

Next morning the sky was clear, the sun was brilliant, and except for a few puddles on concrete surfaces, no traces of the previous evening's storm remained. Roswell appeared to be a clean, dynamic, midsized town. Joe Bauman was my reason for being in Roswell; and his home was in an older section consisting of small, tree-shaded bungalows on quiet streets. In front, two older American cars were parked. Both built like tanks, they were, like the man who drove them, big.

Joe took me into the backyard and we sat on the shaded patio while he told me about his career and his life. At 6'5", Joe looked to be a few pounds over his playing weight, but was darkly tanned. Though he moved slowly, it was without the stiffness of age. He smoked constantly as we talked, and the smoke wafted up to blend visually with his silver-colored hair. While we were talking, Joe's wife Pat returned from an errand, and came back to say hello.

"Do you want to bring your dog out of the pickup?" she asked, referring to the sign in back of the truck. The backyard already had two cats and one dog, each of whom looked as if it moved about once a day.

"Well, I don't really have a dog," I explained. You don't want to start an interview by lying to the wife of a man who once hit seventy-two home runs.

Joe's name is well known in baseball circles as the man who set the organized baseball record for most home runs in a season. Beyond that season, though, his shortened career (Joe played in only nine minor league seasons, and except for one at bat with AA Milwaukee, never swung at a pitch in competition above Class A) is little known. Returning from a second long absence from organized baseball in 1952, Joe put together four seasons of sustained slugging that no other player has ever equaled. None have ever even come very close.

Joe was born in Welch, Oklahoma, only a few miles from Mickey Mantle's home town of Commerce, but his family moved to Oklahoma City when he was about one. He played high school baseball at Capitol City High, south of town. At nineteen, Joe was offered a contract by the Little Rock Travelers of the Southern Association. His signing bonus was an impressive $2500, good money for the tight-fisted prewar years. The Travelers sent him to Newport, in northeastern Arkansas, for first year seasoning. George Kell, the future Hall of Fame third baseman, became his roommate and friend that season. They boarded in an old Victorian house and took their meals together in the train station. The year bore few portents of seasons to come, however. Joe's mother died in that summer and his mind wasn't on the game. He hit .215 with three home runs at Newport, and played in barely half the team's 117 games in the class D four-team league. His roommate showed promise, though. George Kell led the Northeast Arkansas League with 143 hits that season.

While World War II interrupted many baseball careers, it may have served obliquely to keep the big first baseman in the game. Joe joined the navy and spent three years playing baseball in Norman, Oklahoma. A high-level team was developed there, including several major league and AA players. Joe's assessment was that it was the second-best navy baseball team in existence during the wartime period. Lieutenant Charlie Gelbert, a shortstop with nine years solid major league experience, ran the team.

"I learned more baseball there than in any other stretch," Joe remembered. "I was better off than working my way up through the minors."

"How did you hit against the major leaguers you faced while you were on the navy team?"

Joe thought for a moment, trying to envision long ago at bats. "I don't remember having any trouble hitting them," he answered.

After the war, Joe was still under contract to the Little Rock Travelers. Little Rock farmed him out to Amarillo in the class C West Texas-New Mexico League for the 1946 season, and Joe's navy apprenticeship began to pay off. He hit .301 and led the league with forty-eight home runs. Next season at Amarillo, Joe formed a fearsome one-two punch with Bob Crues. Hitting right-handed, Crues hit fifty-two home runs while Joe, from the opposite side, contributed thirty-eight. Balls flew through the southwest air in those days; Bill Serena of Lubbock hit fifty-seven home runs that year and kept both Crues and Joe Bauman out of any top offensive categories. In 1948, after Joe left Amarillo, Crues tied the organized baseball record of sixty-nine home runs in one season to give his former teammate something to aim for.

In 1947, Boston paid $10,000 for Joe's contract for their AA Milwaukee team, who in turn farmed him out to Hartford, in the class A Eastern League. Away from the Southwest and playing irregularly, Joe had a subpar season. Ray Sanders, the Boston Braves' first baseman, was at Hartford on a rehabilitation assignment much of the season and Joe alternated with him at first base, accruing only 276 at bats and hitting .275. "Sanders would play if he felt like it," Joe said, "and if he didn't I would be in the lineup."

After the season, the Braves' farm director offered Joe a cut of $200 per month less than he had made the season before. Joe balked, and in the days before Curt Flood challenged the reserve clause, was left with only two options. He could play ball for less than what he thought he was worth, or get out. There was no arbitration and no effective way to negotiate.

"Put me on the voluntary whatever-you-want-to list," Joe told him. "I could make more selling shoe-strings on the corner."

From 1949 through 1951, Joe was out of organized baseball for the second time since his playing days started. He became co-owner of a service station on Route 66 in Oklahoma City, and landed a part-time baseball job in Elk City with a semiprofessional team. The team paid more than the Braves had, and Joe didn't have to work, just play three or four games a week in the western Oklahoma town. In 1949, Joe refused a contract to play with the Southern Association (AA) Atlanta Crackers because he had given the Elk City manager his word that he would finish the season.

If Joe's first four years away from professional baseball during the war had been either beneficial or at least benign, the years from 1949 through 1951 were pivotal in a negative sense. Joe spent his late twenties playing a reduced schedule at a less than professional level. These are typically the "big" years for offensive players, who by then have experience and maturity but still possess sufficient drive, stamina, and reflexive quickness to make their marks. Joe's independence cost him, though how much will never be known.

"In hindsight, I made a mistake but I'm not resentful. It's just that if I had it to do over, I would have taken what they offered to see how far I could go in baseball."

Boston called again and wanted Joe to play the 1952 season for the Atlanta Crackers, but he had made another important contact by then. A doctor whose name Joe no longer remembered, then somehow affiliated with Artesia in the class C Longhorn League, offered to buy Joe's contract from Boston and bring him down to play baseball in New Mexico. Joe agreed, saying, "Okay, but if they charge you more than a jock strap, you're getting took." They struck a deal whereby Joe could buy back his contract for $200 if he didn't like Artesia, and Joe Bauman was back in organized baseball.

In four full Longhorn League seasons, Joe hit home run totals of fifty, fifty-three, seventy-two, and forty-six. His combined batting

219

average over that period was .371, and he averaged 164 runs batted in per season. In his record-setting 1954 season of seventy-two
home runs, Joe had 456 total bases in 498 at bats for an all-time
high slugging average of .916. Babe Ruth's best was .847.

"How was your fielding?" I joked.

Joe answered seriously, after considering the question as he ha-
bitually did. "I would say that I was an above average first
baseman."

On his travels through the Longhorn League cities, Joe fell in
love with Roswell, New Mexico. He loved the big skies and the clear
air and the fact that you could see forever across the desert. "There
are no chiggers on the desert," he told me. "That in itself would be
enough reason to move here." After the 1953 season, Joe exercised
his option and bought back his contract so he could move upstate
and play for the Roswell Rockets. He became a community fixture,
opening Joe Bauman's Texaco Service and hitting the ball farther
and oftener than ever. Roswell was then an independent team, fi-
nanced by the city.

"We only had fifteen or sixteen guys on the roster. The team bus
had six bunks built in the back, a double bunk across the back and
two down the sides at the back."

"Who got the bunks?" I asked.

"The five oldest guys and the next day's starting pitcher."

There was no radio coverage for the team, but New Mexico
newspapers reported each game. Attendance in the low minors was
drying up during that period, and all the home run records were
like the bright flare of a roman candle just before it burns itself out.
Artesia drew 42,972 in 1952, and in 1953 Joe played before
40,042 home fans. When the Longhorn League was reclassified as
a C league, attendance picked up a little. Roswell drew 53,280 for
Joe's big year, but slipped to 39,911 in 1955. In his last year, which
ended on June 8 because of an ankle injury, Roswell drew only
18,367 even though it had shifted to the higher level class B Southwestern League.

"I played before television, during, and after it became popular,
and the crowds were different. Not just in size, which went way
down, but in their interest in baseball."

Joe's own declining interest in baseball seemed to parallel that of the minors in general.

"I tried to retire after that 1954 season," Joe said, "but a bunch of the town's businessmen talked me into coming back."

"WHAT? You hit seventy-two home runs and wanted to retire?"

Joe grinned at my surprise. "What was I going to do? Come back and try to hit eighty home runs? Ernie, I had found the town I wanted to live in the rest of my life, I had a good business going and by then I had fallen out of love with baseball. The San Francisco Giants invited me to spring training after the '54 season but I didn't go. I had been playing to get out of baseball that year, not to start something new in it. And I couldn't leave my business all summer. I wouldn't have had a monkey wrench to come back to."

Playing against his wishes in 1955, Joe's offensive output declined. Nonetheless, he hit forty-six home runs and .336. The following winter, Joe stepped out on an icy porch and felt something twist in his ankle. By spring, it continued to hurt when he ran. Not long into the season, X rays showed bone chips floating around. He finally had a legitimate excuse to quit without letting the townsfolk down. Hitting off a bad ankle, Joe had seventeen home runs that year in just 167 at bats. He still managed to hit a home run in about every ten times at bat.

Around noon, we decided it was time to start looking for lunch and Joe offered to drive by the ballpark. It was just south of town, next to the rodeo grounds. Printed sources usually used the name Park Field, but Joe called it Fair Park Field. Before baseball it had been a park for town fairs.

The park was much altered. Right field was still 329 feet from home plate, but the ten-foot-high painted wooden fence had been replaced with easier to maintain chain link all round. The clubhouses and central grandstand were gone, and the wind blew through the grounds unimpeded, trapping sagebrush against the fence.

Until September 1, 1954, Joe Bauman's big season had attracted little national attention even though he had sixty-four home runs. That night, however, 524 fans saw him hit four home runs and a double as Roswell beat Sweetwater, 15–9. With a week left in the regular season, the record of sixty-nine home runs set by Joe Hauser in 1933 and tied by Bob Crues in Amarillo in 1948 was within reach, and the Associated Press picked up the story.

Next evening, Rocket manager Pat Stasey put Joe into the lead-off slot to get him more at bats. Joe had two doubles and a single, but didn't hit one out. The playing manager Stasey, who had put himself into the cleanup slot, had three home runs.

On September 3, photographers from *Life* and *Sports Illustrated* joined local coverage and shot away every time Joe came up to bat. In the bottom of the eighth, with Midland and Roswell tied 4–4, Joe lifted number sixty-nine over the right field wall and beat Midland 7–4.

According to Joe, the eight-team league consisting of Roswell, Artesia, and Carlsbad in New Mexico and Big Spring, Midland, Odessa, San Angelo, and Sweetwater in Texas, had only one band-box ballpark, and that was in Big Spring. The oddly arranged schedule had them playing the next two games in Big Spring before finishing the regular season at Artesia. They bussed over with the press in tow, waiting for Joe to break the record.

Joe never got a chance to break the record in Big Spring; they pitched around him. Even hometown Big Spring fans booed as he drew walk after walk in situations where they should have been pitching to him. On Sunday, September 5, the season ended in Artesia with a doubleheader, and Joe's last chance to break the record came down to one day. Before the game, Artesia NuMexer manager Pat Adair came over to talk to Joe. "I heard what happened in Big Spring. We're gonna pitch to you here. Whatever happens, we aren't going to walk you."

Artesia had an odd-shaped old ballpark with the longest distance running directly down the right field foul line at 360 feet. Also bad for Joe's uppercut swing was the fact that the wind was blowing in from right. In the first inning of the first game, NuMexer pitcher Jose Galardo threw Joe a fast ball and he hit it through the wind and over the tin fence to set a new season home run record for organized baseball. In the second game Joe hit two more home runs, one off Jose Galardo's uncle Frank, just in case the Galardo family didn't feel bad enough already. Artesia, who finished on top of the league with ninety-two wins that season, was overwhelmed 17–0 in the nightcap, succumbing to the fanfare and Roswell's unstoppable hitting magic.

The bat Joe used to hit number seventy went on a traveling bat show and is now in Louisville at the Hillerich and Bradsby plant. They gave him a black bat with gold engraving in exchange.

"I didn't make any real money from the record," Joe said. "Lot of ham, though. We got a free ham that year for every home run we hit."

Joe knew a small cantina on a quiet street in Roswell, and we went there for lunch. Over green chili enchiladas and *Carta Blanca* beer, I asked him how he did it.

"Hell, I don't know how I did it. I didn't have a slump all season, but I don't know why. Ernie, the ball looked that big all year." Joe made a circle the size of a canteloupe with his large hands.

"That last big doubleheader gave you a .400 batting average for the year. Were you aware of that at the time?"

He sat for a moment, trying to put the day together in his mind, and finally said simply, "That was secondary."

The sky was on fire in Artesia. Refineries were everywhere, and flames shot out of pipes that pierced the sky with unending burnoff. I had stopped to see the ballpark in Artesia after leaving Roswell, and it was still just as Joe had described it. The eccentric configuration had straightaway center field at 355 feet, while the right field foul line was 360 feet away, and the left field power alley measured in the 340s. The fences were still covered in tin, and the wind was blowing in from right field. In a direct line from home, over second base, beyond dead center, a pipe several blocks away extended up about fifty feet, and an orange flame licked the perfect blue of the sky.

15

Exit at El Paso

BECAUSE OF TEXAS LEAGUE scheduling at my final two planned stops, San Antonio and El Paso, I had to drive across Texas at night to be in San Antonio for the last two games of a home stand. About three in the morning I pulled into a rest stop, slept for a couple hours in the back of Sweetspot, and was driving again by daylight.

Somewhere in Northern Texas about midmorning, at the junction of an interstate and another major highway, I pulled off to buy a bag of ice. When I returned to the truck, a man was standing near the end of the vehicle looking at the SOONERS license plate. As I neared, he drawled out the words, "Sooooners, shee-it!"

He didn't look exactly menacing, but he wasn't smiling either. He probably had been a football player at one time because he didn't have a neck. His body, if it had ever been normal looking, had expanded outward until it resembled a fat cylinder.

I shrugged and walked past him; it wasn't the sort of comment calling for conversation. As I threw the ice into the cooler on the front seat, he drawled and twisted the same phrase twice more, each time increasing the number of syllables until it became "Soo . . . ooo . . . ooo . . . ners, shee . . . eee . . . iii . . . ttt!"

I started the engine and watched in the rearview mirror as he finally walked toward the front door of the convenience store. Then I backed out and timed it so that I passed within about five feet of him as he started through the store's entrance. When Sweetspot was alongside I yelled through the open window, as loudly as I could, "TEXAS, MY ASS!," then swerved toward the highway and quickly merged into the traffic. I caught a glimpse of him standing open-mouthed as I turned onto the road, looking like a human fire hydrant. Actually, I felt no animosity toward Texas, or toward Texans, as a general class of people who lived south of Oklahoma, but I had to say something when my license plates were insulted. I hate it when I run into immature people like him.

I pulled into San Antonio in a driving rainstorm about four in the afternoon, bleary-eyed and skeptical about the possibility of a ball game being played that evening. After checking into a commercial campground, I called and confirmed that the game was off. I had good Mexican food for dinner, then slept for thirteen hours.

San Antonio was a second homecoming for me, of sorts. I had lived here on three different occasions, though the most recent had been thirty years ago and I no longer knew a soul in the city. The most noticeable change to the city was its new waterfront. City planners had "extended" the San Antonio River by digging a new channel and diverting part of its sluggish flow around a horseshoe-shaped bend.

When I lived in San Antonio, the *paseo del rio*, or river walk, was picturesque and had a neglected sort of appeal, but was unsafe. Now it was a well-lighted, flower-filled celebration of the city's 140-year Mexican heritage. Mariachi bands played, restaurants blended into each other so closely that sometimes you didn't know where your black beans and margaritas would come from, and the city, one level above the river, receded into another plane altogether. Some things do change for the better.

The San Antonio baseball club was one of the charter members of the Texas League in the 1880s, and the city had fielded a team in most seasons since. Their most famous ballpark was Mission Stadium, located south of the city on Mission Road. The old road had linked five eighteenth-century missions established by Spain in an attempt to extend her dominion north from Mexico. The missions ran from the Alamo, the northernmost post, south along the San Antonio River to San Francisco de la Espada, about ten miles south of the city. The ballpark had been located just a block from the beautiful Mission Concepcion.

I drove down the old road to see if anything remained of the ballpark, which had been torn down in 1974. I had attended at least one ball game at Mission Stadium in the late 1950s, and probably more than one, but remembered little except the unusual entrance to the stadium. As an enlisted man in the military service in the late 1950s, my pay had been $78 per month, before taxes. To stretch this meager sum, we usually started weekend passes with a tour of the Pearl Brewery. After the tour you could drink free beer, and in those more tolerant days, return for five or six refills of the yeasty, mellow stuff before they started looking at you with distaste. Any ball games would have followed these educational detours, so I'm understandably foggy on the details.

The architect of Mission Stadium had picked up the shape and structure of the classic mission church down the street. A handsome example of Spanish baroque architecture with Moorish elements, the church had twin bell towers capped with finials at the ends of a blocky, fortresslike front. At Mission Stadium, the craftsmanlike detailing was missing, but the entrance building's twin spires successfully echoed its namesake and gave the park a unique character.

The baseball park had been bounded by Steves Street, Mitchell Street, and Mission Road. Now the land was occupied by an Orwellian building that served as a detention center for juvenile offenders. Nothing remained to suggest that a minor league baseball park had ever been tenant there—no standing facade, no plaque, no marker. Minor league baseball parks die like paupers, lying there in unmarked graves.

In 1993, another Texas League park began its ride off into the sunset. Home field for the Missions since 1968 had been V. J. Keefe Memorial Stadium, located on the campus of St. Mary's University. According to writer Bill O'Neal in *The Texas League*, the arrangement had been the first time a professional baseball team had permanent tenancy on a college campus field. The park had been improved over the years, but a new one was being built now near the interstate in the northwest section of town. Team publicists were calling 1993 the "adios season" at Keefe.

When I arrived at the park my second day in town, the grounds crew and most of the front office staff were on the field, working

227

frantically to get the sodden basepaths in shape for that night's game. Keefe was a patched-together arrangement. Fences were 325 feet down each line, 401 feet to center, and trees overhung the power alley in left center. All the seating was crowded into the stands behind home plate, which climbed precipitously upward. Large trees, growing inside the park's concourse, framed the grandstand. Everything seemed to have a little rust and corrosion on it; even some of the outfield fence signs were fading. The press box leaked, and electrical equipment had to be removed after each game. But even small crowds, concentrated into a cozy seating space, promoted a feeling of comraderie. As fans began to arrive, the loudspeaker began blasting out a song called "Missions Baseball," sung to the tune of "La Bamba." Keefe looked and felt like a minor league park, and was a worthy place to watch a ball game.

For most of the game, I sat behind home plate amidst an army of scouts who had converged on this game because they had mid-season reports due. These gnarled, baseball-wise ex-players form an intelligence network that is essential to upper management. They are easily spotted in any park because they always (1) sit directly behind home plate; (2) carry a brief case that holds a JUGS gun, a timer, and ratings forms; and (3) talk to each other like this:

A: You know this guy?
B: Left-hander, just up, 85, 86.

That cryptic exchange occurred when a relief pitcher entered the game and scout A couldn't find him on the stat sheets. Translated, B's reply meant that the player was a left-handed pitcher, just promoted from the class A farm club, and had a fast ball with maximum velocity of eighty-five or eighty-six miles per hour.

Keefe had one irresistible feature. A young man sat atop the right center field fence under a hand-operated scoreboard during the game. I walked around to see if he would let me take a look from that perspective. The counts and outs were flashed electronically from the press box, so his work between innings was sporadic and occasionally team officials had to remind him to post the inning totals.

When the center fielder shaded over for a left-handed batter, I

228

could hear him, from the scoreboard, arguing almost every pitch at a conversational level, so it didn't carry to the infield umpires. ("Hey, that was a strike, dammit. Give him a break. You're calling that a ball? You're crazy. Jesus!") And on he went, muttering his way through pitch after pitch, having his one-sided say about unfairness in the national pastime.

The campus proper sat on a slight rise above the ballpark. I had attended St. Mary's University for one semester the last time I lived in San Antonio, and could see my old classroom building from the park. I remembered reading and excitedly discussing James Baldwin's *The Fire Next Time* in one class. J.F.K. and R.F.K and M.L.K. were alive then, and the hopes for a fairer America were coming to life in that Texas classroom. A short distance off campus the large old house where my wife and I had our first apartment still stood, though much the worse for wear. The house had been divided into four apartments, occupied by three young married couples and the elderly woman who owned it. Now the house stood in something called the Monte Vista Historical District. This trip seemed determined to convince me that I was an anachronism.

The fast way from San Antonio to El Paso is Interstate 10, 558 miles of concrete and boredom. I took US 90 out of the Alamo City, a straight, flat, and empty push through west Texas, leaving early in the morning to keep the sun at my back as long as possible. I rode through Hondo, by Uvalde, and then past Bracketville, where John Wayne filmed Hollywood's version of *The Alamo*. I drove through Del Rio, across the border from that magnetic attraction of my restless youth, *Villa Acuna*. There on brief weekend passes we walked the dusty streets of Boy's Town on sweltering Saturday nights, swigging tequila, consorting with bordertown Mexican maidens, eating tough beef jerky from little carts, and proving, conclusively, that we were men.

At Del Rio, US 90 turns north-northwest, following for awhile the International Amistad Reservoir, a body of water made by damming the Rio Grande. On top of the hump where the Coahuila province of Mexico seems to take a large bite out of Texas, I stopped to rest in the small town of Langtry. There, in a little hip-roofed hovel called the Jersey Lilly, the volatile and unpredictable Judge Roy Bean had dispensed his "law west of the Pecos." The little building stood well preserved in the dry Texas heat, a monument to an obsession. Today, we would call the judge's fascination with actress Lilly Langtry a psychiatric disorder. In the Jersey Lilly, though, they just called him "Your Honor."

Besides the Jersey Lilly, Langtry had a post office, a few shabby, one-story buildings and a dive that served the best Texas-style barbecue I ever tasted. Bud's Place was small, plain, and functional. I ordered a long-necked Lone Star beer and a barbecue sandwich piled so high with beef that it seemed to weave and threatened to topple. The sauce was hot but savory, with a delicacy that let the flavors swarm around and then explode in my mouth. West Texas was hot, and Bud's had a few fans to push the air around, but the heat wasn't the strength-sapping species of the middle South. Everything moved slowly, however; even the flies in the little restaurant seemed to slip around in slow motion.

Another 175 miles west and I stopped in Marathon, Texas, for the night. I decided to spend a rare night in a hotel, as preparation for the last few days of hot, dry driving through the Big Bend country and up to my westernmost stop, El Paso. A small but classy yellow brick hotel sat behind shade trees and flower-lined fountains on US 90, Marathon's main street. Marathon is in the heart of cattle country, and the Gage Hotel was originally built as headquarters for a cattle baron, Alfred Gage of San Antonio.

"He was a big landholder," the desk clerk told me when I checked in.

Knowing how Texans exaggerate, I asked "How big?"

"He owned six hundred sections."

"How much is that in acres?"

"That's 384,000 acres."

"Hmm," I said, trying not to sound impressed.

I intended to loop south, spend the night in Big Bend National Park, follow the Rio Grande north to Presidio, cut through the Chinati Mountains, and rejoin Highway 90 again at Marfa. Before leaving, I checked my plans at the visitor's center. Sweetspot's touring range was just over two hundred miles and I was entering a remote area with few services. Assured that gasoline would be available at a convenient midpoint, I turned south on US 385.

Little more than a century ago, Comanche war parties came from the north into the Big Bend, raiding settlements on both sides of the Rio Grande. Highway 385 follows their route, the great Comanche War Trail, down into what is now Big Bend National Park. The remoteness of the Big Bend area settles onto you quickly after leaving the little towns along Highway 90. No jets leave contrails in the sky, and almost no cars pass on the few roads. I tried the radio and found the reception from a few Mexican stations very poor.

It was too late in the year to see the desert bloom, but it was still ablaze with color. Green ocotillo cacti, orange rock formations, purple mountains in the distance, and always the brilliant blue sky spotted with fleecy white clouds. The land was raw and powerful, and toward late afternoon, after a brief rainstorm pelted the high desert miles away from my route, I saw a rainbow make a perfect geometric half-circle around a mesa.

That evening I camped in the Basin in the Chisos Mountains, a park service campground. My campsite was surrounded by an escarpment rising dramatically on all sides, capped by Emory Peak at 7,825 feet. Driving out the next morning, I watched a collared peccary, or javelina, amble slowly into the brush beside the road. These wild pigs were so ugly both sexes must loathe the arrival of mating season, but somehow they looked just right for this tough country.

I left the huge Big Bend National Park at Study Butte, drove through the ghost town of Terlingua where I stopped at a rocky, windswept cemetery to read the tombstones of miners who had once lived there, and at Lajitas picked up Texas Farm Road 170. From Lajitas to Presidio, the two-lane road ran through a narrow valley alongside the Rio Grande. Having only seen the river in bordertowns, where it was little more than an open, channeled sewer, I was unprepared for the beauty of the wild, free stretch of rapids-strewn water hundreds of feet below. Across the valley in Mexico, the Chihuahua mountains rose as sheer precipices to heights of two thousand feet. At one point on the road, engineers were left with

231

no room to work, and had to build Farm Road 170 up the slope of a crag at a fifteen-degree grade.

After driving through Presidio and turning north toward Marfa, I passed through two blockades set up by the border patrol to intercept illegal aliens. This made a total of four I'd seen since entering the Big Bend country. The officers were very interested in Sweetspot, as the back looked like an ideal hiding place. When they discovered it was set up for more mundane purposes, they asked about my trip in a friendly way, and we talked awhile. This was lonely country.

Driving several hundred miles through the Big Bend country, the sight of other cars had been so infrequent that occupants invariably waved, probably more so because I was driving the local vehicle of choice, a pickup. This had quickly become habitual, and driving west on US 90 I tossed out three unanswered waves before the habit was broken.

At Van Horn, Texas, US 90 ended at Interstate 10. I intended to take the interstate northwest only a short distance, then cut through one of the emptiest, most desolate corners of west Texas and stay the night at Hueco Tanks State Park, thirty miles west of El Paso. The plan was fine, but before leaving Van Horn, I made a Texas-sized mistake.

Maybe the Texas sun had penetrated my Nashville cowboy hat and baked my brain. More likely, it was three months of watching hundreds of batters swing at thousands of pitches, and not ever feeling the sensations myself. At any rate, a combination baseball-golf driving range appeared roadside and some force I couldn't control pulled Sweetspot into a parking place. I walked over to a batting cage with a fistful of quarters.

The balls were hard rubber, and had been pounded into misshapen masses only vaguely resembling spheroids. I set the machine on what I thought was a hittable seventy miles per hour and took a few warmup swings. The balls thumped out of the mechanical arm at what seemed at first to be blinding speed, and because of the weird shapes, they did unpredictable things. They sailed in, broke away, and even at a constant speed, kept me offstride. After four or five swings my timing improved and finally I met one with that contact that seems to move the bat through the ball with only a slight, satisfying resistance. The ball was lined solidly out into the dry rocky field and I coiled to do it again, to send the next one even farther. The pitch came in and lurched impossibly up and away, and before my jerky follow-through was completed I felt a stabbing pain in my lower back. The slightest additional movements caused spasms to shoot through my torn back muscles, and I racked the aluminum bat, limped carefully back to the truck, and painfully lifted myself into the cab. Batting practice was over.

Half an hour up the interstate at Sierra Blanca I turned north on a rough-looking ranch road. Almost fifty miles lay between Sierra Blanca and another principal highway to the north. The road was paved except for a few stretches, but in parts the paving was in bad repair, and even in the smooth-riding pickup, the bumps transmitted a sharp message to my damaged back muscles. About halfway along the back road, sweating profusely, I stopped.

I put a lawn chair in the shade beside the truck, took a few aspirin, fashioned an ice pack from a plastic bag, and wedged it between my back and the chair canvas. Even in late afternoon, the sun was fierce and I had to refill the ice bag within twenty minutes. To the west I could see a prominent peak, the Sierra Blanca, at about seven thousand feet and to the east, Dome Peak, a few thousand feet lower. The only moving things I could see were hawks, soaring on air drafts far above the high desert floor.

Sitting on my third ice pack, a startling thought occurred to me: I didn't really have to go to El Paso! I could take County Road 1111 back to Sierra Blanca, ease onto the interstate, and by the time of tomorrow evening's game between the El Paso Diablos and the Midland Angels, a good chunk of the drive home would be behind me. I had been to El Paso once before, so it wasn't as if I would miss seeing a new city. More immediately, County Road 1111 looked like a washboard, and the muscle spasms in my back had worn away most of my energy.

On the other hand, El Paso had been the mark from the start. "Going all the way to El Paso," I had been telling people all across the South. El Paso wasn't just one more ball game and one more city, it was, as the psychologists say, closure. It was the most distant

233

western point where you could still make the case that you were in the South.

I hadn't put words to it, but had been feeling a strange combination of gladness and gloom ever since arriving in Texas. It wasn't because Texans hated my SOONERS license plate, but because the trip was almost over. I wanted to be home, to see my wife, pick up my life, and write about fresh, vivid memories. But the road was bewitching. For months, every day had provided choices that depended on me alone, and the incredibly limp and tattered Rand McNally atlas on the front seat had provided the means. Going home meant trading a steering wheel for a desk. I didn't even have a job anymore, and that would require some adjustment. I would have to do things I wasn't looking forward to, such as selling Sweetspot to help pay for the trip. The old truck had been in the family for more than two decades, and had been so reliable and trustworthy that I no longer gave a thought to being stranded, even stopped in the middle of the desert. Poor reward, to take her home and sell her.

"You should know when to give it up," the logical side of my brain said. "Could be a good game tomorrow," said the other side. The questions I had begun the trip with had by now been answered. I had wondered whether the Old South of myth and lore was still there, or its regional subculture had gone with the winds of the twentieth century. After three months, I was sure that the traditional values and rules of the South lay quietly but strongly throughout the vast territory. The symbols of southern tradition were under attack, but counterattacks were in evidence everywhere. Writers like humorist Lewis Grizzard, a defender of the folkways of the traditional southern white male, were selling well across Dixie. Advertising for impersonal fast food chains had been regionalized, offering "skat-through" service. When the state of Alabama lowered the Confederate flag from state property, opinion in Georgia and Mississippi favoring keeping the stars and bars seemed to become more entrenched.

Even the mesmerizing southern speech held sway except in larger urban centers or increasingly popular sun belt retirement areas, penetrated *en masse* by Yankee refugees. Early in the trip, before I became accustomed to different, slower cadences, I had failed to understand that "bald" peanuts had been cooked by boiling, that a "born" baseball game was one the speaker found boring, or that a suggestion to take the road to "your right" did not mean going to the village of Yorerot. The South may no longer be a monolithic regional subculture, but the old ways are visible to anyone who drives the less-traveled roads.

The other question had to do with changes in minor league baseball. I had predicted that the southern minor leagues would remain true to the classic baseball formula of diehard fans and gritty, straightforward, all-or-nothing baseball. I had been wrong. Southern minor league baseball had evolved into a new form of entertainment. The obsessed fans, like the gentleman in Chattanooga who shouted instructions to players over a megaphone, were still there in small numbers, but a club that opened its doors today with no promotions or giveaways would attract only a handful of these relics and no others. I had found southern minor league baseball to be different from the old days, but with an appeal and charm that still reflected the simplicity and purity missing from the big league game. In Columbia, South Carolina, I had seen the dugout empty, not to engage in a tedious, irrelevant brawl with opponents, but to watch a young boy tap dance on the dugout roof. In Asheville, North Carolina, I watched two young boys' eyes grow wide with wonder when the Spartanburg manager slipped them used baseball equipment. In Little Rock, I had noted that players approached autograph signing as a privilege, and smiled as they signed their names. My attendance at ninety games had not resulted in disappointment at failure to find the experiences of my youth, but in a slow conversion. I had felt safe, comfortable, secure, and happy in the South's minor league parks, and didn't regret a mile of the summer's journey. Besides, I had been right on 50 percent of my pretrip predictions, and a .500 batting average was nothing to be ashamed of for a season.

I climbed slowly into the pickup cab and started the engine. Out of habit, I looked into the rearview mirror, though I had been sitting there for over two hours and not a single vehicle had passed. County Road 1111 was really too narrow for turning around any-

235

way, so I drove off in the direction I was pointing, heading for El Paso. Could be a good game tomorrow, I decided.

In El Paso, I called the Diablos' office, asked a few perfunctory questions, and arranged to pick up some written material before the evening ball game. My lack of enthusiasm had nothing to do with the organization, nor with the city of El Paso, but rather with the fact that I couldn't completely straighten up because of the pulled back muscles and felt silly. Early in the afternoon, I parked Sweetspot near the international border and walked across the bridge into Juarez to kill some time. At the apex of the heavily trafficked bridge, a small crowd had formed to watch the activities below. A man was running a crude ferry service over from Juarez, in plain view. He had rigged a wooden platform over a big inner tube, and had attached a lead rope to it. I watched while he put a passenger on the raft and waded him over. The Rio Grande was little more than a concrete-lined drainage ditch at that point, and the passenger scurried up the bank on the United States side and slipped through a hole in the chain link fence.

About thirty yards upstream a railroad bridge spanned the river, with a barricade at midstream. While we watched, two men scaled the barricade and strolled over to the U.S. side along the railroad tracks. Maybe they were just avoiding the few cents' toll for pedestrians on the walking bridge, or maybe the population of the United States had increased by three in the five minutes I watched. In either case, so much for border security.

As I walked along the streets in Juarez, every corner teemed with taxi drivers who offered rides. When I refused, they invariably whispered, "You want ladies?" I waved one off by saying, "It's too hot." He drew himself up and said haughtily, "I have air con-di-tion' ladies."

On Juarez's main street, I stopped at a cantina with sidewalk seating and drank a couple of Carta Blancas, watching the foot traffic stroll slowly past in the heat. I got a little hungry but didn't order anything to eat. The name of the place, El Coyote Infirmido, the sick coyote, didn't make me that eager to try the *hamburguesas*.

The Diablos' new park was not in the city, but up US 54, the

236

Patriot Parkway, in the suburbs. It was new, sleek, and accessible, with a name, Cohen "Sportsplex" to give true baseball fans the willies. The entrance building, the fences, and practically everything else in sight were painted and textured to look like adobe, even structures that would never be made of mud and straw. The Diablos' (Devils, in Spanish) staff were all dressed in red.

The playing field provided more of a challenge for hitters in the thin dry air than had old Dudley Field, the home-run-happy park used by the Diablos before 1990. Cohen's lines were 340 feet, and dead center was 410 feet. The park held almost ten thousand and the club was drawing well. In 1992, attendance was second only to Tulsa in the Texas League. Invariably, though, as stadiums get bigger, signs seem to get grumpier. On one door: "ABSOLUTELY NO ADMITTANCE." At the concession stand gate: "No Beverage or Food Beyond This Point—OR YOU WILL BE CHARGED!"

By the bottom of the sixth, El Paso led 8–1. I was sitting in the far left-field corner so I could watch the ball game and the sunset behind the Franklin Mountains at the same time. The game was a laugher and I was having trouble finding a comfortable position in the hard seat because of back pain. Innings were clipping along through a predictable pattern and heroics seemed very unlikely. Then a magnificent play occurred.

With two out and none on, a left-handed hitting Diablo player sliced a long, twisting drive toward the left-field wall. Midland's left fielder, shaded over toward center, had broken toward the left-field line before I even picked up the flight of the ball. He was running full out and tracking the ball, and you could see that he wasn't going to play it off the wall for a safe double. The ball sung past my seat not fifteen yards in front of me, bending toward the foul line; the Midlands player was a blur of gray in pursuit. He left his feet, too late I thought, and flashed horizontally across three outfield signs, stretched thin as a pencil from glove to spike. The ball was past him, slicing wickedly, when he flicked his gloved right hand and snared it scarcely in the web. He got a spiked foot down, then the bare hand, tucked his left shoulder and somersaulted twice before finally planting two feet solidly, coming up with a raised gloved hand to complete the rite, to show the ball and get the call.

237

The umpire's clenched fist was the first acknowledgment, and then six thousand fans were on their feet. They may have come for the promotions or because they had free tickets, but at that moment they were baseball fans, and they were applauding a professional. He ran in, head down, no emotion showing, and disappeared into the dugout.

I checked the media guide later. The player who had made that eloquent catch might as well have been wearing NP, no prospect, for a uniform number. He was twenty-six, already old by minor league standards, and had never played higher than AA ball. He had spent the last three years shuffling between the parent club's class A and AA teams. The game hadn't been on the line, the percentage play was off the wall for a double. Why, then, this strange gift?

I tried to remember my youthful experiences with baseball as movement, with the exhilaration involved in arresting the flight of a bright white sphere, or driving it out in a different direction with a bat. I thought of the relaxed feeling that grew with a game of catch, the rocking, rythmic use of large body muscles, and I recalled the pump of energy that fueled a headlong sprint to first base. Those joys had been learned before baseball meant status, required dedication, or entailed commitment. They were the pleasures of baseball as play. And my sore back was evidence that the years hadn't veiled those senses, no more than they had in the flying Midlands' left fielder.

Beneath baseball as business, as pageantry, or even as nostalgia, there is that irreducible essence. It is beyond reason but is sensed by the multitudes, whether they perform the act or spontaneously rise to applaud in its presence. A young Willie Mays, asked to analyze the meaning of baseball, put it in words once: "They pitch it, I hit it. They hit it, I catch it."

A half moon hung over the Franklin Mountains as I left the ballpark. The mountains looked dark against the deep purple sky, like a crudely cut first grade art project, jagged black construction paper tacked to a purple backdrop, and over everything a yellow cutout moon, which was far too bright and shiny to be real.

238

Suggestions for Further Reading

Each of the following books contains descriptive or statistical material on baseball in the South:

Benson, Michael. *Ballparks of North America: A Comprehensive Historical Reference to Baseball Grounds, Yards and Stadiums, 1845 to Present.* Jefferson, NC: McFarland & Company, Inc., 1989.

Blake, Mike. *The Minor Leagues: A Celebration of the Little Show.* New York: Wynwood Press, 1991.

Brooks, Ken. *The Last Rebel Yell: Baseball's Forgotten Alabama-Florida League.* Lynn Haven, FL: Seneca Publishing, 1986.

Johnson, Lloyd, and Miles Wolff (eds.). *The Encyclopedia of Minor League Baseball.* Durham, NC: Baseball America, Inc., 1993.

Lamb, David. *Stolen Season: A Journey through America and Baseball's Minor Leagues.* New York: Random House, 1991.

O'Neal, Bill. *The Texas League: A Century of Baseball 1888–1987.* Austin, TX: Eakin Press, 1987.

O'Neal, Bill. *The Southern League: Baseball in Dixie 1885–1994.* Austin, TX: Eakin Press, 1994.

Sullivan, Neil J. *The Minors.* New York: St. Martin's Press, 1990.

239

Southern Minor League Baseball Clubs

TEAM	LOCATION	PARK	SEATS
Florida State League (A)			
(West)			
Charlotte Rangers	Pt. Charlotte, FL	Charlotte County	6,026
Clearwater Phillies	Clearwater, FL	Jack Russell	7,384
Dunedin Blue Jays	Dunedin, FL	Dunedin	6,214
Fort Meyers Miracle	Ft. Meyers, FL	Lee County Sports	7,500
St. Petersburg Cards	St. Petersburg, FL	Al Lang	7,004
Sarasota White Sox	Sarasota, FL	Ed Smith	7,500
(East)			
Daytona Cubs	Daytona Beach, FL	Jackie Robinson	4,900
Ft. Lauderdale Red Sox	Ft. Lauderdale, FL	Ft. Lauderdale Sta.	8,300
Lakeland Tigers	Lakeland, FL	Joker Marchant	7,000
Osceola Astros	Kissimmee, FL	Osceola County	5,100
St. Lucie Mets	St. Lucie, FL	Thomas J. White	7,400
Vero Beach Dodgers	Vero Beach, FL	Holman	6,474
West Palm Beach Expos	West Palm Beach FL	Municipal	4,400
South Atlantic League (A)			
(North)			
Asheville Tourists	Asheville, NC	McCormick Field	3,500
Charleston Sternwheelers	Charleston, WV	Watt Powell Park	6,000

TEAM	LOCATION	PARK	SEATS
Fayetteville Generals	Fayetteville, NC	J.P. Riddle	3,200
Greensboro Hornets	Greensboro, NC	War Memorial	7,500
Hagerstown Suns	Hagerstown, MD	Municipal	4,500
Hickory Crawdads	Hickory, NC	L.P. Frans	5,100
Spartanburg Phillies	Spartanburg, SC	Duncan Park	3,900

(South)

Albany Polecats	Albany, GA	Eames Sports	4,200
Augusta Pirates	Augusta, GA	Heaton	3,800
Charleston Rainbows	Charleston, SC	College Park	6,000
Capital City Bombers	Columbia, SC	Capital City Park	6,000
Columbus Redstixx	Columbus, GA	Golden Park	5,000
Macon Braves	Macon, Ga	Luther Williams	3,700
Savannah Cardinals	Savannah, Ga	Grayson	8,500

Carolina League (A)

(North)

Frederick Keys	Frederick, MD	Harry Grove	5,200
Lynchburg Red Sox	Lynchburg, VA	City Stadium	4,000
Prince Wm. Cannons	Woodbridge, VA	County Stadium	6,000
Wilmington Blue Rocks	Wilmington, DE	Legends	5,500

(South)

Durham Bulls	Durham, NC	Durham Athletic Pk.	5,000
Kinston Indians	Kinston, NC	Grainger Stadium	4,100
Salem Buccaneers	Salem, VA	Municipal Field	5,000
Winston-Salem Spirits	Winston-Salem, NC	Ernie Shore Field	6,280

Southern League (AA)

(East)

Carolina Mudcats	Zebulon, NC	Five County Sta.	6,000
Greenville Braves	Greenville, SC	Grenville Muni.	7,027
Jacksonville Suns	Jacksonville, FL	Wolfson Park	8,200
Knoxville Smokies	Knoxville, TN	Bill Meyer	6,412
Orlando Cubs	Orlando, FL	Tinker Field	6,000

(West)

Birmingham Barons	Birmingham, AL	Hoover Met.	10,000
Chattanooga Lookouts	Chattanooga, TN	Engel	7,500

TEAM	LOCATION	PARK	SEATS
Huntsville Stars	Huntsville, AL	Joe W. Davis	10,200
Memphis Chicks	Memphis, TN	Tim McGarver	10,000
Nashville XPress	Nashville, TN	Herschel Greer	17,000

Texas League (AA)

(East)

Arkansas Travelers	Little Rock, AR	Ray Winder Field	6,083
Jackson Generals	Jackson, MS	Smith-Wills Sta.	5,200
Shreveport Captains	Shreveport, LA	Fair Grounds Field	6,200
Tulsa Drillers	Tulsa, OK	Drillers Sta.	10,722

(West)

El Paso Diablos	El Paso, TX	Cohen Sportsplex	9,765
Midland Angels	Midland, TX	Angels Stadium	5,000
San Antonio Missions	San Antonio, TX	V. J. Keefe	3,500
Wichita Wranglers	Wichita, KS	Lawrence-Dumont	6,723

American Association (AAA)

Louisville Redbirds	Louisville, KY	Cardinal Stadium	33,500
Nashville Sounds	Nashville, TN	Herschel Greer	17,000
New Orleans Zephyrs	New Orleans, LA	Privateer Park	4,700
Okla. City 89ers	Oklahoma City, OK	All Sports	15,000

International League (AAA)

Charlotte Knights	Charlotte, NC	Charlotte Knights	10,000
Norfolk Tides	Norfolk, VA	Harbor Park	12,000
Richmond Braves	Richmond, VA	The Diamond	12,500

Seating capacities listed in *Baseball America's Directory*, 1993 and 1994 editions.

Index

245

About the Author

ERNEST J. GREEN was a professor of sociology until 1993. After returning from his trip through the South, he said goodbye to academia and officially retired. Since completing *The Diamonds of Dixie*, Green has been writing his next book, a history of the Chesapeake and Ohio Canal. He has contributed baseball articles and reviews to several publications, including *Nine* and *The Encyclopedia of United States Popular Culture*.